Phenor

"June 17, 1967 -

MW00573824

"David Hearne, an OCS classmate, fellow artilleryman and decorated Vietnam War Veteran, has written a compelling and compassionate book about war: its scope and many dimensions. Above all, it is about the human component and raw emotions of those brave soldiers in the fight. David takes us on a personal look at small unit leadership and the human cost for those on the field of battle and those back home. He also reminds us that, along with the physical scars of battle, there are the emotional scars. Those scars often linger long after the sounds, sights and smells of the battle are no longer readily apparent.

In David's own words "a war of attrition as the main strategy of a war is not a strategy at all. Attrition, unfortunately, is simply part of the very nature of war." Clausewitz posited that war was politics by another means. There must be more logic applied to the prosecution of wars and more thought of what our actions will cause. Our institutions must do a better job of defining who we are and for what we stand. When we define those boundaries, we cannot continue to allow people and factions to stray outside of them. We have been involved in "incrementalism" to a fault since the end of WW II. David Hearne's book is a heartfelt and thoughtful recount of a Vietnam battle that should serve as a constant reminder of what is at stake when our nation calls. Our soldiers are willing to give their all. We should expect that our senior military and civilian leaders are willing to do no less."

Major General Morris Boyd, USA (Retired)
Vietnam 1966-1968 and 1970-1971
The Gulf War 1990-1991

"It is an excellent account of fighting and dying in Vietnam complete with enough background information of individual soldiers to more than sustain a reader's interest. Even though a combat infantryman and former RTO myself, your vivid descriptions created pictures easily viewed by even the most the inexperienced reader. You accurately captured living conditions of the Vietnam soldier, from boredom to sheer terror, all within a twelve hour period. No one can adequately explain the intensity of battle but you came as close as anything I've read. Your book does a great service to the men who fought the families who lost loved ones, the men who died and soldiers everywhere. I dare say, it was obvious to me that you were there! Thank you for a fine contribution to the exhaustive history of the 28th Infantry Regiment. Black Lions Sir!"

Mike MacDonald
President, 28th Infantry Regiment Assn.

June 17, 1967
Battle of Xom Bo II

David Hearne

SUBTERFUGE PUBLISHING

Subterfuge Publishing

Copyright

Published by Subterfuge Publishing
PO Box 8008
Lumberton, Texas 77657
www.subterfugepublishing.com

www.david-hearne.com/xombo
ISBN13: 978-0-9755976-5-1

Library of Congress Cataloging-in-Publication Data
is available on request.

Dedication

This book is dedicated to all the men who fought in the battle of Xom Bo II back on June 17, 1967, and especially to those brave young men who perished there in the mud of LZ X-Ray. When called upon by our nation, these men gave their all. This book was written to celebrate their lives and recognize their ultimate sacrifices.

Their names are listed below:

Alpha Company 1/16th

SGT Edward E. Heyer
Prichard, AL
SGT Alan J. Roese
Lancaster, NY
SGT Frank G. Romo
Azusa, CA
SP4 Carl T. Johnson
Houston, TX
PFC John A. Brantley
Chicago, IL
PFC Emanuel K. Brickhouse
New York, NY
PFC Jerry R. Cook
Alpharetta, GA
PFC Ronald D. Edenfield
Grand Ridge, FL
PFC James M. Elchert
Toledo, OH

SGT. Howard A. Mucha
Willoughby, OH
SP4 Stephen M. Noggle
Minneapolis, MN
SP4 Wayne A. Pettersen
Seattle, WA

PFC Robert T. Harris
Earle, AR
PFC Charles P. Kelly
Fullerton, CA
PFC Robert S. Maguire
Atascadero, CA

Bravo Co, 1st Bn, 1/16th

PFC Paul E. Kelly
Smyrna, GA

PFC Edward A. Smith
Newport, KY

HHC, (Recon) 1/16th

1LT Douglas A. Logan
Crane, MO
SP4 Sammy L. Holmes
Miami, FL
SP4 Charles W. Hook
Friendsville, MD
SP4 Martin L. Plotkin
Lynbrook, NY

PFC William N. Cole
Clairton, PA
PFC Gary J. Ernst
Perryville, MO
PFC Wallace G. Nye
Minneapolis, MN
PFC Leroy Reed
Lake Charles, LA
PFC Douglas D. Wallin
Rochester, MN

Bravo Co, 2nd Bn, 28th

SGT Bobby Minton
Elizabeth, IN
SP5 John H. Stout
Luxora, AL
SP4 Michael J. Morrow
New York, NY

PFC Alan W. Denney
Phoenix, AZ
PFC Alan J. Farhat
Lansing, MI
PFC Victoriano P. Sosa
New Braunfels, TX

SP4 Guy W. Clinger
Lewistown, PA
PFC Richard A. Anderson
New York, NY

PFC James E. Starks
Cameron, SC
PFC John J. Rieck JR.
Cleveland, Oh

Alpha Company 2/28th
PFC Lloyd C. Wohlford
Des Moines, IA

Alpha Battery 6/27th
SSG Samuel Lee Modesitt
Manila, AR
CPL Charles M. Roach
Harvey, IL

I also wish to mention and thank my two sons who have served in Iraq and Afghanistan

SGT Scott
Army - 1 tour in Iraq

Corpsman Alexander
Navy - 3 tours Afghanistan

Table of Contents

List of Illustrations

Photographs and Maps

Foreword

The Vietnam of 2016 is a far different place than what First Lieutenant David Hearne and I flew into back in the Sixties. Since those days, the population has grown from thirty-five million to over ninety million. Many of the rice paddies on the outskirts of Saigon—now Ho Chi Minh City—that were the scene of firefights have metamorphosed into condos and golf courses. Sleepy fishing villages of 1967, once a haven for Viet Cong trying to control the waterways, have turned into luxury resorts. Primitive marketplaces in Hue, Lai Khe, An loc, Loc Ninh, and other villages now have modern shopping malls replete with a Starbucks or other American franchises, including McDonalds, Burger King, Subway, Pizza Hut, Dominos, and KFC. This land I once fought in has healed much of itself. The death and agony that was once Vietnam's daily norm is now but a fading bad memory for most Vietnamese.

When David asked me to write a foreword for his book, I hesitated for only a second before I said, "Yes." The battle of Xom Bo II holds a special significance to me, just as it does for David, because we both were intimately involved in it back in the summer of 1967. We both lost comrades that day when the Black Lions and the Rufe's Rangers clashed with the PAVN 271st Regiment on that afternoon of June 17, 1967.

When I arrived in Vietnam in 1966, I was assigned to the Second Battalion, 28th Infantry, also known as the Black Lions. My first job with the Black Lions was platoon leader with Alpha Company, commanded by Captain Donald Sawtelle. A few months later I was given the job of executive officer of Alpha Company, and soon thereafter I was moved to a Battalion staff job as Assistant Battalion S-1. By June 1967, I was the Battalion S-1. I attribute much of what I have accomplished since then to the time I spent with the 28th Infantry. I doubt that if I had not experienced a year with the Black Lions or had the chance to be a part of the 1st Infantry Division's officer corps, my lifetime of service would not have been the same. Since that tour in Vietnam, I have always held a special affection for the men I served with in the 1st Infantry Division and especially the men of the Black Lions. We were all living together, serving together, and fighting together and that created a bond of brotherhood.

David's book is a poignant book about a generation of young men who did what their country asked of them and did it well. It's a sobering read about the brutality of war, about the violence young men had to live through and had to perpetrate to survive their tour in Vietnam. It is a book about the life of men on the battlefield juxtaposed against those who stayed safe and sound back home during the Summer of Love, an era of drugs, free love, and rock and roll.

David's book is a Vietnam War story mainly about the men who fought in the battle of Xom Bo II. He gives a minute-by-minute narrative of the action, the horrifying experiences, the chaos the men lived through, the loved ones they left behind, and their dreams and hopes of their future—if they survived to that magic DEROS day.

The stories are told from the perspective of the soldiers who fought in these bloody battles. David deliberately concentrates on the men...who they were and their personal experiences. He leaves the geopolitical analysis for others to write about.

David and I were both 1st Lieutenants serving with the 1st Infantry Division's Black Lions when the battle of Xom Bo II raged. He was an artillery officer in the field, and I was an infantry officer at battalion headquarters serving as the S-1. Now almost half a century later we have come together again, to help make sure that what happened that afternoon of June 17, 1967, is finally told.

It is written with the violence and fury that attempts to convey some of the horrors and realities of a real battle. War is brutal, and Hearne does a great job at describing it while also paying honor to those heroes who served their country.

June 17, 1967, is a poignant reminder that many of the stories of the Vietnam War have yet to be told. Hearne's book assures that the brave men who fought and those who died at LZ X-Ray will never be forgotten.

— Major General Troy Oliver USA (RET)

Preface

Xom Bo II was one of the bloodiest battles fought in the summer of 1967, but it never gained the notoriety of battles like Ap Gu or Ong Thanh. The battle of Xom Bo II had 189 casualties versus Ong Thanh, which had 141 and Ap Gu which suffered 119. Our rumble in the jungle ended with 39 men dead and a hundred and fifty more wounded. Two great books have been written about the bloody battle of Ong Thanh, and two books were written to tell of the battle of Ap Gu, but no book has been written about the battle of Xom Bo II until now.

I hope my book "June 17, 1967, The Battle of Xom Bo II" will correct this slight. What little that has been written about the battle portrayed it as a battle where only one battalion was involved or that we actually assaulted the LZ by helicopters, but those assertions are totally incorrect. Companies from the $2/28^{th}$ Black Lions and the $1/16^{th}$ Rangers fought in this battle, and they all suffered men killed and wounded. We were not transported into the LZ by air as Wikipedia entries suggested, but marched into LZ X-Ray from LZ Rufe. The battle was so fierce that Alpha Company and the recon platoon of the 1/16th were declared combat ineffective and had to be replaced by elements of the 1/18th. Bravo Company of the Black Lions was also declared combat ineffective because of its large number of casualties.

The book is about what my comrades did, saw, and suffered during the battle of Xom Bo II. A bloody battle fought during the pinnacle of the Summer of Love where our generation back in the world was experiencing a country in turmoil embroiled with race riots and war protest. A time where the unquestioned respect for parents, politicians, teachers, and the police had eroded to the point where many purposely did whatever they could to show their disdain for society's rules. It was also a time for the birth of new sounds in music.

We were the sons of Second World War and Korean War veterans. Many of us wanted to be like our dads, uncles, and brothers who had served our country in previous wars. They had come home as heroes to a grateful country. They were welcomed home with ticker tape parades, cheering crowds and speeches about their bravery and valor. Many of those who returned would become captains of industry and leaders of our country. In 1967 even our President had previously served in the military and his predecessors President Kennedy, Eisenhower and Harry Truman had also served.

My story is about my comrades who unhesitatingly served their country, and returned to a nation indifferent to their courage and the sacrifices that they made for our country. It is about those who paid the ultimate price and the rest of us who were able to survive the killing, but came home scarred from battle, both physically and mentally.

To write this book, I interviewed many of my comrades, or their loved ones and friends. What was going to be a short two-thousand-word article for the Vietnam Magazine became a lengthy book that would tell the stories of hundreds of men who fought June 17, 1967, at LZ X-Ray in the battle of Xom Bo II.

I hope my story of what happened at LZ X-Ray sets history straight and does justice to all my comrades who fought so valiantly that hot, rainy afternoon of hell.

Acknowledgements

This book would never have been written if not for the help of the many men who served with me back on June 17th, 1967. I am so grateful that all the company commanders were still of this world and could tell me their recollections of what happened that day at LZ X-Ray. Donald Sawtelle, who was my boss and Commanding Officer of the Black Lions Alpha Company, Bill Williamson, the Rangers Alpha Company commander, Don Ulm the Rangers Bravo Company commander, and John Turner the Black Lions Bravo Company commander. I need to thank Richard (Dick) Dalton, who was another FO from 2/33rd. Then there were men like Jose Garcia, who told me of what he remembered as he fired his M60 machine gun during those many hours of the battle back half a century ago. Frank Limiero was another big contributor to the info of what went on that day. Gregory Murry, whose own book, "Content with my wages," which told of his experiences during the battle provided another plethora of facts.

I need to thank these good soldiers for all of their input, like Linsley R. Moore, Ray Gilbert, Wes Canute, James Berry, David Cordeau, Ed Chrisman, John Phil Vessello, Joe Hare, Don Rawls, Neil Skiles, Peter Clark, Michael Patrick Arias, Dennis Soricelli, Felix Vallejo, Leonard Mathis, Fred Atkins, Richard Ancira, David Oshel, William Buonanno, Ross Philips, Wayne Wade, David Aldridge, Dwight Krebbs, Ronald Moreno, Douglas Ikerd, Mike Stubbs, Tom Waldron, and I am sure I am missing someone and I apologize for that.

I also have to thank some of the officers who were involved in the battle that provided me with more insight of what went down. These were men like Troy Oliver, Bobby Roberts, Tony Jezior, Hono Yacapin, and Paul Wenzel.

A special thank you to Robert Youngberg, who helped me find and contact many of the men who were in the battle. He was my most helpful detective in finding many of the men I needed to talk to. Poet, Gary Jacobson, the author of "My Thousand Yard Stare," graciously provided me the use of his words to describe the job of a point man.

I also got to hear stories from the spouses, girlfriends, siblings, and friends of men who fought in the battle and some who gave their all. I thank Sue Canute, Karen Smith, Patricia Ward, Sharon Spear, Gail Bowers, Troy Bowers, Mel Hennemann, Marleen Wesson, Carl Mucha, Thomas Wohlford, Cynthia Kelly, Stanley Noggle, Cheryl Callahan, and again, if I missed anyone, please forgive me.

I especially want to thank Lillian S. Rowan, the mother of Private First Class Ronald D. Edenfield, who was killed in the battle of Xom Bo II. Lillian was gracious enough to talk to me about her memories of her son who died so many years ago.

There were many individuals that helped me with my book. Katie Carlisle did a great job of formatting the book. Jon Van Zile did the bulk of the editing. Also, I have to thank others who vetted my work, Pamela Truax, Vickie Hernandez, Karen Fuljenz, Don Sawtelle, and my wonderful wife, Stacie.

The book was helped along by the wonderful online resources that are now available to writers. The Coffelt Group's database was of great help by providing me all the names and background information of the men who were killed each day in Vietnam. Google's vast repository of information was also greatly appreciated.

Many people helped me with this book, and if I missed anyone, please forgive me – it was not intentional. Finally, I wanted to thank my super wife, Stacie for her support and understanding, without it the book would've never been finished.

Chapter 1
Good Morning

When the killing started, it was slow and deliberate. They were killing us...and we didn't even know it. A single shot would ring out, and the life of one of our men would cease. Seconds later another crack of an AK-47 would echo over LZ X-Ray, and somewhere in the tree line, another soldier would fall dead. This would repeat, and another soldier would suddenly collapse, a geyser of arterial spray exploding from his lifeless body.

The battle had started, but we hadn't even realized it. It was one of those couldn't-be-happening situations. It was our own little Pearl Harbor. You could see it happening, but it just couldn't be, because we were two battalions strong, and had artillery and deadly air support. What sane Viet Cong commander would subject his men to an inevitable slaughter?

That is what we thought at noon on June 17, 1967. But we were mistaken—by about 3 P.M. that day, more than 30 of our men were dead, and a hundred or more wounded, and the battle still raged on. None of us was immune to the savagery of that battle, and as we descended into a maelstrom of bullets and shrapnel, my name was added to the casualty list.

It happened as I was sprinting to a new location on the west side of a huge clearing we called Landing Zone X-Ray. I was running and heard a voice calling, "Lieutenant, you're hit, you're bleeding!" I think it was my radio operator uttering those words. All around us, Vietcong bullets were cutting through the air, some slamming into the ground and flinging up clumps of muddy earth, others burying themselves in trees, and a deadly few finding flesh.

Because of this battle, the date June 17, 1967, has always been indelibly imprinted in my mind. It was called the battle of Xom Bo II, and it was a part of Operation Billings. The events of that day were the most devastating fighting I endured during my Vietnam tour. I would venture to say that all of those who fought and survived that battle still find it haunting their thoughts and dreams. I don't have nightmares of what happened, but I often think about it and wonder how I survived.

In most history archives covering June 17, 1967, the battle of Xom Bo II is not even listed. The most significant event that day was China's surprise entry into the exclusive club of thermonuclear armed countries. Their successful creation and detonation of a hydrogen bomb 150 times more powerful than Little Boy, the bomb dropped on Hiroshima, made Little Boy appear just that: little.

China exploded its hydrogen[1] bomb at about 7 A.M., and while they were still celebrating their success, I was standing with a cluster of other officers and senior NCO's receiving the operation orders for the day. The temperature was already in the eighties and a thin fog hung over the muddy ground of our two battalions strong NDP – night defensive position. The meeting was probably conducted by Lieutenant Colonel Rufus Lazzell, the 1/16th battalion commander. His battalion was also referred to as the Rangers.

This new mission that we were about to embark on was a part of 1st Infantry Division's Operation Billings, which was conducted between June 12, and June 26, 1967, in War Zone D. The area of operation was about forty miles northeast of Saigon, between the villages of Quon Loi and Phuoc Vinh. Lieutenant Colonel Lazzell was given the operational control of our upcoming excursion. He would be in command of his battalion, the Rangers, and also the 2/28th, often referred to as the Black Lions. Basically, he was tasked with moving the Rangers and the Black Lions to LZ X-Ray, which would serve as the center of our new area of operations.

The new mission would consist of two battalions marching 2.4 kilometers into a landing zone, named LZ X-Ray. The LZ was a large clearing, the size of five or six football fields surrounded by a triple canopy jungle that was rumored to be a stronghold of numerous VC units.

Normally we would move from one location to another by use of aircraft, but this time, we were directed to march from our current NDP through the jungle to LZ

X-Ray. The reasons behind the odd order were rumored to be a lack of available helicopters, while others had heard that some general high up the chain of command thought that our two battalions could surreptitiously march to LZ X-Ray without the Viet Cong ever knowing we were coming.

We had little intelligence about the enemy we would soon face, but we did know that we were in the Viet Cong 9th Infantry Division's stomping ground. The 9th Infantry Division was made up of the 271st, 272nd, and 273rd Viet Cong regiments. They controlled much of this area. Their regiments had storied histories and consisted of seasoned soldiers who had fought side-by-side in numerous battles. Their cunning and ferocity during battle prompted Brigadier General James Shelton to praise them as "some of the best soldiers in the world."

There were also conflicting stories that the 271st Viet Cong Regiment had been annihilated during the battle of Ap Gu. In fact, even to this day, a Wikipedia article describes the 271st regiment as destroyed during the April 1st Ap Gu battle. A contributor to that article stated, "I remember that we had destroyed the 271 VC Regiment and that there were over 600 dead."[2] Unfortunately for our men, they weren't destroyed and would engage American forces in numerous more battles during 1967.

One other rumor of why we marched to LZ X-Ray instead of flying in was that Lieutenant Colonel Lazzell or higher-ups knew that Dan Rather's CBS News crew was interested in reporting on Operation Billings. "Either a

CBS or NBC news team goes on every patrol with us," Black Lions, Specialist Fourth Class Tom Waldron, of Charlotte, North Carolina wrote to his parents on June 21, 1967. The decision to hike through the jungle might simply have been a ruse to make our operation less tempting to news crews. Would they want to lug their equipment 2.4 kilometers through the jungle? Probably not. For us, they would have presented an additional responsibility, and you'd never know how they might portray the troops or the event. However, apparently there was the possibility that CBS might just end up covering some phase of our operation. If that happened, Major General Hay, 1st Infantry Division commander, would've wanted to ensure that the news report was positive and showed our troops as highly motivated, well trained professional soldiers. In the summer of 1967, it would have been critical for us to present the most positive impression possible to CBS's viewers because the war wasn't only fought in the jungle; we were also waging a public relations battle back home. Major General Hay would have taken precautions to ensure that any enemy resistance could be quickly eliminated. We were four companies strong which made an attack very unlikely, but just in case it would have been comforting to Major General Hay to have air, gunships, and artillery immediately available if needed.

The morning of June 17, 1967, was pretty much like any other morning for infantrymen in a Vietnam combat zone. Their DEROS dates were one-day closer, and they had lived through one more night. For me, it was two days before my wife Gayla's birthday, and I wondered if my last-minute birthday wishes would get to her by June 19. There wasn't much I could do about it.

Breaking camp and moving to a new location was at the top of the agenda for that rainy Saturday morning. Before that could happen, the four infantry companies involved in this operation—two companies of the Rangers 1/16th and two companies of the Black Lions 2/28th—would have to bring in the men manning their outposts on their perimeter. They would also have to attempt to return their part of the encampment area back to its original state. Our NDP, or night defensive position, had been christened with the name LZ Rufe, which was the nickname used for Lieutenant Colonel Rufus Lazzell, the commander of the Rangers 1/16th. His troops were often referred to as "Rufe's Rangers."

We had occupied LZ Rufe for three days, and during that time seven of our men had been killed. On June 14, the second day of our operation, six men were killed and sixteen wounded in a battle referred to as Xom Bo I.[3] We had also endured numerous VC mortar attacks resulting in more soldiers killed or wounded. In fact, the VC were firing 60 mm mortars at us both day and night, which was a new experience for me and probably most of the other men. Mortars were randomly exploding around us all day, which was very unnerving to say the least. It was more than harassment because men were killed and wounded in these attacks. In fact, the day prior to our march to LZ X-Ray, 19-year-old Private First Class John Edward

Camino, from Brownsville, PA of the Black Lions was killed during one of the mortar attacks.

Chapter 2
Our Night Defensive Position

Before we could leave LZ Rufe, a lot of cleanup work would have to be accomplished. All the fighting positions would have to be filled back in. The men would have to empty their sandbags, dumping the muddy dirt back into the holes they had lived in during the previous days. The LZ would have to be cleared of all debris that the VC could use against us. Batteries, tin cans, glassware, clothes, garbage, and anything else that was not coming along to our next position would be buried or burned.

In addition to all the cleanup work, everyone needed to assemble their gear for the hike to the new LZ. We would each be loaded down with ammo, rifle, flak jacket, fragmentation grenades, smoke grenades, and a rucksack. The rucksack contained a change of socks, underwear, toiletries, fatigues, secret snacks, and at least three or four boxes of C-rations. And don't forget toilet paper!

We also each carried a poncho that served as protection from the rain as we hunched over eating our C-rations and a thin bed at night to protect us from the mud and bugs as we tried to sleep. It would also be what our comrades would wrap us in, if we were killed to shield their eyes from our corpse.

We would also be carrying canteens full of water, water purification pills, a compass, bandages, and a gas mask. The mask was carried in a case strapped to the leg, along with one atropine syrette. The atropine syrette was meant to save us if the Viet Cong attacked us with chemical agents, like nerve gas. In reality, it was usually used to save men who had been bitten by the bamboo viper, also known as the many-banded krait. This snake was so poisonous that venom from one bite was enough to kill twenty grown men. We called it the one-and-a-half-step snake or two-step snake because if you were unable to use your atropine syrette by the time you took a couple steps, you were very likely on your way to being dead. Those claims might be a bit of an exaggeration, but the snake could kill a man if the atropine syrette was not used and appropriate medical help given.

Many of the men carried heavy bundles of empty sandbags that were sodden from muddy water. They would use these bags at the next NDP to help fortify their fighting positions. Everyone also brought a bottle of nasty yellowish colored bug juice that was supposed to keep us safe from ravishing mosquitoes. A good number of us also carried Bibles. The military would provide you one free if you asked. Medic Ray Gilbert was a soldier who carried one of the government issued Bibles around all the time. Between his medical knowledge and that of scripture, you had an excellent chance of recovery. The majority of the men also brought a few packs of cigarettes, and some I'm sure had a lid of Mary Jane stashed away in their rucksack.

Many men carried M1942 machetes to hack their way through the jungle. On this hike, many of the infantrymen would lug two 81mm mortar rounds for the mortar squad. They carried them in two sandbags draped over their shoulder. The mortars added another 6.5 pounds of gear to carry to the next LZ. Just about everyone carried an M7 bayonet in their M8A1 scabbard, which was another 1.4 pounds. Finally, add another two pounds for all of those who carried the M1943 foldable entrenching tool.

Most riflemen carried two ammo belts of a hundred M60 rounds, worn Pancho Villa style adding another 14 pounds to their load. If they hadn't yet collapsed to the ground from the weight, then a couple M18 claymore mines, 3.5 pounds each, and trip flares were added to their load.

My extra gear consisted of an M16 rifle and ammo, in addition to my standard-issue .45 caliber pistol. I also carried my area terrain maps, code translation book, binoculars, and a flashlight with a filter lens.

Chapter 3
The Job of Forward Observer

God fights on the side with the best artillery.
– Napoleon

I wasn't an infantry soldier, but an artillery officer, assigned as a forward observer to Alpha Company 2nd of the 28th, known affectionately as the Black Lions. Lieutenant Colonel Jerry S. Edwards was the Black Lions battalion commander.

Most of the guys called me Dungeon Niner-Seven, which was my call sign and contained the ubiquitous niner designation that was coveted in the artillery jargon. My parent unit was Battery C of the 2/33rd artillery, a 105 mm howitzer battery located in a fire base five or six miles away at Chi Linh Special Forces Camp.

As a forward observer (FO) I served as the eyes and ears of my artillery battery. I was part of a three-man artillery team that consisted of a radio telephone operator (RTO), a sergeant, and me, First Lieutenant Hearne. Our job was to provide artillery support to the 2/28th Black Lions Alpha Company, commanded by Captain Donald Sawtelle, a 1961 West Point graduate who had already spent about eight months in the field.

The six 105 mm howitzers that made up Charlie Battery of the 2/33rd artillery would be at Alpha Company's disposal whenever Captain Sawtelle needed them. My job was to make that a reality. As the saying goes, "The infantry claims to be the queen of battle. The artillery is the king of battle, and the king always puts the balls where the queen wants them."

Being a forward observer was dangerous and one of the most challenging positions on the battlefield for a variety of reasons. A forward observer had to be highly skilled and exceptionally intelligent. We had to foster skills in reconnaissance and have the ability to think quickly under extreme stress. Our missions were always critical, and any errors made under stress could bring massive firepower smashing down on friendly forces instead of the enemy. It overwhelmed me sometimes that I had been given such tremendous power. I could flatten an entire village with my artillery or wipe out hundreds of men. If I called in a fire mission, I could obliterate trees, buildings, animals, and men. I could blow them to pieces so badly that you wouldn't be able to recognize what was left; body parts mixed with branches and entrails of dead animals, tossed together with tons of dirt and mud until it was a massive ocean of debris; a piece of a skull, a hand, a rifle melted down to just the barrel, burnt tree limbs, armies of ants looking at their new landscape and all their new food, a leg bone, dead monkeys, swarms of flies, and blacken stumps of trees that once stood proud and tall in the battle field. I could set a village ablaze with white phosphorus. I could burst rounds high in the air above the enemy and shower them with deadly shrapnel, or I could pound a forested area so long with high explosive rounds that it turned into a shrapnel-infused plowed field.

I needed to deliver this power in battle to uphold the words of men like Stalin, who said, "Artillery is the God of War," or as General George S. Patton quipped, "I do not have to tell you who won the war. You know, the artillery."

I was twenty-four, and I had this onerous power to kill and grotesquely wound huge numbers of men without seeing the blood and gore I caused. As they say, artillery is king on the battlefield and I was one of the men who could unleash the King on the enemy.

Being an FO in Vietnam was not a desk job. In fact, a forward observer had to be able to work for extended periods of time under constant pressure, as battles often lasted many hours or days. I humped the jungle with the infantry on all of Alpha Company's operations. My team participated in the same firefights and endured mortar attacks, booby-traps, and we'd shit in the woods, just like the regular grunts. Our job was grim, not solely because of the difficulty in performing it, but also the weight of knowing we had one of the shortest life expectancies of any category of soldiers in Vietnam. We were a coveted kill for the VC. If a forward observer was spotted by the enemy, his life expectancy was about fifteen seconds. We weren't alone: the same was true for snipers, scouts, and machine gunners. If Charlie saw any one of us, we would become their target practice.

I was a 6'4" target who was typically holding a radio handset to my face as I ran tethered to my RTO, who carried a PRC-25 radio on his back. His radio, with its waving antenna, told the enemy that we were prime targets. Worse yet was the fact that we usually moved in tandem with the company commander, Captain Sawtelle, who also held a handset to his face and was also attached to a radio riding on another man's back.

Chapter 4
Breakfast at LZ Rufe

On the morning of June 17, the men grabbed a breakfast of C-rations, some of them heating breakfast over a slice of C4 explosive. We didn't have sterno, but C4 was a great substitute in the field. If a soldier was lucky, he might have scored a C-ration of ham and eggs or beanie weenies. My breakfast often consisted of beanie weenies drowned in Tabasco sauce accompanied by a can of peaches or fruit salad. I actually got used to C-rations and didn't find them as bad as many people make them out to be.

Breakfast was also time to light up if you had them. Smoking was prevalent during the Vietnam War. Probably 75 percent of the men smoked. In fact, the government actually included little packs of cigarettes in our C-Rations. They were miniature packs of the real thing. There were brands like Marlboros, Salem, Camel, Lucky Strike, Newport, Winston, Pall Mall, Chesterfield, Kent and maybe some others. Everybody was trading with others for their brands and guys like me who did not smoke could trade my allotment for cans of fruit. If you look at combat pictures of men in Vietnam, you will invariably see a cigarette dangling out of their mouth.

Some days we actually got something closer to real food flown in on our re-supply choppers or sometimes our company's cooks would scramble up some eggs and fry a little bacon right out in the field. They would bring to the field these big containers of what was called coffee. However, it was so strong it could have been used instead, as a chemical weapon. Twenty-one-year-old Felix Vallejo of Austin, Texas remembers his friend Sergeant Bobby Minton of Elizabeth, Indiana was one of the men who brought out the hot meals, but on Operation Billings, Minton had been assigned as a rifleman.

The re-supply choppers would bring in other niceties such as large blocks of ice for our soda pop and beer, mail from home, and in the evening chopper runs, they would often deliver freshly cooked dinners in large thermos containers.

Breakfast on the morning of June 17, however, consisted solely of shitty coffee, c-rations, and a few smokes. For some, this simple meal would be their last.

Chapter 5
Monterey Pop Festival

While we were preparing for our excursion to LZ X-Ray, thousands of people my age back in the world were gathering for the Monterey Pop Festival in Monterey, California. It was Saturday morning in Vietnam, but back in California, seven thousand four hundred miles away it was still Friday night.

It was a cool gray Friday evening when the three day Monterey Pop Festival kicked off with the folk rock group called The Association. Their opening song was a ballad titled "Enter the Young" proclaiming how the young were about to change things. It was a little pretentious, but it captured the feelings of the youth in 1967. We were going to make changes to the world.

The song was written by Terry Kirkman, one of the stanzas goes like this:

Here they come
And some are doing, some are trying
Some are selling, some are buying
Some are living, some are dying

Some are living. Some are dying. Those words certainly rang true for us. While thousands of our peers experienced one of our generation's quintessential happenings under a haze of pot smoke, we were experiencing the "some are dying" line in the sweltering jungle as a steamy mist floated about us. In the last few days of operation Billings we had sustained at least seven young men killed and twenty or more wounded.

Two major events would take place in the next few hours whose differences were as great as their geographical distance between them. On one side of the big pond, thousands of concert goers would experience a historical festival of rock and roll giants while back in Vietnam we would soon live through an epic event of kill or be killed. The differences were of such magnitude that neither group could truly comprehend the experiences of their counterparts. These vast differences in life experiences were a major part of the huge societal disconnection for the returning Vets. Our former classmates back in the states were living the Summer of Love and experiencing new lifestyles, religions, sexual freedom, music, fashions, drugs and more. In fact, the Monterey Pop Festival concert's banner proclaimed "Love, flowers, and music," which said it all. The changes were so great that upon our return it was like some alien world we had entered.

A few hundred miles north of the Monterey Pop Festival in the City by the Bay was the true epicenter of the Summer of Love. There in San Francisco's Haight-Ashbury district thousands of hippies, dropouts, visionaries, musicians, followers and the curious were attempting to create a new utopia. Visitors to the Haight-Ashbury were greeted by young women with flowers in their hair, guys with a joint to share, and the constant sound of music everywhere. It was truly a unique time.

The music of 1967 evolved along with the times. Most of the top songs of 1967 prior to June 17 were beautiful inspiring music with a focus on love and fun, but by the Summer of Love new groups were hitting the scene with lyrics that spoke of the unrest, war, and racial divide. Songs that were previously too contemptuous, too controversial were now mainstream, songs like *I Feel Like I'm Going To Die Rag* by Country Joe and the Fish.

That summer the Haight-Ashbury's fame reached its peak as it became a haven for top psychedelic rock performers and groups. Acts like Jefferson Airplane, The Grateful Dead, and Janis Joplin all lived a short distance from its epicenter. They were a big element in immortalizing the Haight-Ashbury scene in song.

Another well-known neighborhood presence at that time was The Diggers. They were a local "community anarchist" group known for its street theater and its free food and free health care program that they provided to the Haight-Ashbury's residents. They also would become a major part of the anti-war movement.

Chapter 6
Leaving LZ Rufe

June 17 would not be a day of love, flowers, and music for our men. Even though our temporary base camp LZ Rufe provided us a sense of relative safety, its accommodations were more primitive than that of Montagnards, a primitive tribe living in the Vietnamese highlands. It was muddy and as Private First Class Douglas Ikerd who was new in country, aptly recalled it as that LZ that was "Simply one big mud hole." Specialist Fourth Class Thomas Waldron with Bravo Company of the Black Lions told his parents in a letter that, "it was the worst jungle I've seen. It's an old jungle with what is called triple canopy. Many trees tower 100 ft. high also much bamboo as tall as 60 ft." Waldon was right, and it was very hard to move through the dense jungle.

The preceding night I had attempted to sleep lying on the muddy ground wrapped in my poncho. June 17th fell within South Vietnam's wet season, and we were constantly drenched in rain. It was hard to stay warm at night in the jungle when the ground was soaked with water. If you tried to dig a foxhole, it would quickly fill with water, and you would end up sitting in a pool of muddy water.

Our II field force commander, General Bruce Palmer Jr., knew that his adversary General Thanh of the Viet Cong 9th Infantry Division would take full advantage of the rain and mud of the southwest monsoon season to hedge their offensive plans in War Zone D and C.[4] Rain often interfered with the efficient use of air and artillery power, leveling the playing field a bit for the combatants in the big unit battles.

The other issue was that LZ Rufe was very hard for the men to dig in: it was full of roots and thick clay type earth making digging terribly time consuming.

After we were loaded up and had cleaned up the site, the men in each company had to wait around for their turn to exit our NDP and start marching through the wet jungle to our next location, LZ X-Ray.

The first company to leave LZ Rufe was the Rangers 1/16th Alpha Company commanded by Captain Bill Williamson, a 1961 West Point graduate. Behind him came part of the Rangers headquarters company, including Battalion Commander Lieutenant Colonel Lazzell and his entourage. Next came the Rangers 1/16th Bravo Company, led by Captain Donald S. Ulm from Seattle. Finally, the Rangers recon platoon left LZ X-Ray and quickly disappeared into the Jungle. The recon platoon was commanded by First Lieutenant Douglas Logan.

As the Rangers Alpha Company marched out of LZ Rufe, First Lieutenant Richard Dalton from Dalton, Wisconsin, started blocking fires East of the company's route of march. Dalton had been in country for about eleven months and was an experienced artillery forward observer from Bravo Battery 2/33rd. Although we were both from the same artillery battalion, we had never met. Similar to my own history, Richard had first been an enlisted man before he received his commission. In 1965, Dalton went to Officer Candidate School (OCS) at Fort Sill, Oklahoma, and graduated with the class of 11-65. The following July of 1966, he was off to Vietnam. Interestingly, his hometown of Dalton, Wisconsin was named after his great grandparents, John and Jeanette Dalton back in 1911. It's now a small hamlet of 200 in the midst of the growing Amish community of Wisconsin.

While the Rangers marched toward the new LZ, Captain John Turner's Bravo Company of the 2/28th, Black Lions also set out. Our company, Alpha, would stay put until Bravo Company arrived at the new destination. Luckily, the commanders of all these units were experienced, level-headed officers. Captain William R. Williamson was a West Point graduate who had served as a platoon leader with the 82nd Airborne Division and for the past eight months as the Rangers' Alpha Company commander. He had seen action in numerous battles. Captain Ulm was a seasoned company commander who had fought in the battle of Prek Klok and received a Silver Star for his part in that action. On June 14, 1967, Captain Ulm and his company had fought a pitched battle with elements of the PAVN 271st Regiment that cost him six men killed and sixteen wounded. The story of the battle appeared on page six of the June 17, 1967, issue of *Stars and Stripes* newspaper under the headline, "Operation Billings—GIs Kill 68 Reds." The article claimed that sixty VC were killed in the fight. It read, "U.S. losses Wednesday were six killed and twelve wounded. Total U.S. Losses were so far seven killed and twenty wounded." I am not sure where the number sixty-eight came from in the headline.

Captain Turner of the Black Lions Bravo Company was also a seasoned company commander who had been in-country for almost a year. My company commander, Captain Sawtelle, was a West Point graduate and had graduated from the same class as his good friend Captain William Williamson. Captain Sawtelle had his baptism under fire his very first night at our base camp in Lai Khe. His hooch had been hit by a VC mortar round, blowing him out of his bed and virtually deafening him for the next few days. Luckily, he was hit only by the blast and not by shrapnel or other flying debris.

Marching along with the Rangers' Headquarter element was AP correspondent and photographer Henri Huet and his assistant, according to Specialist Fourth Class John Phil Vessello, an RTO for the 2/33rd artillery liaison officer assigned to the Rangers.

The morning was full of steaming mist that kept our fatigues from drying and added to the misery of humping through the jungle. When we had down time, many of us occupied ourselves with letters from home. Letters from home were better than gold as far as we were concerned; they were so important to keeping up our morale. It was our connection to the real world. The army made it simple for us to mail home. We didn't have to buy a stamp for the envelope, all we had to do was write "free" on it, and it would get delivered back home. The ability to send mail home for free was one of our best perks. Pay wasn't great, but for a first lieutenant with three years of service, I received $532.80 base pay, combat pay of $65, and a separation allowance of $30. I also received a $120 housing allowance. That came to a total of $747.80. In 1967, the average monthly earnings back in the States were $608.33, or $7,300 annually. So I was earning more than the average pay while I was in Vietnam.

My wife, Gayla, was very frugal, probably as a result of growing up as an army brat. She was used to the meager wages soldiers were paid and had seen her mother exist by making the dollar stretch by buying from the commissary, Post Exchange and not being caught up needing to buy brand name products.

To put my pay into perspective, in 1967, you could score a White Castle hamburger for 14 cents, a 2 cents increase from 1966. If you wanted to go out to dinner, and lived in Berkeley, California, you could eat at Oscar's, and for a mere dollar, you could buy a double-decker hamburger with French fries, salad, and a dessert of ice cream. For only thirty cents more, you could get a complete fried chicken or shrimp dinner (also with fries and salad). Pie was only thirty-five cents a slice, an ice-cream sundae was forty cents, and coffee or a soft drink cost a dime. If you wanted to grab a quick bite at a lunch counter, you could get a hot dog and a Coke for forty-nine cents. Like so many institutions of what was once a part of the sixties, Oscar's closed in May 2015.

You could buy a loaf of bread for twenty-five cents, a three-course Morton's TV dinner was only fifty-nine cents, and hippies could buy an ounce of grass for a mere ten dollars.

Most PFCs in Vietnam had less than two years of service, which qualified them for a base pay of $128.70 per month, plus combat pay of $65, separation pay of $30, and a housing allowance of $60. Their pay totaled $283.70. Somehow soldiers and their families survived financially.

Chapter 7
Communicating with Home

My wife, Gayla, was very aware of how important mail was to a combat soldier and wrote to me every day...well, almost every day. When the choppers came in with the mail, I would often receive a handful of her letters and packages. Many of them contained pictures of her, which I inserted into my collage of pictures of Gayla on the back of my map case. She was a striking petite woman who resembled Natalie Wood. In June, she was six months pregnant with our son, Scott Hearne. She would spray her letters with perfume, and that extra touch made them even more precious. Most soldiers took a few of their letters with them into combat—including me. I stuffed a few of mine into my helmet liner.

I probably read each of her letters ten times or more, always looking for some new nugget or meaning and loving her promises of love for evermore. Captain Sawtelle considered his love letters from his wife Jo—with news of his first child, Stacy—the highlight of each of his days in Nam. Letters were our primary connection to the world we left behind.

For many the letters became a type of a diary of what went on in Vietnam. The many letters Specialist Fourth Class Wes Canute sent home to his sweetheart, Sue, were squirreled away as treasured mementos of their relationship before they were married. Now a half a century later they tell the story of what Wes endured back in 1967 as a 1st Infantry Division soldier.

As uplifting as these letters from home could be, they could be just the opposite if they happened to be the dreaded, caustic "Dear John" letter. The most devastating communication a soldier could receive was a "Dear John" letter. They were even worse than a notification of a loved one's death. The "Dear John" letter meant you had been betrayed and your loved one, nine thousand miles away, had deserted you while you were sleeping in mud. Many a man committed suicide after receiving one or did some insane heroic act in a battle that would lead to his death, hoping it would fill his lover with guilt for eternity.

The one way most of us communicated with family back home was by mail. There wasn't any internet, or face time, and virtually no phones. During the Vietnam War, there weren't any landlines or cellular telephones, so calling back home to your family or your loved one was near impossible. The army did have the MARS (Military Affiliate Radio Service) stations. The MARS system used "phone-patch" telephone connections over short-wave radio. In the majority of cases, MARS was the only way soldiers could call home. Occasionally someone would get lucky and get a chance to call home, but in 1967 that was an expensive luxury.

About two weeks before our excursion into LZ X-Ray, one of the young men who fought in our battle took advantage of Lai Khe's MARS station. Private First Class Edward Smith of Newport, Kentucky, called his twin sister, Karen, reaching her in the middle of the night. His call that evening was a total surprise. The sound was terrible, but she could make out what he was saying. He was excited that his R&R was coming up. He had been in-country since February 8, and his unit, Rangers Bravo Company, was scheduling him for an R&R. Edward told Karen it would be nice if their mother could loan him some money for his vacation away from the war. The staticky call lasted only a few minutes, but it was important because it would be the last time anyone in Edward's family would ever hear his voice.

Some soldiers used small reel-to-reel tapes to make recordings to send home. First Lieutenant Douglas Logan, leader of the Ranger's recon platoon, sent his wife, Sharon, cassette tapes expressing how his life and the war was going. He also commented on how upset he was about the protests that were happening across America while he was doing his country's calling. Doug found it exasperating and discouraging that huge groups of protestors were actually taking out their dislike for the war on returning military men. It was demoralizing.[5]

Another member of the Ranger's recon platoon, Private First Class Wallace Nye, also availed himself of the new technology and made tapes for his loved ones. He found it was a great way to correspond with the folks back home. His sweetheart, Gail would be the recipient of some of his tapes. In a recording made while he was in Lai Khe, you can hear artillery going off sporadically in the background as he talks about his life in Vietnam. One interesting tape had him telling Gail about the confusing world of military jargon and acronyms:

He was explaining to her what FO, RTO, MFO and an FO RTOs meant.

I have never seen so many letter stuff in my life.

Like some guy who was going out with us.

Of course that sounds a little weird too.

When we go out on patrols we bring an artillery guy with us who calls in artillery if we need it. See?

Well, he is called a forward observer or FO. Because he is for the artillery, he is an AFO, and if he was a forward observer for mortars he would be an MFO.

Well, this guy was standing there with a radio on his back who is the AFO's RTO, because a radio operator is a RTO.

Well, I asked our sergeant who he was and he said he was the AFO's RTO.

Just about sat down and cried. I don't know what these people are talking about.

News from home sometimes came by way of the Red Cross. They didn't contact you unless it was very important news, something very bad or something very good. Captain Sawtelle was one of those men who experienced the unnerving circumstance of receiving a notification from the Red Cross two weeks after arriving in Vietnam. Sawtelle was in the Tactical Operation Center (TOC) for the Black Lions in Lai Khe when a man from the Red Cross came banging on the locked command center's entrance door. At that moment, Captain Sawtelle was on the radio with Danger 77, who was Major General William F. Depuy, commander of the Big Red One. Sawtelle was giving Depuy the Black Lions' situation report.

The knocking at his door from the Red Cross Representative was unsettling and a bit ominous. When he heard the knock, he gave Major General Depuy a "Wait Out," which is military parlance for, "Hey, got to put you on hold while I take care of something MORE IMPORTANT." Captain Sawtelle then ran to the locked door, asked the man from the Red Cross what was so important, and learned that he was now a father of a baby girl named Stacy. Sawtelle quickly returned to the radio and reconnected with the General to complete his report. Later that evening, 3rd Brigade Commander, Colonel Sidney M. Marks, counseled Don Sawtelle on the hazards of giving a Major General a "Wait Out." The protocol faux pas proved to be a non-event, however, and soon after that Captain Sawtelle was given command of the Black Lions Alpha Company.

Chapter 8
Who Fought in the Vietnam War

On the date of the Xom Bo battle, I was already twenty-four years old, an old man compared to most of the troops. In fact, the Vietnam War of 1967 was fought by an American military force with an average age of twenty, according to most historical sources. Sixty percent of the men killed in Vietnam were between seventeen and twenty-one, a total of 35,198 men.

One out of every four men killed in Vietnam was age twenty, making it the most dangerous age for an American soldier. In all, 14,095 men aged twenty paid the ultimate price. It was ironic that so many of our armed forces consisted of men too young to vote or even legally drink, yet they were old enough to be conscripted to fight in a war with an enemy who had no way of even reaching our shores.

It was not until 1971 that the federal voting age was dropped to eighteen years old. The change came about in response to the strong movement whose common slogan "Old enough to fight, old enough to vote" finally convinced Congress to lower the age.

President Johnson, who succeeded President Kennedy after his assassination, increased the number of combat soldiers in Vietnam from a low of 16,000 to around 500,000 troops by 1967. As more soldiers poured into Vietnam, our casualties count soared. The count of Killed in Action went from 122 in 1963, Johnson's first year in office, to a high of 11,363 in 1967; an average of 31 men killed each day. In 1968, the deadliest year of the war 16,899 men were killed which averaged 46 Americans slain by Viet Cong per day.

The men in our units came from all walks of life. Private First Class Gary Joseph Ernst was a 20-year-old young man who came from the farming community of Perryville, Missouri. Mel Hennemann, a high school classmate of Gary's, said they graduated from Perry High in May of 1966 and Gary joined the service shortly thereafter. Hennemann described Gary's hometown as a uniquely predominate German Catholic or German Lutheran part of Missouri. Lingering German accents can still be heard there. The county is dotted with small German bergs. It's a beautiful area of well-tended farms on what some call the Ozark Plateau of rolling hills, dairy, corn, and soybeans.

Private First Class Ronald D. Edenfield was a teenager of 19 when he entered LZ X-Ray. He was from Grand Ridge, Florida, a tiny town of about 450 citizens. It took up all of 2.5 square miles of Florida land but had its own post office and its own zip code of 32442.

The smallness of Private First Class Edenfield hometown makes my hometown of Charlestown, New

Hampshire look huge in comparison. Charlestown was over 15 times as large. It was one of those picturesque New England towns with a real main street lined with stores, churches, monuments and frequented by people who knew everything about their neighbor. It was a wonderful place to grow up in. It had a population of about 2,700, and sent more than its fair share of men to the Vietnam War. Just my high school class of 1962 probably had half of our males signing up or being drafted. My classmate and friend Calvin Fisk, brother of Major League baseball player Carlton Fisk, got his invitation from Uncle Sam about the same time Operation Billings started. Calvin had just been drafted by the Baltimore Orioles and had started spring training in Florida when he received a draft notice that would send him to Vietnam. When First Lieutenant Calvin Fisk returned back to the states after serving with the 25th Infantry as an S1, he was considered too old to play professional baseball.

Our town also lost one man to the war. Twenty-year-old Private First Class David Gardner, who had lived a half a mile from my home, had been in country less than three months when he was killed by a booby trap. The tragedy occurred during an operation in Dinh Tuong Province with the 2/39th. His death happened just two weeks before Christmas. Along with him, fifty-one other Americans perished that day in Vietnam casting a pall on the holidays for many families. The horrible news of his death reached his wife, Linda, and David's parents Leona and Ernest Gardner two days later. David was awarded posthumously a Purple Heart and a Bronze Star with a "V" for valor. He also earned another Bronze Star for Merit.

We, of course, had a lot of guys from the big cities fighting in the battle of Xom Bo II. They came from cities like Houston, New York, Seattle, San Francisco, Chicago and more.

One man, Specialist Fourth Class Carl T. Johnson of Houston, Texas, proved city boys were just as manly as country boys. He was one of those young guys who would demonstrate his bravery, toughness and his willingness to do anything to help his comrades survive.

Even President Johnson's two son-in-laws served tours in Vietnam. Marine Captain Charles Robb served two tours as a company commander with the 1st Marine Division and Patrick Nugent an Airman First Class served a tour. In short, the men who fought in the Vietnam War came from all walks of life.

Joining the army and doing a tour in that far off land of Vietnam had become almost part of the youth culture by 1967. Jan Fredrickson, who had dated and fallen in love with Private First Class Douglas Dewey Wallin of Rochester, Minnesota recalled how she and her friends viewed their boyfriends being drafted.

"A friend off to the DRAFT, was something that all the guys did, and then they came back, and I really didn't think anything about it being a danger, but just a time away, of missing someone. Life went on as usual. Maybe that's the reality of most everyone, of those days. Little did we know the severity of the stint over there, until it hit home, and then it hit. I think everyone I know, now—

can tell about a friend, relative, or someone they knew in the neighborhood, that was killed in Vietnam. It became 'normal'—but not when it hit close, it was a sledge hammer to the heart that never left."

Chapter 9
Operation Orders

Early Saturday morning on June 17, we would have had a meeting about our day's objectives, but I have to admit that I have no recollection of the meeting or the overall plan. I am positive we would've made sure that all of us were in agreement on the day's secret challenge word and response word. We also would have made sure we all were using the right radio frequencies and encryption codes for the day. The frequencies changed day to day, along with the encryption code. Often in these strategy meetings we were presented with more current terrain maps. We didn't have GPS back then, so an accurate map was critical. From the effects of our Agent Orange defoliation, or the tremendous speed at which the jungle retook clearings and deserted villages, it was often difficult to find yourself on some of the older maps. Regardless, reading the map and knowing where you and your friendlies were located was paramount in staying alive.

The overall command of the operation was given to Lieutenant Colonel Rufus Lazzell. He was the commander of the Rangers and had been their commander during the July 9, 1966 battle of Minh Thanh Road, where he had been wounded and sent back to the States to recuperate. Luckily doctors at Walter Reed Hospital were able to put his damaged elbow back together so he could use the wounded arm. Lieutenant Colonel Lazzell returned to Vietnam in November 1966, and Major General Depuy gave him command of the Rangers again.[6] Operations Billings would be his last offensive before his DEROS, or return back to the States. In other words, Lieutenant Colonel Lazzell was a very short-timer during Operation Billings.

Our unit, Alpha Company, was slated to move out of NDP Rufe last and march to LZ X-Ray. Although I don't recall this either, I'm sure I would've drawn up some plans for walking fires and got an okay from Captain Sawtelle.

Chapter 10
Our March Begins

About 10:30 A.M. we got the word that Black Lions Alpha Company was to saddle up and move out. That meant I would need to start up my walking fires. "Walking fires" was the practice of shooting artillery parallel to or in front of our path of march. We hoped the fire would harass or frighten off any VC lurking along our route to LZ X-Ray. It also provided a quick reference for me to rapidly employ blocking fires or close-in contact fires if needed.

Before we left our NDP, it was always prudent to take a nervous piss or answer nature's call because there wouldn't be any bathroom breaks along the way on this type of outing. When loaded down with all our equipment, it was an onerous and even frightening task to relieve oneself. Anyone under fire with a full bladder found it very difficult to concentrate on their job. Believe me, when anxiety is high, it's a true blessing to have an empty bladder.

The platoon leaders lined up their men and our hike through the woods began. It was stifling hot by the time we started. The temperature was somewhere in the high nineties, and the high humidity made it seem like over a 100°F. We were also receiving scattered showers that cooled you one moment and then virtually turned to steam the next. Our march through the jungle would be a single file, behind the point man. To me, the point man's job was more dangerous than any other job in the company. He was the eyes and ears of the column. He was also the most likely to be the first soldier killed during the march to LZ X-Ray. My job was supposed to be dangerous, but I felt like his job as point man trumped mine. The one good thing about the job of point man was that you didn't have to do it day after day.

A few lines from Gary Jacobson's "Dawn Patrol" illustrates the danger the point man faced.

> Do you want to walk the point
> Way out front of all those other jerks.
> Think of all the perks...
> You get to be the first
> To see where the Vietcong lurks
> You get to be up where the action is!
> See firsthand
> Where the bullet with your name on it is!
> Just pray Charley doesn't see you first...
> Might ruin your whole day
> With an AK-47 burst...
> That would take all the fun out of this little
> fray
> This Vietnam passion play

That we offer our lives for…
That we pound the jungle floor for,
Sicken our very souls for…
But what ya gonna do,
You don't want to live forever, do you?

Chapter 11
A Hike in the Jungle

I had over five months in-country, mostly in the jungle. I had learned a lot about survival in this God-forsaken land. I knew that the small things that some men took for granted were the kinds of things that could keep me breathing one more day. The most important thing was for me to take care of my job and watch out for my men, because their lives and mine intertwined, and survival depended on us fighting together as one.

We all marched along wordlessly single file, probably ten feet apart. And as we marched we listened intently for any unusual noise. The jungle was dark green, wet from rain. Droplets of water dripped from branches as we passed under. There were strange vines dangling from high branches, and thick clumps of shrubs flourished all along our path. Strange dark moss grew on the sides of trees, and patches of ferns stretched up to seek rays of sun.

As we marched along, we would occasionally hear birds bickering high up in the trees. The chatter of monkeys often floated down to our ears. At least we thought it was the sound of monkeys. Monkeys were common in Vietnam; we even had them in our base camp as pets. Then there were the tokay geckos, or as we called them the "fuck-you lizards." This little creature made strange noises that sounded like he was saying, "Fuck you." Some thought it sounded more like "Fa choo." It was just another of the sounds you filed away in your head as normal ambient noise. Then, of course, there was the constant crunch of twigs and leaves underfoot, produced by hundreds of boots.

Leaving the security of the LZ was nerve wracking. For the new guys, the twinks, the cherry boys, they probably could hear their hearts beating like drums in their heads. Guys who had been in-country and seen action before were hoping and praying this would be a waste of time. They knew that once we were outside the LZ's perimeter, we were in the Viet Cong's back yard. They would be watching us leave the LZ, probably counting the men in the column, taking note of our weapons. But we wouldn't see them.

Some of our guys with strong religious beliefs felt a bit more secure in the jungle than others. They were confident that God would remove them from harm's way. One of those was Arturo Garcia, a devout Catholic. His mother had sent him three rosaries to wear around his neck to keep him safe and ward off evil. Arturo gave one of those rosaries to his friend, Wes Canute, who wasn't Catholic, but that wasn't going to stop Wes from wearing such a strong talisman. As Arturo and Wes marched into the jungle on June 17, they both were wearing their rosary beads.

Arturo got through the battle of Xom Bo II safely, and so did Wes, except for some minor wounds. Were the rosary beads responsible for their good fortune? Hard to say. Those of us who had strong religious beliefs felt that each day we survived was a sign of God's grace, and each passing day reaffirmed and strengthened that conviction.

On October 17, 1967, Arturo Garcia would march into the Battle of Ong Thanh, but his luck would run out, and he would be killed along with sixty-three other men.

Chapter 12
Booby Traps

Through all this foliage, our eyes constantly searched for trip wires or prongs sticking out of the ground. Each of us tried to follow in the steps of the man we followed. If he didn't suddenly explode, we could assume that where he stepped was a safe spot for our foot.

The jungle was full of terrible death traps waiting for an unsuspecting soldier. In a previous mission, we were searching an idyllic looking orchard when one of our men heard the frightful click of a Bouncing Betty mine being activated under the weight of his foot. He heard the click and froze on the spot and started screaming in terror for help. If he removed his foot or even shifted his weight, the Bouncing Betty would launch out of the ground and explode at hip level. It would blow off his legs and rip open his torso, spilling his intestines and pulverizing his manhood. If he wasn't instantly killed, he was destined to live a life as a paraplegic or worse.

War is terribly callous, and in this particular instance, the bulk of my unit moved on, leaving a medic and a small contingent to try to save the soldier or call a medevac to rush him and his body parts to the nearest Aid Station. That was about the only choice we had. I never heard if they figured out a way to save him, but I did hear an explosion just a few minutes after we moved out of the area.

The VC were experts at creating booby traps. They knew that death or injury by a booby trap had a long-lasting psychological impact on soldiers. Some of their barbaric booby traps consisted of things like punji stakes, bear traps, crossbow traps, spiked mud balls, double-spike caltrops, scorpion-filled boxes, and the use of deadly viper snakes.

When you were stomping through the jungle, you had to be aware of all those dangers. A bullet from a VC was not the only way you might die, but it was probably the preferred way if the shit hit the fan. In fact, a bullet or hunk of shrapnel tearing through a soldier's head or heart would kill so fast that he would never know he had been hit.

High caliber bullets create "vicious flesh destruction...shatters ribs and blows bone fragments into lung tissue." A well-placed bullet tearing into the body would usually result in instant death.

But on these hikes through the jungle, you might just as easily find a green viper snake lashing out at your face as you brushed past some shrubs. The VC would tie green viper snakes to low-hanging branches or vines they knew would be in our path. The snake, already agitated by its predicament, would lash out at any living thing that came within its reach. Its bite would cause tremendous swelling and rotting of flesh. If the soldier was to live, medical care was needed promptly.

Sergeant Richard Ancira with the Rangers Bravo Company was one of the unfortunate ones who had the bad luck of being impaled by punji stakes. During a search and destroy mission on April 1, 1967, nineteen-year-old Ancira of Austin, Texas was serving as his squad's point man. He was cautiously moving down a trail looking for any signs of VC, when all of a sudden the earth gave out beneath him. It happened so fast that he couldn't stop from falling. What he had fallen into was a hole that was studded with bamboo punji stakes. One on the punji stakes tore into his left leg between his ankle and knee. It tore into the calf and he was trapped. Luckily his comrades were right there and immediately grabbed him preventing him from falling over onto the other punji stakes. They lifted him off of the stake and medevacked him to a nearby MASH unit. Richard had been in country only about four months, but had already earned two purple hearts. After a few weeks of healing, he was released back to active duty.

The fear of booby traps was a constant threat that added to the mental fatigue of combat. If a soldier had the misfortune of seeing one of these medieval instruments of death like a spiked mud ball slamming into an unsuspecting comrade, impaling him, lifting him off his feet, and trapping him like an animal; it would haunt him forever. The bamboo spikes would punch all the way through the body, often puncturing the lungs, intestines, face, and neck. Removing an impaled soldier from the bamboo spikes was excruciatingly painful. Its horrendous wounds were often fatal. This type of weapon was dreaded by the men and unnerved many. Booby traps were an enemy you could not strike back at. The feeling of impotence was infuriating, and these objects of death were everywhere.

Chapter 13
Environmental Hazards

Booby traps and VC weren't the only enemies...there was also the constant heat and moisture. Many men carrying sixty pounds or more in one-hundred-degree heat could succumb to heat exhaustion or worse yet suffer heat stroke. Because of the water we traipsed through daily, along with the wet socks and boots we sometimes wore for days, terrible foot infections became another enemy. The problem was so bad that sometime parts of a foot would have to be amputated. The infections could develop into trench foot or immersion foot, with symptoms so serious that when an afflicted soldier tried to remove a sock, a strip of skin and a layer of flesh would often tear away from the foot. The skin between the toes would turn to mush and become open, oozing lesions. The foot would emit a sickly smell. Leg cramps, pain, and swelling of the foot would usually accompany the infection. As foot soldiers, immersion foot was a serious condition to contend with. It made tromping through the jungle, rice fields and swamps very difficult or impossible for any afflicted soldier.

As the condition worsened, open sores led to fungal infections, then to jungle rot or tropical ulcers, and eventually gangrene that required the amputation of toes, the heel, or other parts of the foot—and sometimes the removal of an entire foot.

In the company I was assigned to, Alpha of the Black Lions, we had our share of men suffering from immersion foot. One of them was Specialist Fourth Class Wes Canute whose infection was so severe that he almost lost a toe, but the doctors were eventually able to save it. However, the condition ended his time in the jungle, but not before the battle of Xom Bo II.

Trench foot wasn't the only health issue that we had to worry about; actually, there was a huge list of nasty health issues that could quickly reduce a soldier's combat effectiveness. The multitude of parasites that loved to live inside of us included pinworms, round worms, tapeworms, and more. The Cryptostrongylus Pulmoni, or lungworm, was a nasty little worm that according to some accounts, hooked a ride to Vietnam from Australia via some soldier's intestines and found Vietnam very welcoming. The worm would enter the body through food touched by an infected person and then begin to explore. It would travel from mouth to ass, take a hike up to the lungs, and then back again to the intestines. These worms would reconnoiter the body just like we did the jungles of Vietnam.

Probably half of the men in our column had a pound or more of these parasites wiggling around inside of them. While we were humping along the jungle trails, they were peeking out our sweaty ass. This caused an irritation around the anus, so we'd stop to give a little scratch and then a few minutes later wipe sweat from our faces with the same hand delivering a couple of fresh worm eggs right onto our lips to be licked off seconds later.

The worms and other parasites would often cause dysentery, which could put a soldier out of commission for days. Dysentery in Vietnam was so bad that men died from it, but if treated it usually lasted just a few grueling days. It was a great way to lose ten to twenty pounds quickly.

Another deadly disease our men had to contend with was malaria. We were constantly feasted on by mosquitoes, and it is astounding how few of us were stricken with malaria. However, we did have our fair share of victims. One man from our company, Private First Class Michael Patrick Arias came down with one of the most virulent strains of malaria and ended up spending six weeks in a field hospital in Long Binh enduring fever, chills, headaches, sweating, tremendous fatigue and vomiting.

Medics also had to deal with soldiers contracting various venereal diseases, probably as a result of visiting Lai Khe's Healthland, where you could get a steam bath and a massage. They also offered very pretty ladies who would help you relax if you were a "number one GI." As a door prize for visiting the establishment, our men would usually walk away with virulent strains of venereal diseases. In fact, we broke all previous war records for contracting venereal diseases; an accomplishment we didn't write home about, however.

So that was some of the additional perils we faced during our year long vacation in sunny tropical Vietnam.

Chapter 14
Our Hike Continues

All the time we were trudging through the jungle, mosquitoes swarmed around us, excited by the aroma of sweat we exuded. Between the 100-degree heat and the anxiety and fear that was our constant companion, our clothes stayed drenched in sweat. Many of us actually wore and slept in the same damp clothes for days, so we were surely very aromatic to our flying friends. We had become feral and deadly.

I was with the command group in the middle of the column. The command group consisted of the company commander, Captain Sawtelle, our medic James Callahan, Specialist Fourth Class James Berry, Sawtelle's RTO, a couple other RTOs, and me. Our position in the column provided us a false sense of security, and at the same time created additional danger to the men who were close to us. Those soldiers feared that the VC would wait for a command group to present itself before they would attack. This was not too farfetched because this is exactly what happened to us on a previous mission. We were singled out by the VC and attacked with a claymore mine. Most of the command group was blown through the air. I was sent sailing and knocked unconscious, and when I came to, I found myself lying behind a huge termite hill. Besides some broken teeth, miraculously, I was not seriously hurt. However, as I remember it, a sergeant assigned to us as a photographer, was ripped up badly.

Black Lions Alpha Company was spread out in a very long column, making the command group easy to recognize. I am sure the VC could hear our men tromping through the jungle. My walking fires easily announced to our enemy that we were on our way; the almost hundred and fifty men stomping through the jungle only reiterated the fact. To make our location even more obvious to the VC, we were forced to pop a smoke grenade and ask an air observer for our coordinates because the luxuriant growth of plant life prevented us from knowing our position. Specialist Fourth Class Thomas Waldron with the Black Lions Bravo Company wrote his parents that, "it was the worst jungle I've seen. It's an old jungle with what is called triple canopy. Many trees tower 100 ft. high - also much bamboo as tall as 60 ft." Waldron description was right on the money. Its denseness made it virtually impenetrable, but with constant hacking, with a machete, we slowly moved through it.

Landmarks in triple canopy jungles are virtually nonexistent; there are simply trees and more trees, huge termite mounds and huge swarms of mosquitoes. It is very easy to get lost chopping through the undergrowth and bamboo.

We didn't know it then, but our lead element getting us lost was an incredible stroke of luck. If we had attempted to enter LZ X-Ray at our designated entry point, we would have most likely collided with the entire Viet Cong regiment. If we hadn't veered off course, I probably wouldn't have been around to write this book. As Candace Bushnell said in her quote,

"Maybe mistakes are what make our fate...without them what would shape our lives?"

Chapter 15
Signs of Viet Cong

Earlier that morning, when elements of the Rangers were marching to the new location, they discovered a well-worn trail about two hundred meters south of the new LZ. During the march, the keen-eyed Donnie Gunby, an assistant gunner with Alpha Company, first spotted the suspicious trail about 3 meters to his right as he meticulously surveyed his surroundings. It was obvious to Gunby, a Georgia country boy that it had recently been trampled down by a large group because it was devoid of grass and even leaves. According to Jose Garcia's recollection, who was a machine gunner with Rangers Alpha Company, it ran parallel to the Rangers' line of march.

The path's discovery caused the 2nd platoon to temporarily halt their march so they could investigate their find. They were the lead element which meant the long column of men snaking behind them, would be stopped and the men would be wondering what was going on. The column would become one big dangerous traffic jam.

The path was reported to their platoon leader, Second Lieutenant Sermuskis. Once the Lieutenant saw how fresh and used the trail looked, he contacted Captain Williamson, who came strolling up to check out the find. Meanwhile, Lieutenant Colonel Lazzell was fuming over the delay in the march. He was pissed-off that the march had halted and wanted to know why in the hell Alpha Company had stopped.

Lazzell hadn't heard any shooting or explosions, so he radioed Captain Williamson for a sitrep. After Lazzell had been told what they discovered, he and his contingent moved up to the front to take a look. According to Garcia, Lazzell wasn't alarmed much by the trail, but did call in an airstrike to the east of LZ X-Ray. The fact that we were a bit behind schedule seemed to bother Lazzell more than the evidence of a large unit's presence. He told Captain Williamson to move out, and almost instantly the column began its march once again.

Chatter on the radios also confirmed that more trails running north and south were discovered on the east side of the clearing, along with freshly dug fighting positions. If this had been a Hollywood movie, a barrage of chaotic menacing sounds would have accompanied the scene, evoking a feeling of dread and foreboding of the chaos and bloodshed that would soon befall the men.

Even with this new information of enemy activity, we marched on. I wondered if these paths were worn down from hundreds of VC leaving the area or from hundreds of VC marching in to attack us. I tried to dismiss my concern, my trepidation with the old, *"The higher*

Brass are the experts. They know what they are doing. I need to trust that they know what really is going on."

The ominous feeling of dread of knowing this was the purported home of the VC's 9th Infantry Division made it hard to feel really safe.

Chapter 16
Premonitions

Some soldiers believe they will never be killed in combat, others are more realistic and recognize their mortality...but some are cursed with premonitions of their own death in combat. As a soldier, this is a terrible burden to carry; the feeling that death is always awaiting at the next battle. The famous World War II correspondent Ernie Pyle was haunted with a premonition of his death, and a Japanese machine gunner made it a reality.

There were certainly men in the Rangers and in the Black Lions that were haunted by these feelings. According to Marleen Wesson, Private First Class Charles Patrick Kelly, an automatic rifleman in the Ranger's Alpha Company, had been plagued for months with a feeling of doom. It was more than just a feeling in Private First Class Kelly's mind; it had evolved into a certainty. In fact, just two months prior to Operation Billings, Kelly flew to Hawaii for his RR. However, he didn't stay in Hawaii, instead he hopped a plane and flew to California and met with his girlfriend, Marleen. He wanted to see her one last time, and to try to convince her that she needed to forget him and move on with her life because he knew he wasn't returning home alive. He'd even brought back his father's pistol which he'd promised to return after his tour ended. During his short stay with Marleen, he surreptitiously put the pistol back on the shelf in the closet of his parent's home where it had sat for years.

Just days prior to Operation Billings, he wrote once again to Marleen about his premonition of death and again suggested that she forget him and move on with her life. It would be her last letter from him.

Black Lions Specialist Fourth Class Thomas Waldron sensed something malignant about the operation. He wrote to his parents, "I could tell it was going to be a bad operation from the beginning. So true. It's been nothing but trouble from the beginning.[7]"

The fear of death was experienced by all of us. We were young men who had much to live for, and the fear of our sudden demise was something that constantly festered in the back of our minds. It was hard to plan for our future when a part of our brain kept telling us that, "Hey buddy, you have a good chance of not getting home alive so don't make a lot of future plans." Also, recalling that before we came to Vietnam, we filled out forms for whom to contact as our next of kin in case we were killed added even more doubt to our belief of immortality.

Reality collided with our joie de vivre of youth. Something was wrong because we were eighteen, nineteen, twenty and twenty-one, a time when we were supposed to really live. A time where we would first taste love, feel grown up, own a car, be a part of all the changes that were happening so rapidly across America. We were the generation that was going to the moon, our ladies were taking the pill, our music was revolutionary, every home had a television, and we were going to bring equality to America. These young years were the years we felt so alive, so exuberant, we actually felt immortal and truly as the generation that would finally change the world to something better.

In Vietnam, those feelings and beliefs quickly evaporated as General Westmoreland's attrition scoreboard kept listing more and more dead Americans. It reminded us daily that we were not in America, but on the dark side of the planet where we would do a one-year sentence and then if alive be released back into the real world. Every day, however, more men throughout Vietnam would be added to the list of KIA's. Some days only twenty or thirty, other days a hundred or more. Not very comforting, but when you come down to it, kill or be killed is what war is all about.

Our war game was not some pansy sports game like baseball or football; we played a game with virtually no rules. We didn't have timeouts, halftimes or equal sized teams and no umpire to make things fair. In our game, anything was okay if it ended in killing your opponent. Shoot the opponent, stab him, beat him to death, fry him or blow him up, and as an artillery officer, that of course, was my favorite. Death by high explosive rounds, gone in one big bang. The trouble, of course, was that the Viet Cong also had no rules and a lot of ways to kill us. They could shoot us, stab us, garrote us, booby trap us, blow us up or beat us to death. Knowing all that made us very aware that death could be right around the next bend in that trail in the jungle.

Chapter 17
Joining the Army

I was another one of those soldiers who had joined on my own, but that was to avoid the draft and have some say in my future with the army. Xom Bo II happened just about three years after I had joined the Army while living in Livorno, Italy.

I was an army brat, living with my parents and perfectly content with my life as a fledgling guitar player and singer on the Italian night club circuit. My sheltered, secure life was drastically and forever changed by our country's infamous lightly threatening letter from my draft board back in Newport, New Hampshire, proclaiming the end to my civilian status. In essence, the letter gave me the prerogative to join the U.S. Army in Italy and have free transportation back to the States or be drafted and be forced to pay my own way back. Well, I took the free transportation choice, but not before I received advice from my father, a Warrant Officer, and various written promises from Camp Darby's premier enlistment sergeant. Most of the promises that I received from the Sergeant were fulfilled. I enlisted at Camp Darby outside of Pisa, Italy. The military flew me back to the States for basic training at Fort Dix, New Jersey. After those eight weeks of fun, I received orders to report to Redstone Arsenal for AIT Advanced Individual Training as a Radar and Nike Missile repair man. That school was an entire year, and as soon as I finished that training, I went to OCS, Officer Candidate School, in Fort Sill Oklahoma. A huge sprawling military base that taught me what I needed to know as an Artillery Officer. I graduated from OCS on March 29, 1966, with the class of 5-66.

One year later, I found myself getting paid to hike through the lush green forest of Vietnam.

Chapter 18
False Sense of Security

On the June 17th hike, I think most of us in command had underestimated what we might run into. We knew we were entering an area reportedly very active with elements of the Viet Cong 9th Infantry Division, but at the same time, we were four infantry companies strong, augmented by a recon platoon with the support of two battalions. Would the VC try to attack a unit so large?

Even with this comforting doubt, we were still looking for monsters in the shadows and praying the Grim Reaper was elsewhere this late morning. At least that was my feelings. I am sure that the twinks, who had never been in combat, saw things much differently. They were probably envisioning every possible horrible scenario as they trudged along the newly hacked out jungle path. When you are new in-country, every tree has a VC hiding behind it. That odd branch protruding from behind a distant tree is an AK-47. If birds take flight, an attack is imminent. If the jungle is silent, an attack is imminent.

That afternoon, however, their keen sense of danger should not have been dismissed.

I think many of us were jaded and felt secure because our force was so large. We just couldn't comprehend why the VC would really want to fight a battle with our four infantry companies and recon platoon. We were around five hundred men with artillery blasting its way ahead of us. Surely the VC wouldn't dare attack a fighting force as large as ours. We were just out on a Saturday morning stroll, another boring search-and-destroy mission. We might receive some harassment fire, and a few snipers might take shots at our men, but with a force as large as ours, we felt we had less chance of getting killed than a protester at the Newark, New Jersey race riots.

Chapter 19
Race Riots in America

On Saturday, June 17, 1967, it was Atlanta's turn to be ripped apart by racial violence. The Atlanta chaos would continue for a couple days, but not with the destruction and mayhem that Newark, NJ would soon experience. Those two riots were just part of a series of violent racial disturbances that blossomed throughout the States that long, hot summer, the Summer of Love. Now, almost a half a century later, race riots still fester like some incurable cancer.

The days preceding June 17 had seen huge changes in the status of African Americans. President Lyndon B. Johnson had appointed Thurgood Marshall as America's first African American Supreme Court Justice. Right around the same time, the Supreme Court ruled that whites could marry African Americans with no fear of legal repercussions. This ruling came as a result of a white man, Richard Loving, who had tried to legally marry Mildred Jeter, a black woman. According to Virginia law, their marriage violated the 1924 Racial Integrity Act, which prohibited mixed-race marriages. The Supreme Court felt different, and by a unanimous decision, ended all race-based legal restrictions for marriages in America.

Even as racial turmoil divided communities in the States, the military units in Vietnam were very integrated. My infantry company was very mixed, and I never noticed any overt racism. Many of our sergeants were African Americans who were career military men.

We were isolated from most of the political and racial strife going on back in the States, but a few of the new rulings would eventually affect some of us. The Supreme Court's ruling ending all raced-based restrictions on marriages in America would be a welcomed blessing to Sergeant Linsley R. Moore. Moore was an African American in the Black Lions Alpha Company. When he was stationed in Germany he had become smitten with a young German woman named Angelika. She fell in love with him, and it wasn't long before they were talking marriage. But it was 1965, and being African American and very young created a terrible dilemma for Linsley Moore and Angelika.

Coincidently, about the same time they were getting married, a 13-year-old named Janis Ian wrote a song called "Society's Child." The song was about a relationship similar to Moore and Angelika's; it spoke of the feelings of a young girl who witnesses the humiliation that her African American boyfriend received from her own mother and the taunts the couple endured from classmates and teachers. In the song, the girl finally succumbs to society's pressure and ends the relationship. Here is a sampling of Ian's lyrics:

> They say I can't see you anymore baby,
> Can't see you anymore.
> One of these days I'm gonna stop my
> listening,
> Gonna raise my head up high.
> One of these days I'm gonna raise up my
> glistening wings and fly.
> But that day will have to wait for a while.
> Baby, I'm only society's child.
> When we're older things may change,
> But for now this is the way, they must
> remain.
> I say I can't see you anymore baby,
> Can't see you anymore.

Society's pressures did not stop Moore and Angelika. On January 22, 1965, Linsley and Angelika became Mr. and Mrs. Linsley R. Moore in Bamberg, Germany. Their love was real, and they were still married over a half century later.

On June 17, 1967, "Society's Child" made it onto the Billboard's top 40 list, and within the next couple weeks, it would be number one in many American cities.

I had lived in integrated communities and gone to integrated schools, so an integrated unit seemed perfectly natural to me. However, years later I learned that some of the African American soldiers who had come from segregated communities felt uncomfortable in an integrated military. They weren't sure what the policy was for mingling with Whites. On the battlefield, however, a comrade's race meant absolutely nothing. A soldier was not measured by the color of his skin, but by his bravery, reliability, and performance under fire.

Chapter 20
Trudging Along

About halfway through our Saturday afternoon jungle outing, it started raining. The humidity increased and we waded through mud. I continued to shoot my artillery into the jungle to the west of our location. The woods stayed quiet except for the sounds of birds, the drip of rain, and the steady shuffle of hundreds of boots.

During these marches in the jungle, many of us would daydream about home and the loved ones we had left behind. We dreamed about what we would do when we returned back to the world. I would occasionally steal a glance at the back of my plastic map case to refresh my memory of what Gayla looked like and wondered how she was handling being pregnant all alone back at Fort Sill, Oklahoma. Captain Sawtelle was probably having flashing Technicolor images in his head of his wife Jo and their new baby girl, Stacy. Sawtelle was a short-timer. He only had to stay alive a few more weeks before the big silver bird would fly him back to the world, where he would be a student at Purdue University. Sawtelle would later remark that, "Joining the free spirits of the late '60s in the classroom was more challenging than the academics."

Ed Chrisman was another soldier about to return back to the world to experience the free spirits of the Sixties. He would be assigned to Letterman Hospital in the Presidio, located in San Francisco, the epicenter of the hippie movement.

Sergeant David Cordeau, a squad leader for First Lieutenant Jerry Wilson, was probably thinking about his wife, Nolia. She had been his high school sweetheart back in Port Arthur, Texas, and they had been going together since eleventh grade. Only eighteen years old, Cordeau had fourteen men under him, a daunting responsibility.

Chapter 21
Our Arrival

At about 12:30 P.M., the rain ceased, and we started spilling into LZ X-Ray. The center of the clearing was a jumble of men and activity. The clearing was large, probably about the size of six or seven football fields. Sergeant Cordeau with 1st platoon remembers the swaying grass and how deceptively peaceful and inviting the LZ looked.

I know I felt a sense of relief at having arrived at our destination without encountering any contact with our enemy. It was a hot sunny afternoon as we marched up to the perimeter we would soon secure. If I recall correctly, Captain Sawtelle, me, and our respective RTOs went to the center of the clearing to talk to the other commanders.

Two areas in the clearing were already staked out to be used as Command Posts "CP" by the Rangers. One was about fifty meters from the northeast edge of the LZ's tree line, which was used by Alpha Company's command group. Their entourage consisted of Captain Williamson, his two RTOs, Clark and Henderson and medic Specialist Fourth Class Duckwiler, Also in the group was First Lieutenant Richard Dalton the company's FO from 2/33rd artillery accompanied by his RTO and his recon sergeant.

About 50 meters south of Captain Williamson's CP was the battalion's CP where Lieutenant Colonel Lazzell was setting up his headquarters. His group consisted of his RTO's, an artillery Liaison officer and his RTO Specialist Fourth Class John Phil Vessello, Also accompanying Lazzell was his battalion's operation officers, Major Tony Jezior, and Captain Bobby Roberts the assistant S-3.

As we were entering the LZ, Lazzell's security squad and his RTO's were setting up his staff's communication equipment including a tall jungle antenna. The LZ was a beehive of activity; some supplies had already been delivered by hueys and now large Chinooks laden with ammo and equipment, were circling over the LZ waiting their turn to land. Everything was quiet; there wasn't any sign of Viet Cong. Short timer, Peter Clark, Captain Williamson's RTO stated, "The light rain which had sprinkled us during the morning had stopped and, pretty much, things were as good as they got in the field. There were no signs of any current enemy activity or presence that I could detect, and I considered myself pretty good at that business."

Before our arrival, leaders of the other companies had spread their men around the huge perimeter to temporarily secure it until permanent positions were assigned and our company, the Black Lions Alpha Company, could move into its sector.

Captain John Turner was the commander of Black Lions Bravo Company, while Sawtelle commanded the Black Lions Alpha Company. We were supposed to relieve the Black Lions' Bravo Company in the northwest quadrant while they moved down the western perimeter to secure the LZ's southwest quadrant.

That part of the plan never happened.

Fighting positions weren't being dug yet because no one was in their final assigned positions. Most men had found some kind of temporary cover, including termite mounds, clumps of bamboo, or trees they parked themselves under. The men were stretched thin, with each outpost of two men separated by about 60 to 150 meters. The distance between outposts was so great that it was impossible for most of the men to see or communicate with the next outpost. The men had also entered the tree line to varying depths; some were thirty meters from the tree line, and many others were fifty or more meters from it. The jungle was so thick that men could easily become disoriented and find themselves firing in the wrong direction.

Worst of all, however, the fear of contact with a large VC element had pretty much dissipated for many of the soldiers. In fact, some men had settled down to eat lunch or read old letters while they waited for someone to tell them what to do.

LZ X-Ray was much nicer than their previous location. It was higher and drier, and Sergeant Leonard Mathis of the Rangers recon platoon was looking forward to taking off his boots, letting them dry out, exposing his bare feet to a little sun and finally putting on dry socks now that they were out of LZ Rufe's mud.

While we were getting our briefing at the command center, much of Alpha Company was still on the path into the LZ. By the time the last squad's men were finally stepping into the LZ, the firing had started. Specialist Fourth Class Wes Canute, a member of that final squad, remembers bullets flying and dirt spitting up into the air as they entered the clearing. Men dove into the knee-high grass, trying to be as invisible as possible. Bullets flew over their prone bodies. One man near Specialist Fourth Class Canute was shot in the side while hugging the earth.

In a letter to his wife on June 24, Canute wrote, "He was in my squad. He was a real good man. As far as I'm concerned, he died for nothing. He was lying flat on the ground when he was hit."

The man's name was Private First Class Lloyd Wohlford. Wes was so strongly touched by Lloyd's death that in January 2005 he and his wife Sue visited Lloyd's sister Margaret in her hometown of Decorah, Iowa, where she owned and ran Margaret's Boutique dress shop. Wes had known Lloyd quite well—in fact, they had spent the night before the battle talking about life back home in the world.

At the first lull in the fire, Sergeant Bivens, who was a hundred meters or so to Specialist Fourth Class Canute's front, motioned for the squad to follow him to a location closer to the wood line, near where Captain Turner's Bravo Company had spread out.

At the same time, the three Alpha Company's platoon leaders were getting instructions from Captain Sawtelle on where to move their men and what their responsibilities would be.

The battle was starting.

Chapter 22
Preparing for Battle

At the most northern position of the Black Lions' perimeter, Private First Class Victoriano Perez Sosa and Private First Class Richard Anderson were manning their two-man outpost. Things were quiet there, and Private First Class Sosa was probably daydreaming about his beautiful two-year-old daughter, Cynthia, who he often bragged about. Twenty-two-year-old Sosa had been in-country less than three months and was fortunate to have a wife, Lydia, who habitually wrote letters and sent him food packages. Victor often shared his good fortune with his comrades, so Lydia's kindness made her a favorite among Victor's friends. Sosa's partner, twenty-year-old Private First Class Richard Anderson of Brooklyn, New York, had been in-country for just over three months.

Before the battle began, they were waiting to be relieved by men of the Black Lions' Alpha Company so they could move to a new position further south on the western perimeter of LZ X-Ray. That move would never happen.

While all this was going on, a few choppers circled above us with supplies. They had mail, ammo, food, and other supplies.

A few hundred meters from our command group, two Viet Cong machine guns lay hidden in the thick brush, taking aim at our men. One machine gun was on the east side and one on the clearing's north side, according to Ronald Moreno[8], Don Koch, and Fred Hill.[9] Other VC waited patiently and silently in the brush and in fighting holes that had been prepared the previous day. VC snipers were also sitting high up in trees with a clear line of sight into the clearing. Their preparations were elaborate: the Viet Cong had created a web of crisscrossed wires hidden in the thick vegetation covering the jungle floor. The wires linked their field phones together around the LZ's perimeter, providing communications between the VC commanders in charge of the ambush.

The commanders of the Viet Cong regiment knew that the Americans would prep the area with bomb runs and artillery prior to their insertion into the LZ, so the bulk of the VC troops had left the area after it was prepared for the ambush. They had moved a safe distance away from the LZ so they could rest up for the impending battle. A few VC lookouts stayed behind to observe and report any activity happening around the LZ to their commanders. Other VC continued to observe the American units back at LZ Rufe.

Around noon of June 17, a steady stream of Viet Cong stealthily moved into the jungle surrounding LZ X-

Ray. They arrived from a staging area north of the LZ. They were armed with RPGs, AK-47s, recoilless rifles, grenades, claymore mines, carbines, 60 mm mortars, and even .51 caliber machine guns. Still unobserved by us, the VC companies set up their mortar tubes and sent their forward observers closer to our perimeter.

As the VC's 271st units set up, their men waited nervously in their concealed positions. They watched American soldiers eating C-rations, taking a smoke, reading letters, taking a piss, and some even cleaning their weapons. The seconds ticked by and each moment brought the scythe of death a bit closer to the Americans and Viet Cong in wait.

Chapter 23
12:25 P.M. and We See VC

It was just about 12:25 P.M. when a soldier from the Black Lions' Bravo company 3rd platoon spotted five VC moving north, but they disappeared into the brush before they could be engaged. At about the same time another soldier from the 3rd platoon spotted three Viet Cong attempting to climb a tree. This time, two M-79 grenades were fired at them, but they scurried off into the jungle probably unharmed.

At 12:42 P.M. one man in Bravo 1-16 Infantry spotted 2 VC east of the perimeter and shot and killed them. Almost immediately two more were spotted in the same area and he killed them also. Then VC sniper fire started. You could hear the crack of the bullets which were mostly aimed at men of the Ranger's Bravo Company who were spread out on the East side of the perimeter.

The men of the VC's 271st regiment were cleverly concealed around the LZ X-Ray's perimeter that they had reconnoitered the previous day. With camouflaged positions, they were virtually invisible. Unfortunately, most of us never saw the men lying in wait for us, but all of us felt their wrath. Many of those who did see them wished they hadn't.

The initial sniper fire was a bit more disturbing, but it did not really alarm most of us to anything big because we would rarely enter a haven for VC without being shot at by snipers. Still unknown or unfathomed by us was the fact that we were surrounded by VC. They were not just harassing us, but had begun systematically shooting and killing our men almost from their very first shot. I remember thinking those shots were coming from somewhere up near the northeast side of the clearing. As units recognized what was happening the chatter on the radios started to sound ominous. The talk was frantic.

Chapter 24
Same Time Back in the States

Back in the world, it was midnight Friday and hundreds of young men 17, 18 and 19 gaped in horror as they watched blood spewing from victims as "The Plague of the Zombies" flickered away on the huge outdoor screen of the 1500 car Sheridan Drive-In just a few miles south-west of Chicago. It was the first Friday night of summer vacation and hundreds of teenagers cuddled in cars as they watched the Triple Horror Rama of scary movies, Dracula Prince of Darkness, The Plague of the Zombies and The Last Man on Earth. It was a busy night because these kinds of movies were the perfect excuse to hold your date close and cop a few feels or more. Drive-ins were big in June of 1967.

While some school mates of a few men in our units were humping their latest flame in the back seat of 67 Pontiac GTOs, Camaros, Mustangs and Thunderbirds, our young soldiers were humping into the tree line to set up a temporary perimeter. There was a large amount of confusion of what everyone was supposed to do. It had been planned that the unit I was with, Black Lion's Alpha Company was going to replace Bravo Company up in the North West quadrant of the clearing, but that plan changed as contact with this elusive enemy escalated.

At that moment I would've loved to been one of those sitting in a car staring at the big screen stretching across the sky with all the action happening in black and white, or just as acceptable would have been sitting on the porch of our house in the stifling 1967 summer heat sipping lemonade and yakking to a friend on the telephone with its cord stretched out through the screen door. But I was caught up in a real nightmare, a living nightmare where I was one of its characters with no knowledge of what the ending was going to be.

There was a palpable tension building as we heard the frantic reports coming over the radio. I wasn't in a position to make any decisions at that point; I was simply a Liaison Officer from the 2/33rd artillery. Captain Sawtelle had decided that his men, for the time being, were to create and maintain a second line of defense on the northwest side of the clearing. He was going to spread his platoons out behind the Black Lion's Bravo Company. Sawtelle had his own premonition that a concerted attack on that sector was imminent. Radio Telephone Operator (RTO) Specialist Fourth Class James Berry, who was also known as Bushwacker Kilo, lugged Captain Sawtelle's PRC-25 radio around. Soon Sawtelle would be using that radio to bark out orders to his platoon leaders to take up new positions.

James Berry was a seasoned RTO. He had been Platoon Leader Troy Oliver's RTO until First Lieutenant Oliver moved into the battalion's S-1 spot. His new job was advisor to Lt. Col. Jerry S. Edwards, the Black Lions' battalion commander, for all matters concerning human resources.

First Lieutenant Oliver would have the unsavory job of supervising the processing of all the men who were killed during the battle and to request replacements to fill their positions. Oliver would also have to oversee the write ups of all the citations for Silver Stars, Bronze Stars with a "V" device and any other medals for bravery. There were a lot of them, and he would also have the duty to get Purple Hearts requested for every man who had been killed or wounded during the battle.

Chapter 25
The Battle Begins: Time 12:55

After the first few shots had been fired and the 4 VC had been killed by a member of the Rangers' Bravo Company, most accounts agree that things seem to have stayed quiet for ten minutes or more. But then at 12:55 P.M., what was thought of as a small skirmish suddenly exploded into the lethal savagery of a full-scale battle.

The fighting then spread like a virulent disease to different areas of the LZ. Now members of the Black Lions' Bravo Company were under a heavy attack along with members of the Rangers' Alpha Company. The Rangers Bravo Company was also receiving heavy fire. Many of the men had not yet set up their positions, so they were at a disadvantage when they came under intense fire. The Black Lions' Bravo Company and the Rangers' Alpha Company would come under tremendous fire from the VC. Men were going to die in this battle. Grenades were being tossed at the men in Bravo and the Rangers' Alpha Company, and casualties mounted. Bullets tore into trees, bamboo, and into many of the young men desperately trying to kill one another. Lives would be cut short on the afternoon of June 17th in Phuoc Long Province Vietnam.

While bullets, grenades, and claymore mines filled the air with death around Captain Turner's Bravo, my company Alpha, maintained our positions in the clearing behind Bravo's platoons. The bullets and shrapnel hissed out of the jungle peppering our locations. Alpha's men had tried to dig into the grass covered clay earth a bit, but few had been very successful. We had to scoop the dirt out lying down or be hit by bullets cracking over our heads. Everyone in Alpha had their eyes fixed on the wood line with their weapons poised in front of them ready to fire. We expected to see hundreds of VC come streaming out of the brush firing AK-47's and tossing grenades at our exposed positions slaughtering us there on the wet Vietnam earth. There was a feeling of not just being ambushed but of being surrounded — by invisible attackers lurking somewhere within the looming dense trees and underbrush that encircled us. Accompanying this feeling was the primal symphony of anguished screams, thunderous artillery, the clatter of automatic weapons, the crack of AK-47's bullets, rustling trees and the frantic cries for "Medic."

The reports coming into Captain Sawtelle about the other companies' situations were dire.

Chapter 26
What the AP News Reported

Henri Huet, a great war photographer of the Associated Press, was on the scene and remembered it a little different. He reported that the first shots were fired by the VC at heavy-duty Chinook helicopters that had started to settle down with ammunition, sandbags, and heavy equipment. The choppers were waved away and within 15 minutes the artillery began to shake the jungle. "It was fantastic," Huet said, "One great rolling sound, then came the jets, bombing and strafing."

Henri Huet stayed with us during the battle, and his resulting photos received much recognition. In fact, as the battle started he requested to move closer to where Jose Garcia was engaging VC with his M60 machine gun. Specialist Fourth Class John Phil Vessello was given the task of escorting him to that location. They had to run through a part of the clearing to get to the path that led to Jose Garcia's position. Vessello said as they approached the area he saw a body lying out in front of Garcia's position. He left Huet and his assistants there and hustled back to the Rangers' Headquarters command post.

A few of Henri Huet's Xom Bo photos became iconic haunting images of the Vietnam War. Some of them were of our medic James Callahan trying to save our wounded and dying comrades while under fire. Personally, I was awed by Huet's bravery as he dashed about in the middle of the battle to record the deadly combat we were engaged in. June 17th was also one day after Cecile Blumental's birthday, the woman Huet loved, so he had reasons to have not been with us, but for him, it was his duty.

The shots on the choppers might have been part of the opening exchange of fire, but for me, the minutes of the beginning of the battle are just a collage of memory wisps that passing time has faded to vagueness. Since his recollection was reported in the news of June 18, 1967, the day after the battle, it probably is an accurate account of what he saw and heard from his vantage point.

Chapter 27
The Battle Escalates

By 12:55 P.M. the Black Lion's Bravo Company, and Alpha of the Rangers were receiving heavy automatic weapons fire and small arms fire from the north. The heaviest volume of fire was concentrated on the northern most platoons of each company.

I had started Artillery fire just north of our sister company Bravo, but an Air Observer requested that I temporarily relinquish my six 105 howitzers to him because he felt he had a better view of the battle and knew which unit most needed the artillery support. He was right because as bad as our situation was, the Ranger's Alpha Company was being totally over run and their platoon leaders were requesting artillery just meters from their own positions. My howitzers were quickly redeployed and their rounds started falling on the new coordinates to the east. Exploding ordnance and shrapnel started tearing up the attacking VC, and unfortunately probably wounding or worse yet, killing some of our own men. The requests for close end artillery by the platoon leaders were last-ditch efforts to try to disengage from an overpowering Viet Cong force that had a superior number of men.

Forward Observer, First Lieutenant Richard Dalton, hunkered down with Captain Williamson a few meters from the tree line and listened to the terrible news coming over the radios. Dalton could hear the firefight raging just fifty meters or so from his position. In fact, bullets were ripping into the trees nearby and snapping over his head constantly. Williamson shared with Dalton the dire situation his platoons were in and requested the artillery be brought in even closer. The Viet Cong practiced a tactic of getting as close to our men as possible to make the effective use of artillery virtually impossible without endangering our own soldiers. The tactic referred to as, "Grab their belts to fight them," was employed during the battle and complicated Dalton's fire missions.

With the enemy's close proximity to Alpha's positions, First Lieutenant Dalton would experience a Forward Observer's worst nightmare of being forced to fire dangerously close to the men he was trying to protect. Under these extreme situations, an FO can only hope and pray that his fire missions will produce more good than bad.

Chapter 28
The King of the Battlefield

By 1 P.M. the Second of the Thirty-third's 105mm howitzers were pounding the area containing the Viet Cong. At first, the Air Observer's perspective from above allowed him to adjust the artillery with more acuity and speed than we could have from the ground, but as the battle progressed the smoke from the hundreds of exploding rounds obscured his vision. White phosphorus rounds were being fired into the area along with high explosives ordnance. The white phosphorus set trees on fire and the explosions of the other 105mm rounds spread the burning debris to other trees. Quickly the smoke from the exploding ordnance, burning trees, and other debris floated above the triple canopy jungle blotting out even the tops of towering 100 foot trees. Hundreds and hundreds of rounds were sailing through the air. It was not just 105 rounds, but also 155 mm, 175mm and 8 inch rounds that were raining down in the jungle around us. At first, you could hear the distinct whine of them slicing through the air above us, but quickly the din of battle merged their sound into the discordant roar of combat.

The responsibility of adjusting the fire of my artillery battery returned back to me, and I struggled with moving my rounds that were being fired by 2/33 Charlie battery to areas of our perimeter that would benefit Alpha Company of the Black Lions and the other units involved in the battle. I could not see the rounds land, so I had to determine how far out the artillery was by ear. Over my PRC-25 radio, the FDO or Fire Direction Officer located in a bunker at a fire base miles away would give me the expected time of impact for my rounds, and I would attempt to distinguish their detonations from all the rest of the ordnance exploding around us. Adjusting artillery during a multi-company battle was exceedingly difficult and dangerous to the men you were supporting because their movement was so fluid that rounds could easily fall too close to friendlies. The kill radius of a 155mm howitzer round is 50 meters from the point of impact. A 105 round which I was firing had a kill radius of 30 meters, and the few 8 inch rounds that were fired in support of our engagement had an 80 meter kill radius.

In much of the battle, I would be laying prone on the ground communicating with the FDO back at the firebase as they fired the requested rounds. The FDO's voice emanating from the static of the radio "Dungeon Charlie 52" would call out, "Dungeon Niner Seven Shot" meaning rounds on the way. Seconds later I would hear him utter a "Dungeon Niner Seven Splash" and I would count backward from 10 to 1 and then the rounds would explode, I hoped, somewhere to the front of me. As I waited for my rounds to impact, I would feel this great foreboding or sense of anxiety that they would not land where I had intended them to land. I would envision them exploding right in front of me or behind me in one huge thunderous crack blowing Captain Sawtelle and me away forever. During the battle, I had moved artillery in so close to our position that branches and spent shrapnel did fall upon us. My feeling of constant doom was somewhat justified because in heavy combat situations many things can happen to cause incoming rounds to crash on top of our men instead of the enemy. That was a heavy weight that affected me virtually all the time as I adjusted the artillery fire. Minor changes in weather, wind direction, or a rain storm miles away could cause the rounds to fall short. The men on the guns changing from one source of rounds to a different lot could have a devastating effect on my fire mission. Wet powder in the bags, overheating of the howitzer's tube or human error in the frantic calculations of elevation and azimuth during the fire mission, were all factors that could lead to a deadly barrage of rounds blowing up our own troops.

Chapter 29
The First Assault Continues

The battle was now a huge cacophony of sounds, the pungent smell of gunpowder, burning trees and the chaos of hundreds of men killing and maiming one another supposedly for God and Country. But in reality, we killed strictly to stay alive and for really nothing else.

Gunships had also arrived and began blasting away at any Viet Cong elements that they saw. Platoon leaders were requested to pop smoke to mark their locations to help the gunships know where not to shoot.

We were being supported by two gunships that were spitting out flames and smoke as they fired thousands of rounds per minutes into the tree lines. Their rapid speed of shooting created a continuous hum or whirl that was as soothing as the purr of a kitten to a cat lover. Whenever the gunships flew over our location, blasting away at their targets, thousands of hot shell casings rained down around me and the other men of Captain Sawtelle's company. The casings were bouncing about everywhere, some landing in the grass others peppering all of us spread out in the clearing. Those foolish enough to not be wearing helmets attempted to cover their head with their arms. The casings stung and were hot, but unless they struck you in your eye or teeth probably did very little harm. The bullets spewing out of their mounted guns, however, were pulverizing anything they hit, grass, trees, bushes, and whoever might have been in the path of the murderous stream of bullets. The guns were ablaze with a deadly torrent of lead that would tear up anything in their path.

Chapter 30
Captain Turner's Battles

At 12:55, the Black Lions Bravo Company was also engaged with an intense ground assault by the Viet Cong. Bravo's front was partially protected by artillery that was tearing up the jungle north of LZ X-Ray, flinging trees and debris into the air. Out of the haze of its roiling smoke, two soldiers—Private First Class Richard Anderson and Private First Class Victoriano Sosa from the Black Lions Bravo Company's northernmost position—saw Viet Cong clad in black pajamas darting in and out of view.

Unfortunately, the VC also saw them and attacked their hastily prepared position with carbines, AK-47s, and grenades. Bullets came in from all directions, and the two-man position was quickly overrun. Captain John Turner's two men were killed. Two of the attacking VC then commandeered Bravo's lost position and used two dead American soldiers' bodies as cover. From their newly won position, the two VC started firing at other Black Lions thinly spread out over the northern perimeter.

More VC swarmed the northern positions of Captain Turner's Bravo Company's 3rd platoon. The deluge of bullets from the attacking VC was intense, and more men from Turner's company fell wounded.

Captain Turner's 3rd platoon's right flank was completely in chaos, attacked from all sides with its ranks in utter disarray.

Chapter 31
Lost in the Battle

In the confusion of a firefight, soldiers are often separated from those in command and find themselves in the enemy's killing field. This is a terrifying situation to be in. During the Xom Bo II battle, men became disoriented in the trees line and had no idea if they were receiving fire from the enemy, from their own comrades, or from both sides. Bullets seem to come from all directions, and the heavy fire prevented them from returning fire on the enemy. They could be killed by friendly fire as easily as by the enemies' bullets.

A few of Captain Turner's men found themselves in this predicament. Private First Class Joe Hare, the RTO for 3rd platoon's Sergeant Gilbert, and the platoon's medic, Felix Vallejo, were positioned just a few meters behind the hastily deployed perimeter. They were pinned down by incoming fire from an unseen enemy and unable to return fire because the dense jungle prevented them from seeing more than a few meters. The close-in friendly artillery was practically falling on top of them, with hot shrapnel hitting all around. Hare got a small piece of smoking shrapnel embedded in his left shoulder, but the wound was minor. Later that evening, Private First Class Hare would serve as Captain Turner's RTO, replacing Turner's former RTO, who had been killed by mortar fire.

Chapter 32
Black Lions Fight Back

The Black Lions Bravo Company's 3rd platoon was the closest element to the Rangers platoon, which was also under attack. With men wounded and some dead, Black Lion's platoon sergeant, Sergeant First Class Billie J. Dodd, moved himself and four of his men toward the northern position to add more firepower to the battle and drive back the Viet Cong over-running the northern perimeter.

As Dodd maneuvered his group closer, the VC started firing on them. Before Dodd's group could take cover, two of them were killed, and Sergeant First Class Dodd himself was badly wounded. His RTO, Private First Class Ben Walker, of Colorado Springs, CO assumed control of the situation. He found cover from the enemy fire and deployed the remaining members of the squad. The men sought makeshift cover behind trees, huge termite hills, and thickets of bamboo. From behind their feeble cover, the Black Lions directed heavy fire into the marauding VC soldiers. The battle was intense, and the

Black Lion's contingent of men was largely outnumbered, yet they held their position.

The scene was a cacophony of combat: the crack of AK-47 rounds snapping by, the explosion of rocket-propelled grenades, the screams of "Medic!", the moans of the wounded, the chatter of VC yelling commands to their comrades, the whirling sound of M-16s unleashing clips of bullets into the attackers, and the yells of the Black Lion's men yelling for ammo. All of this chaos was wrapped in a cloak of thick black smoke from the hundreds of artillery rounds pounding the area, cutting off any new VC troops from entering the battle.

Some of the men from Bravo's second platoon tried to move closer to 3rd platoon to help them hold back the onslaught of Viet Cong assaulting their sector. Specialist Fourth Class Tom Waldron, a twenty two year old team leader from Charlotte, North Carolina, was one of them and recalled edging his way along the tree line on the west side of the clearing and seeing Viet Cong darting about in the shrubs north of him. They were uniformed in black pajamas.

Private First Class Ben Walker of 3rd platoon took the initiative to call in and adjust his unit's mortar fire on the enemy. The jungle north of the battle became a grinding machine of death as round after round of 105 mm artillery exploded, pulverizing the trees, bamboo, and any VC remaining in the impact area. The advancing Viet Cong were unable to maintain their attack because of the thunderous artillery raining down and Private First Class

Walker's close-in precision mortar barrages. The smell of war was all around us.

Chapter 33
We Lived What Some Imagined

While at least fourteen hundred young men locked in mortal combat went about trying to kill one another in a real-life 1967 adaptation of *The Hunger Games*, the music at the Monterey Pop Festival rocked on, oblivious of what was happening seven thousand four hundred miles away in Vietnam.

For the attendees, the smell of pot replaced the smell of gunpowder, burning trees, and death. The music of The Association, The Paupers, Lou Rawls, Beverley Kutner, and Johnny Rivers filled their evening instead of the sound of thousands of bullets, artillery rounds, and the cries of wounded men. The huge dichotomy between these two scenes of that generation of America's youth could not have been more different.

Similar to the fighters in *The Hunger Games*, those of us locked in mortal combat were largely selected by a local committee, in this case, their local draft board. A few men decided on their own to join the service, but the vast majority of the men in our units had been drafted.

We were trained to kill, armed to kill, and given rules of combat to adhere to. Violate the rules and serious consequences resulted.

It is hard to create a mental picture with words alone of what a battle of this magnitude is really like. Things were happening all around LZ X-Ray; everyone was engaged in one way or another. Men were being killed; men were being seriously wounded. Men were fighting to stay alive. Men were killing other men, men were praying, men were crying, men were lying in pools of blood, men were begging for help, men were frantically firing bullets, men were tossing hand grenades at objects moving, and young men were dying.

There's no mercy in war. It's all about killing and maiming. In fact, our empathy and compassion for our enemy evaporated as soon as we saw our men killed or wounded by them. We became devoid of any redeeming emotions for them.

We were not in a movie set; this was the real thing, a real bloodletting in the jungle. As artillery rounds came screaming in and smashed into the jungle, the puddles rippled from the vibrations. The rounds pounded the earth like the huge fists of an angry giant. In fact, you could feel the earth shudder beneath us. It was strange, but as the rain splattered down and the rumble and flashes of artillery continued, it was like the world had flipped upside down and thunder and lightning were bursting upward out of the jungle floor.

In Monterey, the State-side half of my generation was also feeling vibrations, but from Fender bass guitars,

Gibson guitars, Rickenbacker guitars, Epiphone guitars, and the pounding of Ludwig drums. The music was loud, it shook your guts, it made your ears ring—and even after the concert, the ringing continued. There was no smell of napalm or acrid gunpowder and cordite. Instead, the smell of marijuana, incense, flowers, and sweat filled the air. No one was crouching behind bushes or trees in fear of their life...unless they were tripping on LSD. There was insanity in the air of the Cheech and Chong variety, but the concert-goers were safe, grooving with their own. In fact, there were zero deaths, no riots, no injuries, no violence, and no arrests during the three-day concert. It was a happening they would never forget. They would tell their friends and later their kids that they were there and saw all these famous rock bands.

We would never forget our own happening—its smells, its music of AK-47 cracks, the whoosh of napalm spreading across a field, the click of brass cartridges spraying out of a rifle, and the cries for medics and ammo. Our happening would have lots of deaths and even more wounded. The papers wouldn't write much if anything about it, and there wouldn't be any books written about it. And for many of us, it would be years before we told anyone of our June 17, 1967, happening. It was not the kind of happening to talk about, and really it was just too hard to make anyone understand what our happening was like.

Chapter 34
The Rangers 3rd Platoon

The battle exploded at 1:06 P.M. on the northeast and northwest sectors of the perimeter. Captain Turner's men were under heavy attack and trying to hold their sector of the northwest perimeter from a large Viet Cong assaulting force. At the same time, the 3rd platoon of the Rangers Alpha Company was trying to hold back a Viet Cong onslaught on their positions. Third platoon was being attacked by the same VC elements that were attacking the Black Lions Bravo Company. These were mostly hardcore VC in tan uniforms and heavily armed with AK-47s, RPG's, carbines, grenades and more.

Twenty-two-year-old Sergeant Frank Romo and three of his comrades were getting ready to start their digging to construct their assigned fighting positions near a trail leading back into LZ X-Ray. It was lunch time however, and the four decided to take a couple of minutes to eat some c-rations before starting their work. At about that time a couple other men from Alpha

Company moved by their position to go further out into the surrounding jungle.

Nineteen-year-old, Sergeant Dennis (Chip) Giles, was the squad's machine gunner and had already set up his M60 overlooking a well-trodden trail leading back to LZ X-Ray. Giles was from Kipling, Ohio; a small town with a population of less than 200; which was named after author Rudyard Kipling. Giles had been working as a store clerk when he was drafted and by June 17, he had been in country for about nine months.

Twenty-four-year-old Private First Class Don Rawls of Maple Hill, North Carolina was Sergeant Giles assistant and Private First Class Kirley also from North Carolina was the ammo bearer. They had dropped their rucksacks and stacked the belts of M60 ammo close to the gun and then sat down to eat. They had just opened some cans of C-rations when they heard a few shots from the area where the men who had just passed them had entered the jungle. Then a couple more shots rang out and then all hell broke loose. There were VC coming, not just one or two but many of them.

Sergeant Giles jumped behind his loaded M60 and took aim at the horde of Viet Cong coming towards them. Don Rawls took up a prone position to Giles left and started guiding the belt of M60 rounds into the gun. Sergeant Romo with his PRC-25 was to the left of Rawls giving a quick situation report to Specialist Fourth Class Frank Limiero who was 3rd platoon's RTO.

Who shot first no one really knows, but suddenly bullets were flying everywhere. Giles started cutting down the Viet Cong that were moving towards him, but there were so many of them that his single machine gun could not stop them all. Sergeant Romo got on the radio and frantically put out a call for reinforcements and more M60 ammo.

The Viet Cong were firing their AK47's as they advanced toward Romo and his group. Within a short time, Private First Class Rawls was shot in his left hand. The bullet destroyed his left index finger making loading the M60 very difficult. Things were getting very bad as Giles had also run out of ammo and needed Rawls to retrieve another 100 round belt and load it as quickly as possible. Disregarding his mutilated hand, Rawls reached over Sergeant Romo to grab what he discovered was their last 100 round ammo belt. That was when he also discovered that Romo was dead. Shocked by the fact that his comrade beside him was dead, Rawls renewed his effort to reload Giles' M60 and had just finished when two of the bullets pouring in around them slammed into his side shattering two of his ribs and incapacitating him. He was bleeding badly and knew he was in bad shape. Rawls managed to crawl over to a nearby termite mound to get out of the direct line of fire. As much as he was bleeding, he knew there was little chance of surviving, but he still had a little hope. Propped up against the side of the termite mound and cradling his loaded M16 he gazed out into the jungle and faded in and out of consciousness. He knew what VC did to wounded Americans and accepted the fact that he would have to kill any who found him because if he didn't, they would slit his throat.

He told himself he would play dead which is how he looked anyway all soaked in blood. He would end up lying there in a pool of blood for hours before a medic could reach him and get him evacuated.

Sergeant Neil Skiles, a short timer from Industry, Illinois ran through a hail of fire to reach the pinned down squad and discovered that his friend Sergeant Frank Romo had been shot three times in the chest. Skiles had brought with him more ammo for Giles' gun squad which by then consisted of three wounded men and one dead. Private First Class Kirley, who had replaced Rawls as the assistant gunner had been shot in the shoulder almost as soon as he took over the job. Giles wasn't much luckier, he had been shot in the right calf and needed attention. Giles disregarded his wound and kept firing as more Viet Cong kept moving down the trail. Sergeant Skiles, recognizing their serious shortage of M60 ammo, jumped up from his position and dashed back to the clearing for more, taking fire all the way. He grabbed as much M60 ammo as he could carry and worked his way back to Giles. Sometime during the battle, Skiles was also hit, but it didn't stop him. Skiles was just a few weeks from his rotation back home, and he was determined to make it through this battle alive. He and Giles machine gun crew would continue the fight until the Viet Cong finally pulled back. During part of the battle, Sergeant Giles was loading and shooting the M60 by himself. At one time the gun jammed and he had to roll over on his back to get in a position to clear it and thread a new belt into it.

Sergeant Romo's squad was probably the first to receive fire from elements of the PAVN 271st Regiment, which had begun probing our defenses.

The RTO of Rangers Alpha Company's third platoon was listening on the net as the firefight raged between Romo's squad and the attacking Viet Cong. From the staccato sounds of AK-47 fire, the exploding rocket-propelled grenades, and the resounding boom of grenades accompanied by frantic calls for assistance, it was obvious what Romo's team of four was enduring. Twenty-year-old Specialist Fourth Class Frank Limiero, the 3rd platoon's RTO, knew that his location was just a few hundred meters away from the carnage, but the wet jungle hid the brutality of the battle. Only the sounds told him of the savagery taking place, and Limiero knew that the primal horror of war would soon be visiting him. He listened to the radio transmissions until Romo's frantic voice cracked, "God help us, there're hundreds of them."

After that transmission, Romo's radio went dead. That final message would haunt Frank Limiero for the rest of his life. Romo was twenty-two years old when he was shot and killed during that assault. He was from Azusa, California, and had less than four months to go before he was scheduled to rotate back to the world. His father, Rudolph Gonzales, would be notified of his son's death June 20th.

First Lieutenant Johnson was the 3rd platoon's leader, but he was brand new in-country. This intense assault was his baptism to real kill-or-be-killed combat, and unfortunately its brutality and severity unglued him to the point where he was unable to effectively lead his platoon.

Realizing their dilemma with First Lieutenant Johnson from his panicky situation reports, command knew they had to quickly place someone else in charge of 3rd platoon. With few options, Captain Williamson placed his bet on Johnson's RTO, Specialist Fourth Class Limiero to take over the control of the 3rd platoon's engagement with the Viet Cong. Limiero was a good choice because he was experienced in combat, knew how to communicate over the radio, and knew his comrades' abilities. According to Limiero, First Lieutenant Johnson appeared to be in shock from the extreme carnage and was randomly firing into trees at no apparent targets. Some of his men had started to do the same and sporadically fired into the trees, perhaps hoping to frighten away the advancing enemy. According to Limiero, Johnson had not offered any type of defense scenario to counter the attacking, highly experienced Viet Cong.

Limiero quickly took charge of the deteriorating situation. He was faced with multiple issues. His men had not finished digging their fighting positions, neither the forward nor secondary perimeter foxholes, which made his platoon very vulnerable to the attacking Viet Cong. His men took cover behind clumps of bamboo and massive termite mound—or anything that appeared to give them some protection. Limiero was also saddled with the problem of numerous wounded men needing immediate medical attention, which he could not provide until the battle was over. And of course, he knew that the battle's outcome was an unknown. His men might experience the same fate that Romo's team endured. It was unthinkable, but very possible.

Limiero had inherited a platoon that was about at half strength and was not engaging the enemy as a cohesive fighting force. He realized from his position, located by what looked like an ox cart trail, that he had to rally his men to return fire against the advancing Viet Cong or all would be lost.

Hell was breaking out all around him and more men were being hit with shrapnel or bullets. Life-and-death decisions had to be made. Things had to be done quickly, to turn the battle around. If they were to survive, Limiero had to slow down the advancing Viet Cong.

Limiero first felt a bit of panic, anger, and a bevy of other emotions, but then he pulled himself together and stood and yelled at the men in the 3rd platoon. "Stand and fight! Look 'em in eye," he shouted with conviction. "Nobody's goin' to die gettin' shot in the back...unless it's by me!"

His bravado worked, and the men started to fight as they had been taught as soldiers. Miraculously, some sense of control returned to the 3rd platoon.

One of the members of the platoon, Specialist Fourth Class Charles Kelly, positioned himself behind a small berm and began to place suppressive fire on the advancing enemy. Others joined in firing M16's, lobbing grenades and firing M79's at the Viet Cong. The line temporarily held, but ammunition was quickly disappearing with the high rate of fire. Specialist Fourth

Class Kelly realized he was about to run out of ammo and attempted to dash back to the supply point and obtain more. On his way there he observed one of his comrades wounded and exposed to crossfire. He crawled over to him, dragged him back to a more covered area and administered first aid. Charles succeeded in getting more ammo and returned to the line and again engaged the enemy.

The Viet Cong unit assaulting 3rd platoon's position far outnumbered Limiero's men, so the situation still appeared bleak as hell, but there was hope if they fought like demons possessed. And they did.

But even with all the men fighting, including the wounded, the situation continued to deteriorate. Limiero decided to call for close-in air support. Jets were nearby and had already been strafing LZ X-Ray's tree lines, so he requested they do a pass-over near his platoon's position. He moved to the front of his platoon area and popped red smoke to mark his platoon's forward location. Limiero told their pilots to bring fire forward of the red smoke, but unknown to him, another smoke canister of the same color had been ignited behind their unit. The jets saw the 3rd platoon's position as the target instead of the area controlled by the Viet Cong.

Before Frank Limiero could call off the strafing run, the jets came in for a sweep of 3rd platoon's area with their 20 mm cannons blasting away. Frantically, Limiero tried to contact the jets to cease fire, but before he was successful he was hit in the hand, along with his machine gunner who was struck in his side.

The Viet Cong witnessed the confusion and immediately took advantage of 3rd platoon being strafed by their own jets flying above them. The situation was perfect for a final assault down the muddy ox cart trail. The jungle highway filled with Viet Cong, and as the attacking jets flew away from their strafing run, the Viet Cong scampered toward the dazed 3rd platoon. A few dashed towards Limiero's position while he was on the radio trying to get the jets to end its mission. Limiero saw the Viet Cong approaching him with their AK-47s at the ready. With his mind going crazy with anger, desperation, fear, and confusion, he raised his Army-issue Colt 45 and shot and killed the two closest Viet Cong before they could open up with their AK-47s. Miraculously, Limiero's machine gunner had recovered enough from the shock of being hit that he was able to reposition his M60 machine gun and begin firing on the advancing Viet Cong.

Another member of the platoon, Charles Kelly, who'd held his position on the line and kept firing at the Viet Cong was overrun and killed during the large assault. Unfortunately, his premonition of death that he had shared with his girlfriend, Marleen, had come true, but he hadn't died in vain. He had saved one man from sure death and his valiant fight had probably saved others.

Finally, Limiero was successful in ending the jets' strafing run. As soon as the jets ceased firing on the men of 3rd platoon, the remaining men reorganized themselves to continue the fight. Now with the jets aware of their mistake, they shifted their approach and, seconds later, dove toward the earth once more. This time, they dropped two shiny six-foot-long napalm canisters. The shiny objects tumbled through the air like big, deadly eggs stuffed with 130 gallons of flammable, gasoline-based jelly.

They fell through the jungle canopy, then suddenly a strange “wump” was heard as they exploded on impact. A tsunami of flames spread out over the jungle floor, sucking in the surrounding air. A two-thousand-degree inferno engulfed everything touched by the sticky flaming jelly. Limiero and his machine gunner could feel the heat radiating from the napalm and the wind the inferno created as it incinerated any Viet Cong who had occupied the area hit by the napalm. Limiero was sure the napalm hit some of the enemy because he heard briefly the screams of Viet Cong soldiers as they were burned to death.

As the flames of the napalm died out, Limiero and his men held their breath, hoping the close-in air support and the heavy artillery barrage thundering around them had turned the tide.

They had hugged the ground and prayed that the air strikes and their own artillery would not hit them. They knew what short rounds and unguided air strikes could do to their positions.

Suddenly, Limiero heard whistles blow. They were the kind of whistles the Viet Cong used to signal their soldiers to attack or retreat. Third platoon waited to see where the Viet Cong would come charging from, but none did. The whistle had meant retreat. Limiero and his men enjoyed a few moments of relief, but it was short lived because 60 mm mortar rounds started raining down on their area. The retreating Viet Cong used this tactic to cover their retreat. While men in the 3rd platoon kept their heads down, the Viet Cong collected their dead and wounded and disappeared back into the jungle.

The sound of mortars crashing into the jungle was unnerving because you never knew where the next one would land. The mortar rounds exploded in nearby trees, raining down pieces of shrapnel, branches, flurries of leaves, and splinters of bamboo. The men of 3rd platoon took refuge from the falling mortar rounds in any fashion they could. They tried to be as small as possible, covering their heads and praying and waiting and praying and waiting some more. Some promised God that if they were spared from death, they would never do another bad thing ever, along with probably a bunch of other dubious promises. Their prayers appeared to work, because suddenly the mortars stopped. One of the last rounds fell just meters away from where Limiero had taken refuge.

Sporadic automatic weapons fire continued for a while, but then the guns stopped, the explosion of mortars and RPGs faded away, and an eerie silence hung over the ravaged jungle. Men of the 3rd platoon gazed out over the destruction. Termite mounds were half destroyed, clumps of bamboo and jungle foliage shot to pieces, and further out to the front was the blackened and smoldering remains of the Viet Cong's short-lived refuge.

"A thick, choking smoke lingered about two feet above the forest floor from the massive amounts of ordnance that had been fired," Limiero remembered. "Equipment and bodies lay all over."

There were American soldiers and Viet Cong lying dead just inches from each other. The scene was unflinchingly brutal and primal.

Many of 3rd platoon's wounded hobbled or dragged themselves to the rear area of LZ X-Ray in hopes of finding medics or someone to help them. Others were unable to move because of the gravity of their injuries and had to hope and pray that aid would soon come their way. As Limiero said, "It was not a pretty sight, seeing such brave men in the name of so much glory, bloodied and broken."

Specialist Fourth Class Frank Limiero's job was not finished. He still had the task of getting the remaining wounded and dead back to the choppers waiting in the evacuation area. Sergeant Neil Skiles also helped carry the wounded out of the wet jungle. He had been wounded during the battle, but he wasn't going to let a little blood loss stop him from lending a hand to his more severely wounded comrades.

Neil was also, unknowingly, in the middle of another battle that was raging back in America. His father Edward Skiles Sr. was on the verge of losing their 331-acre farm because of lack of help in working it. If Neil was killed, it would mean the family would not just lose Neil but also the family farm. Things were desperate and banks, attorneys and acquaintances were petitioning his case with the military for his early release from the service. Neil knew things were bad back home, but hadn't been told how severe. The draft had grabbed most of the fit young men in McDonough County Illinois and the few left were not farmers. It was only his father and mother tending 296 acres of planted farmland, 550 head of livestock and maintaining all the heavy equipment used on the farm. It was a grueling impossible task for them to work the farm all alone. The Vietnam War was killing them and their farm.

The events back in Industry, Illinois population 500, however, were the furthest things from Neil Skiles' mind. His focus was helping his comrades to safety. During the battle, his friend Limiero had also become a casualty. He had been hit with numerous pieces of shrapnel, one piece actually slicing into his hand. Limiero had also received multiple burns from shrapnel and other ordnance to the point that his shirt became so shredded that he discarded it sometime during the battle.. Even though he was told to stop and get medical care for his own wounds, Frank continued to bring casualties from the battlefield back to the CP. Limiero felt like many other soldiers who, after seeing the gravity of other soldiers' severe wounds, felt a tinge of guilt at taking time away from the medics to treat a minor wound when they had so many near-dead to treat. His refusal of treatment cost him a highly deserved Purple Heart commendation—and still to this day, almost a half century later, the army still refuses to issue it.

Chapter 35
The Rangers 2nd Platoon

Sergeant Gregory Murry and his small squad of men from 2nd platoon of Rangers Alpha Company were desperately fighting for their survival on the northeast side of the LZ. They found themselves right in the path of the major attacking VC force. In fact, the assault that began at 1:06 P.M. would be responsible for most of the men killed in Rangers Alpha Company.

They were positioned to the east of the Black Lions Bravo Company, which was also under heavy attack. The VC had saturated that part of the perimeter with many fighters who were ferociously attacking the American elements trying to defend that portion of the perimeter. The Viet Cong had elements engaging the Rangers 3rd platoon, who were to the front of the Rangers 2nd platoon, but at 1:06 P.M. the VC launched an assault across a wide front that included the part of the perimeter held by the 2nd platoon. Large groups of Viet Cong flowed around 3rd platoon to assault 2nd platoon's positions.

One of the first soldiers to see and engage the VC was Jose Garcia. He was setting up his machine gun under instructions from Murry when he heard and spotted a group of armed VC a short distance away. His assistant, Donnie Gunby, didn't hear them, but Jose's ears had not failed him. Within moments of his pronouncement, the attacking Viet Cong appeared in front of them. Garcia aimed his twenty-three-pound M60 at them and pulled the trigger. The gun lurched, and fire began to spit out the end of the muzzle. Lying prone, he peered down the trail at the advancing enemy and kept firing. Twenty-year-old David Ward of Lockport, NY was Garcia's ammo bearer. He also saw the VC coming and dropped to the ground as bullets cracked over his head.

Bob Pointer was another machine gunner from the 2nd platoon who also started firing at the enemy. A large number of VC armed with AK-47s returned a tremendous volume of fire. They shot in bursts of ten to fifteen rounds, but with so many of them shooting it was a constant cacophony of the cracks of the AK-47 bullets and muzzle blasts. Sometime during the initial assault, Private First Class Robert Maguire from Atascadero, California, firing from behind a large termite hill, was struck by VC bullets and died.

Jose Garcia was sure he was about to be killed by the Viet Cong onslaught. They were so close that he could see his bullets stitching red holes across their bodies. He could watch his tracer rounds float lazily toward a charging Viet Cong, who would suddenly tumble to the wet jungle floor, dead.

Jose did a bit of praying as he raked the advancing enemy in front of him. He had serious doubts that he would ever see his hometown of Houston, Texas, again. He hoped and prayed that his parents and his fiancée Janie would be able to accept his death.

Sergeant Murry was positioned just a few feet behind machine gunner Jose Garcia and observed Sergeant Howard A. Mucha of Willoughby, Ohio, and another rifleman named Haggerty from the Rangers dive into a freshly dug VC fighting position. Both of them started firing at the VC swarming into the area. The attacking VC returned a fusillade of fire, including tossing grenades at them. Howard and Haggerty used their rucksack to try stopping the VC from lobbing grenades into their fighting hole.

A lieutenant and some of the other men from the 2nd platoon yelled at them to fall back. Haggerty jumped up out of the hole and successfully scampered back with other members of 2nd Platoon. Howard, for whatever reason, maintained his position and kept firing at the advancing VC. His position was an obstacle to their advance so they continued spraying his position with AK-47s and lobbing grenades at him.

At this point, there was no way for Howard to exit the fighting hole or escape the bullets and grenades coming toward him. The records state he died of gunshot wounds, but his brother, Carl, said Howard came home in pieces. Machine gunner Jose Garcia said he remembered seeing grenades being lobbed into the fighting hole.

Regardless of how he was killed, he was gone, and his death saddened his family immensely. His brother Carl and sister Carol had already lost their mother and father, and now Howard was gone. Carl was especially affected, because he had been upset with Howard's desire to be a machine gunner. He had warned his brother of the dangers a machine gunner faces and told him how upset he was with him for seeking the job. Carl felt that Howard's chances of getting wounded or killed were greater. Howard had already been an ammo bearer for Garcia's M60 gun crew for four or five months prior to his sergeant E5 promotion and being given his own fire team.

Carl and Carol were notified about a week later that Carl's greatest fear had happened: his twenty-two-year-old brother had been killed.

While Howard tried to hold the VC back, Jose Garcia and Donnie Gunby continued to receive a hail of deadly fire on their position. Jose had finished off one entire belt of ammo and was about to load another when bullets ripped into his position so close that the shots exploded clumps of dirt and rocks into his face. Instinctively he covered his eyes to protect them, but the flying dirt and debris had already temporarily blinded him. Luckily he quickly regained his sight. Blinking with his eyes watering, he looked around and discovered Donnie white-faced and expressing in words what Jose felt. Donnie shouted over to Jose, "Garcia, ain't no way in hell we're going to make it out of this one alive." As he was yelling, the bamboo around them was being whittled down by two VC firing their AK-47s just above their heads.

Garcia knew they had to fight to stay alive. Gunby, only twenty years old, snapped out of his daze and slapped another belt of ammo into the machine gun, and the fight continued. Streams of red tracers whipped over the jungle floor, converging on gray uniformed figures. As Jose stared past his M60's barrel, he watched the colorful pyrotechnics of his tracer rounds bouncing about as they hit trees and other objects and changed course. Steam or perhaps it was smoke lifted off the hot barrel of his gun. Gunby fed another belt into the smoking M60. If they were going to die, they were going to take a lot of Viet Cong with them.

Machine gunners, Bob Pointer and Jose Garcia were firing so rapidly at the advancing enemy that they were both running out of ammo. Murry noticed the dilemma and told Carl Johnson, a native of Houston, Texas, and John Brantley from Chicago, Illinois, to recover the full ammo cans they had left on the trail a short way back.

They immediately responded to Murry's request. Hunched low, Carl shot across the trail and grabbed the four-hundred-round can of ammo. He dove across the trail back to Pointer's position. According to Murry, Carl actually did a flip through the air and landed on his back near Bob Pointer, who was now holding an empty machine gun. Carl righted himself, grabbed the ammo can and within moments was loading a new belt into Pointer's machine gun. John Brantley had grabbed the other can of four hundred rounds and successfully returned to Pointer's machine gun team. John dropped down to a prone position to the right of Bob Pointer and started firing his M16 at the VC and their muzzle flashes that lighted up the shrubs and bushes the Viet Cong were firing from.

Suddenly a cloud of tear gas floated toward the men of 2nd Platoon. Men grabbed for their gas masks, but the filters on most of the masks were so wet they were useless. Sergeant Murry buried his face in the ground, trying to keep the gas from his eyes. The Viet Cong used the gas as a prelude to an intense RPG attack. In seconds, RPGs were smashing into trees and bamboo and the men were getting hit by shrapnel.

Bob Pointer realized that he and his gun crew had become isolated from the rest of the line, so he attempted to pull back. He needed to move back only a short distance. Carl Johnson grabbed the extra belts of ammo and cautiously started toward the new position. That's when they noticed that their twenty-two-year-old comrade, John Brantley, lay face down on the jungle floor. The battle was over for him. He had been hit numerous times by shrapnel and he was gone. The family he had dreamed of with his wife Dorothy Mae would never be. He was another one of our men who had been in-country just three months and would be returning to his home in Chicago in a flag-draped aluminum case.

On the way over to Vietnam, John had flown in a passenger plane and played cards with Robert Harris and T.J. Clement, talking about his wife, Dorothy Mae. The three of them had trained at Fort Polk, Louisiana, then reunited in San Francisco for the long flight to Vietnam.

Robert and John were both assigned to the Rangers Alpha Company and would continue their friendship until June 17, 1967, when twenty-year-old Robert was shot to death and John mortally wounded by shrapnel. Mr. and Mrs. Willie Brantley, who lived right next door to their son John and Dorothy, received the horrible news a few days later that their son was gone.

At the same time, Garcia had weathered the gas attack and the deluge of RPG rounds fired at his position. David Ward, Garcia's ammo bearer, had been hit in the eye, and the bullet had somehow punched a hole through the top of his head, but hadn't killed him. He was lying prone a short distance from Jose Garcia and Donnie Gunby.

Right after the gas attack and the simultaneous RPG attack, Jose and what remained of his crew attempted to fall back a bit. Jose and Donnie grabbed David Ward to pull him back, but as they tried to move him, he started to vomit blood. Under their dire situation, Jose Garcia decided it was best to leave Ward where he was and have him play dead.

Garcia and Gunby spotted a tree large enough to offer them some cover. They quickly began to set up their new position, but before they could finish, more RPGs slammed into the trees around them. Garcia took shrapnel in his left arm and hand. The wound was a major problem because he was trying to set up his M60. To spread out the bipod, he needed both hands, but now his left arm was virtually paralyzed. The barrel of the gun was so hot that he could not touch it without burning the flesh off of his hand. Miraculously, he regained some control of his left arm and was able to complete his task of setting up his M60 without being hit again.

The VC were coming down a trail toward him, firing AK-47s and RPG rounds. Jose positioned his gun against his shoulder and balanced it with his right arm and started to hose down the advancing Viet Cong. Two more RPGs smashed into the trees behind him, peppering him with shrapnel that caused him to yell out in pain from the burning metal searing into his flesh. Every time Jose was hit, David Ward, still laying bleeding from the gunshot wound to his head, was also struck by the shrapnel and let out a groan—but he was still alive.

Viet Cong whistles were suddenly heard around the perimeter. Everyone waited for another assault, but the whistles were signaling a retreat. Just prior to the Viet Cong retreat, Sergeant Murry had started to move his men forward to retake control of the area they had temporarily ceded to the Viet Cong. There were wounded and dead Americans still lying out there, and since the intensity of the battle had diminished, it was time to move forward and try to recover the men still out there. As Murry got his men to start crawling forward, the Viet Cong saw their movement and countered with a barrage of RPGs and a hosing of the area with their AK-47s. It was during this action that Alan Roese was struck in the head with a bullet and killed. Other members of 2nd Platoon were also hit.

Then, suddenly, the attack lost its momentum, and the Viet Cong melted back into the jungle north of us, leaving behind death and misery. A few Viet Cong maintained fire on our positions, but the intensity of the battle lessened into harassment from the bushes and trees instead of a deadly assault.

The LZ was like something from a horror movie where half-dead things come shambling out of the woods. It was a real-life horror scene that we all were a part of. Sergeant Murry remembered one man who was hurt badly trying to drag himself back to the safety of the rear line. One of his arms had been seriously hurt, yet he would lay on his side and push with his legs, trying to snake his way to the rest of the platoon. He occasionally waved his good arm at the men he was crawling toward, then he'd stop to dig his fingers into the jungle floor and claw his battered body a few more inches forward.

Other wounded men continued spraying the wet jungle foliage with bullets as they painfully hobbled back from the front to the rear perimeter.

David Ward was one of the first wounded men recovered from the jungle floor. Unbelievably, this gravely injured man who had endured unflinchingly brutal horror was still alive. For him, the battle must have felt like an eternity as he lay helpless, with bullets and shrapnel smashing all around him. David Ward was one of the miracles of the battle. His survival during that period of pure hell is inconceivable to me. Just imagining being shot through the eye, with the bullet exiting out of the top of your skull is terrifying enough, but enduring playing dead on a muddy jungle floor teeming with ants, leeches, centipedes, millipedes, and snakes is a scene straight out of the most horrific nightmare.

But for David there was still more to endure: he had to stay quiet and not move as Viet Cong swarmed the area where he lay bleeding. Worsening the situation was the irritating cloud of CS gas that floated over him and swarms of flies that took advantage of his helplessness. The battle raged around him and hunks of hot shrapnel from Viet Cong RPGs struck him three more times. Machine gunner Garcia could see him and hear him moan each time he was hit, but David never cried out during his ordeal.

A few days after the battle Ward's parents, Vincent and Margaret Ward received a telegram informing them that David had been seriously wounded. It was months of surgery and healing before the doctors finally discharged him.

Jose Garcia and his assistant Donnie Gunby took stock of their selves. Gunby was one of the very few men of Alpha Company who was not wounded, but Garcia was not that lucky. Jose had been hit three times with shrapnel. He had a piece of shrapnel in his left arm, another in his right leg behind his knee, and a nickel-sized piece of shrapnel embedded in his right buttock.

Garcia got patched up on his arm and leg wounds, but he was a little shy about having the medic dig around in his buttocks looking for a hunk of metal. It burned like hell, but he decided to endure the pain that afternoon. Once back in Lai Khe, he put it off again. In the end, the hunk of shrapnel became a permanent souvenir of the battle of Xom Bo II. It was sort of a pain-in-the-ass reminder of what he once endured in Vietnam. His nickel-sized Vietnam souvenir shows up whenever he has to fly and go through the TSA's full-body scanners. Jose has experienced some exasperating moments with TSA because of the shrapnel embedded in his butt.

Chapter 36
Battalion HQ Involvement

Peter Clark was Captain Williamson's RTO for the Rangers battalion radio net. He had been in-country for almost an entire year and was seriously contemplating extending his time in Vietnam. Clark had marched in with Alpha Company earlier that morning. When they first arrived at LZ X-Ray, he and Williamson were situated on the edge of the clearing, fifty or so meters from the northern end of the LZ. He had heard the start of the firefight northeast of his position, but like most of us he didn't think it was anything big—just a couple VC left behind to harass our men.

As the conflict started, Clark also observed Lieutenant Colonel Lazzell hop into an observation helicopter and take to the air. Lazzell was another short-timer and was still hampered by an elbow that had been badly damaged during a battle the previous year. First Lieutenant Richard Dalton, the FO for the Rangers Alpha Company explained that Lazzell's jeep whip antenna had been blown apart by a .50 caliber bullet and shreds of it were blasted into his elbow. Lieutenant Colonel Lazzell spent months at Walter Reed Hospital recovering from the incident. Later in 1966 he returned and again was given command of the Rangers.

As Clark stated in Gregory Murry's book, "Almost all the useful emerging intelligence about the battle was auditory, and the battalion CO had placed himself where he couldn't hear anything that wasn't coming through his radio headphones in a noisy open chopper."

On the ground were still the battalion S-3, Major Tony Jezior, and Captain Bobby Roberts, the assistant S-3. They were the battalion operation officers.

One of the jobs that twenty-seven-year-old Captain Roberts of Campbellsville, KY was tasked with was coordinating air support during the battle. It was a job of tying in close-air-support with all the other organic fire power – artillery, helicopter gunships, and mortar squads.

It required monitoring the battalion nets and deciding on where to most effectively use the limited assets available. He had four companies and a recon platoon all wanting the support of the gunships, bombers and other sorties he controlled. To make the job more difficult, Captain Roberts had to do his job hugging the ground or get shot. Bullets were constantly whining and cracking over his head as he talked to the forward air controllers (FACs) flying in tiny Bird-Dogs, L-19 somewhere high above him. He would request situation reports from the units on the ground and from their input decide where to napalm, where to drop 500 and 750 pound bombs and where to send the gunships.

The battle was terribly traumatic, but for Captain Roberts even more disconcerting were the desperate cries for help from the Rangers recon platoon. He had been their platoon leader just weeks before. Those cries were coming from men he knew well; men he had become friends with; men he had fought alongside. He desperately wanted to get as much ordnance on the Viet Cong attacking them, but communicating with his old recon platoon was virtually impossible. Viet Cong bullets and grenades had destroyed many of their PRC-25 radios. RTO's had been shot, some were seriously wounded and others were dead. If you can't talk to the men needing the support, you can't deliver deadly bombs, artillery, rockets or other ordnance.

Within minutes after the beginning of the battle, Captain Roberts, miraculously was able to provide gunship support for my unit and others fighting in the north end of the LZ. Soon he would have bombs and napalm smashing down into the surrounding jungle killing many of the attacking Viet Cong. It would be a day he would never forget.

Chapter 37
Prelude to Second Assault

At about 1:25 P.M., the thuds of two or three VC mortar rounds were heard landing among the men of the Rangers Alpha Company and the Black Lions Bravo Company. Anticipating more rounds, the soldiers tried to take cover as more mortars fell and exploded. Five more smashed down into their positions; seconds later, more exploded in their midst. They were 60 mm mortars the VC were firing at them.

The rounds came blasting into the left flank of the Rangers Alpha Company, wounding numerous men. More ka-rumps added to the chaos as the mortar barrage continued. Bright red orange fireballs blossomed wherever they impacted, followed by a shower of leaves, twigs, dirt, and sizzling deadly shrapnel. Men were hurt, yet more ka-rumps echoed around the LZ as the VC continued firing.

Around twenty 60 mm mortars peppered the northern elements of the Rangers Alpha Company and the Black Lions Bravo Company.

The Rangers Bravo Company had also been hit hard in the initial assault and were now trying to collect up their wounded. The Vietcong had furiously attacked Bravo Company, but had failed to penetrate its line. Sergeant Richard Ancira remembers that when it started it looked like hundreds of Viet Cong were swarming towards his position. The VC were firing AK-47's, carbines, RPG's and some tossing Chicom grenades at him and his comrades. Bravo Company returned fire at the advancing Viet Cong. Unfortunately, Captain Ulm's Bravo was down to about 90 men, but they were still able to hold their position and turn back the assault.

Sergeant Ancira, however, didn't get to see his men push the VC back because at the very onset of the battle a grenade landed just a few feet from him. When it exploded, it tossed him around like a feather in the wind. It showered him with shrapnel and one large chunk smashed into his head, knocking him unconscious. Another piece ripped into his left hand destroying two of his fingers. More shrapnel peppered his body, but he didn't feel it, because he was out. This was the third time that Ancira had been wounded, and fortunately, it would be his last. Sergeant Ancira was eventually evacuated from the battle and spent months in the hospital before he returned back to active duty.

Chapter 38
The Second Assault, 1:30 P.M.

The mortar barrage was a prelude to a 1:30 P.M. ground assault. By the time the men of Alpha realized that the mortar attack was over, the VC were in front of the consolidated 2nd and 3rd platoons of the Rangers Alpha Company.

This was a large assault that was coordinated with a simultaneous assault on the Rangers' recon platoon in the southeast and the right flank of the Black Lions Bravo Company. The sections of our perimeter were hit hard by the VC.

The 1:30 assault on the Rangers Alpha Company appeared to be launched by the same VC elements that had attacked them in the earlier assault. Alpha was much more prepared for this second assault. They had consolidated their 2nd and 3rd platoons' lines and had artillery falling close in front of their positions. In fact, fifteen minutes of continuous artillery fire obliterated the jungle in front of Alpha's position. The fire was close in, creating a wall of death the VC would have to retreat through if they wanted to escape the grenades, heavy automatic weapons, and thousands of M16 bullets washing over the landscape.

This assault was turned back, but not before the VC got within thirty meters of the tree line, or fifteen meters from the 2nd and 3rd platoons' line.

A rifleman from the 3rd platoon, Private First Class Daniel J. Phelps, was manning a two-man position that came under attack by a group of ten VC. They wore black pajamas and fired at his position as they moved toward it. Phelps's impromptu fighting position was a large termite hill that was being raked by the approaching VC AK-47s.

When they got within twenty-five meters of his position, Phelps and his partner opened up on them, killing the ten assaulting VC with about two minutes of automatic M16 fire. During or directly after the exchange, Phelps's partner was hit and killed, probably by a sniper. Phelps was now alone in the battle; in fact, he could see no other men from his company, but he maintained his position through the entire engagement. Other VC attempted to crawl toward his position as the battle raged, but Phelps was able to shoot them before they shot him. Some VC were able to drag away a few of their new dead, but the original ten VC killed at the beginning of the assault remained unreachable and were left behind.

Rangers Alpha Company command post had migrated from the center of the company's sector to the area that was being assaulted. Alpha's commander, Captain Williamson, wanted better knowledge and control of the battle and had hastily moved his command post to this new location. He also knew his artillery forward observer, First Lieutenant Dalton, could more effectively adjust the artillery if he was closer to the area being attacked.

While Dalton was adjusting artillery on the VC, Captain Ulm's Bravo Company was being assaulted. Two of Bravo's men, PFC Paul Edward Kelly of Smyrna, Georgia and PFC Edward A. Smith of Newport, Kentucky were firing their M16's and tossing grenades at the advancing VC. They were holding their position, but the fighting was intense. The VC were using snipers in trees to try and kill Ulm's men and were continuously firing rocket-propelled-grenades at Bravo's front line. The RPG rounds were exploding in the trees and raining down shrapnel on the men below.

The VC were intent on breaching Kelly and Smith's position. The two men continued to exchange fire with the VC. They were firing clip after clip of bullets, but the VC were still moving closer and closer to them. Their high rate of fire was exhausting their ammunition and it was obvious that one of them would have to retreat from their position to retrieve more ammo. Unfortunately, before that happened, they were both sprayed by shrapnel from a mortar or RPG round exploding just meters from them. They were peppered by the razor sharp shrapnel, but continued to fight back. The shrapnel wounds, however, were serious and Smith and Kelly were bleeding profusely. No one knows exactly when they died, but the wounds were mortal and before medics could reach them, Bravo loss two of their best. Kelly was only twenty one and Smith twenty when they died. Both had been in country for about four months.

Chapter 39
Captain Williamson Is Wounded

Around 1:30 P.M., Peter Clark, Captain Williamson's RTO reported he and the captain had been wounded. Clark and Williamson were both hit by shrapnel from an RPG round after they moved to their new location. Williamson's wound didn't slow him down much; he remained on the radio, trying to stay abreast of the changing situation. Clark also reported that he saw two VC entering the perimeter. Those two VC were believed to be the only VC that broke through the Rangers Alpha perimeter. Their success was short lived because they were immediately killed.

A medic was summoned to attend to Captain Williamson's wound, while he continued to command his company throughout the battle. First Lieutenant Dalton's artillery barrages were so close to the perimeter that occasional pieces of shrapnel were hitting friendlies. In most cases, the umbrella of bamboo diminished its velocity sufficiently that the still hot shrapnel might sizzle on the men's wet clothes, but didn't penetrate them. The massive close-in artillery fire was a critical factor why the VC were unsuccessful in overrunning Alpha's positions.

The Viet Cong launched another mortar attack and this time some of the rounds struck just meters from Alpha's command group. First Lieutenant Dalton recalled that at least two rounds crashed down into their area. One was just a couple meters from where he was stretched out on the ground with his handset pressed against his face.

At 1:45 P.M., after an intense fifteen minutes of fighting, the assault on Alpha subsided.

Chapter 40
2nd Assault on the Black Lions

During the same period the Rangers were being assaulted, the Black Lions Bravo Company was under a similar attack by the VC. Artillery was pounding down on the area held by the VC, keeping them from advancing. In fact, artillery was falling within thirty meters of the perimeter.

The Alpha Company 2nd Platoon was pinned down in the grass within the LZ's clearing. They were holding a blocking position directly behind Bravo Company, which was under attack. Many of the men from the 2nd platoon crawled south toward a clump of trees to get out of the VC's withering fire. The bullets were being fired at the men in Bravo Company, but the majority of them ended up hitting the area Alpha Company's 2nd platoon was occupying. The heavy automatic fire was so intense that it prevented us from standing up to return fire. Firing into the woods from our prone position would undoubtedly hit the men in Bravo Company.

The sky north of the 2nd platoon's position in the elephant grass was black and furious looking. It boded ominous, with swirling dark clouds of smoke and debris punctuated with flashes of brilliant white, yellow, and red bursting from its darkness. To many, its fury and thundering noise was a welcomed happening. The inability to fight back was frustrating for the men in 2nd platoon, but there was little they could do except wait until we were cleared to return fire. That would come soon. Until then, it was at least comforting to see tons of our ordnance smashing down on the VC's positions. Our artillery and air support were a blessing that provided us an edge over a very experienced adversary.

Chapter 41
David Cordeau's Squad

Sergeant David Cordeau of Port Arthur, Texas, had a squad of fourteen men who were part of the Black Lions Alpha Company's 1st platoon. They were positioned just inside the tree line on the northwest quadrant of the LZ and had been receiving fire since the battle began. Their area had also come under a salvo of VC mortars and RPG rounds. Shrapnel was flying everywhere, and Cordeau's men were being hit. His fourteen men lacked any real cover and had simply dropped to the ground to lessen their odds of being shot.

From their prone position, they raked the jungle in front of them with their M60s, M79s, and M16s. Cordeau, whose call sign was Outlaw 1 on the company's radio net, was engaging an entrenched enemy with everything he had. Even as his men fired toward the source of the bullets cracking over their heads, the Viet Cong's assault continued unabated. The enemy could not be seen from Sergeant Cordeau's position, but they were close enough to toss grenades at him and his men. One grenade came within a couple feet of his position, but failed to detonate. Twigs, leaves, bark, and dirt showered the men as other grenades exploded around them. For some it was more than that: it was hunks of red-hot shrapnel slicing into their flesh. As the battle raged on men were getting hit. Private First Class Heartman got hit in the jaw with shrapnel and a short while later got hit once again. Another man in Cordeau's squad got hit with shrapnel and before the battle was over 6 of his 14 men had been wounded, but they held their sector of the perimeter.

Sergeant Cordeau said, "Shrapnel just kept raining down on us, and there was little we could do about it."

The stuff just kept peppering his men. It was shrapnel from VC mortar rounds, grenades and even from our own ordnance. During a slight lull in the battle, one of Cordeau's men decided to stand up and look around. The man was tall and had been in country for just a few weeks. Sergeant Cordeau said his man was looking around like a big prairie dog. Cordeau jumped up to pull his man back and at that very instant a huge piece of jagged shrapnel smashed into the Sergeant's head. His three pound helmet took the brunt of the blow. It went sailing off of his head, and a large gaping hole was torn into its camouflage cover. The impact knocked Cordeau to the ground and left him dazed for a few minutes. He recovered his helmet and put it back on. If the shrapnel had hit any lower, Sergeant Cordeau would have been killed. Cordeau kept that piece of shrapnel and his helmet for years as a reminder of how close he came to death.

Sergeant Cordeau was only 19 during the battle and had been in country for about 8 months. He was one of Platoon Leader, First Lieutenant Jerry Wilson's, best squad leaders. An eighteen-year-old David Cordeau in 1966 had joined the army on his own straight out of high school. He went to Ft. Polk for Basic and AIT in Fort Gordon, Ga. Before Advanced Infantry Training he married the love of his life, Nolia Lege also of Port Arthur, Texas. By October of 1966, he was saying goodbye to his wife of just a couple months and was off to Vietnam.

David was surprised at how fast he gained rank. He was a sergeant in less than a year and was given a squad to lead.

Now he was in the biggest firefight he had ever experienced and at nineteen years old was saddled with the responsibility of keeping his fourteen men alive. Cordeau accomplished that task, but six of his men still were wounded. Some were hurt bad enough that, after being evacuated, Sergeant Cordeau never saw them again.

Chapter 42
Sawtelle's Second Defense Line

Sergeant Linsley Moore from the Black Lions Alpha Company had his men spread out in the clearing, and they were taking heavy fire. His experiences that afternoon were significant enough that after the battle Sergeant Moore created his own written record of it. That account of his involvement, I found to be a fascinating view of the battle. He wrote that, "The Viet Cong were all in the woods and hanging in the trees, picking off people one by one. We couldn't see any of the people from the 1st Battalion 16 Infantry because they got caught in the wood line."

Linsley and his men had been told to swing around to the north front of the clearing and provide a secondary perimeter, or blocking position, inside the clearing.

"As people moved into the clearing, they would start taking up positions closest to the entrance of the clearing," he wrote. "This caused my squad to have to move all the way to the far end of the field. As we went past the company commander, he stopped me and told me to swing my squad all the way around the far right side of the wood line and take up positions, and the rest of the company would follow. As we moved around the clearing, the intensity of the fire picked up so bad we had to hold fast because they had us pinned down."

Sergeant Moore and his men spread out in the tall elephant grass and dropped to the ground to wait for the Viet Cong to bust out of the wood line and attack them. They listened to the barrage of artillery rounds and the battle raging thirty to fifty meters deeper in the jungle. They heard the crack of bullets zooming by them and the sound of VC mortar rounds exploding all over the area.

While they hunkered down in the tall grass, they were surprised to see a soldier looking like a huge flaming torch come running out of the woods. The soldier was Specialist Fourth Class Dannie Smith of the Black Lions Bravo Company, who had occupied a position close to the one that had been overrun at the onset of the battle. He had successfully held his position, shooting and killing Viet Cong soldiers as they came into view, for most of the first engagement. Then three Viet Cong, one with an AK-47 and two with carbines, started firing at him. He moved to a position behind a tree as the three Viet Cong jumped behind a large termite hill. Specialist Fourth Class Smith tossed a grenade at their position and raked the area with his M16, but they shot back and tossed a Chicom stick grenade at him.

For a short period of time, the three black pajama–clad soldiers and Specialist Fourth Class Smith traded fire and flung grenades at each other, and then suddenly Smith realized that his clothes were on fire. A bullet from one of the Viet Cong rifles had hit one of his smoke grenades. It exploded into fire and smoke and set Smith's clothes aflame. When Smith realized his dilemma, he jumped up and raced to the clearing to seek help. The three Viet Cong soldiers raced after him and continued to fire, but they missed.

When Specialist Fourth Class Smith hit the clearing looking like a flaming meteor, he was yelling and screaming for assistance.

Sergeant Moore's recollection was, "All of a sudden we saw a soldier run out of the woods yelling with a radio on his back, all the smoke grenades set off. You could see he was wounded badly, so we grabbed him and set up a base of fire against the Viet Cong, who were chasing him. Five minutes later, all the firing stopped, so we dragged this soldier back to where the commander was, for first aid. The commander took him from us and had some of his people take him to the medics, who were set up about fifty meters away. He then said, 'Moore, I want you to take your squad straight across the field to that little bush,' it was about a hundred meters away."

Sawtelle told Sergeant Moore, "We are going to cut the field in half and set up a smaller defense."

The fire that had engulfed Specialist Fourth Class Smith had been extinguished and the medics quickly treated him for serious burns. He should have been immediately medevaced out of the field, but the battle was too intense to bring a chopper in. When one did arrive, there would be a lot more casualties to chopper out.

Sergeant Moore believed that Viet Cong were watching them, and he was probably correct. When he and his men fulfilled Sawtelle's orders, they again came under intense Viet Cong fire.

It was about 1:35 P.M. when Sawtelle's east/west line across the clearing was completed. This new line sealed off the two battalions' CPs from VC attacking from the north.

Sergeant Moore recounted what happened next: "Charlie was smart, he saw everything that was going on and he waited until we cut the field in half and then cut loose on us. My squad and half of another one were caught right in the middle. We couldn't move in any direction. The rest of the unit pulled back about a hundred meters behind us and set up, so this caused us to be right in the middle, between the unit and the Viet Cong. We couldn't shoot because the 1st Battalion 16th Infantry was in the woods all around between my squad and the Viet Cong. What a hell of a predicament. I tried to talk to the company commander on the radio to get us the hell out of there and to give us some artillery fire on our right flank, because they were trying to pick us off. The only reason they didn't hit us was because of the bush, which they couldn't see though. The artillery started coming in, but it was way out, so I yelled into the radio to bring it in closer so we could make the Viet Cong keep their heads down while we crawled back."

I was the artillery officer that Sergeant Moore was requesting support from. I wanted to bring artillery rounds in a lot closer to his position, but I couldn't because the Rangers Alpha Company was supposed to be in the area he was receiving fire from. I did adjust the fire a little to give them a little more cover. It was the best I could do without blowing up our own men. "Once we started crawling," Moore continued, "we could see two gunships coming and raking the top of the wood line. They sure were a sight for sore eyes. On the other side of the field were three jets making their runs on the other edge of the woods. I don't know where we would be if it wasn't for them. After I got back to the command post, I got a chance to talk with the artillery officer. He said he really didn't want to shoot so close to the wood line because he didn't know how many men of the 1st Battalion, 16th Infantry were in that area. You could see he was worried about it, but it would still be a while before we found out what the outcome was."

Sergeant Moore's request for the close-in artillery was always a hard choice to make. I would've wanted to fulfill his request, but at the same time, I couldn't fire in another unit's sector unless I was sure they were all dead, or their commander also requested the close-in fire.

Sergeant Moore's men did survive the hail of bullets raking their positions.

His recollection of the battle continued, "An hour later, all the shooting stopped, and we all got up to check the wood line to see how many people we could help. Bodies of one company were spread all over the woods. From what someone told me it was Alpha Company 1st Battalion, 16th Infantry."

During Sergeant Moore's ordeal, Sawtelle also had some of his other men stand up in the elephant grass and fire into the tree line, aiming high to avoid hitting our own men. Sawtelle also had a .50 caliber machine gun set up, which was used to shoot at snipers located in the trees.

Sergeant Mike Stubbs and his squad were responsible for manning the .50 caliber. Twenty-year-old Stubbs was from Charlotte, North Carolina and was with the Black Lions Alpha Company's 1st Platoon. Sawtelle's RTO Specialist Fourth Class James Berry also assisted in setting up the machine gun. Many years later Mike Stubbs was astonished to discover a CBS news clip that captured him and a couple of his other squad members preparing the .50 caliber machine gun for action. The CBS news clip narrated by Walter Cronkite and Dan Rather is a vivid reminder of the battle for any of the men who were there.

Once the .50 caliber was set up it was used to continuously spray high up in the trees on the western side of the clearing with the goal of killing any Viet Cong who were perched in them firing at our men.

During the battle, Captain Sawtelle moved among the men in his platoons, cajoling, comforting, urging, inspiring, and even threatening them to do their best while exposing himself to the same threats they faced. I was his tagalong. Everywhere he went, I went along with our RTO's. Sawtelle didn't let the bullets pouring in prevent him from doing his job.

Some of Captain Sawtelle's men were so close to the tree line that they worried that the napalm being dropped by jets just inside the surrounding woods would also cook them. Twenty-year-old Private First Class Michael Patrick Arias from San Tan Valley, Arizona was one of the men who remembered how close the napalm was falling. Parts of the napalm canisters were landing in the clearing close to Michael. He also recalled that it seemed like the Viet Cong were just fifteen or twenty meters away from him shooting at them from the tree line. Private First Class Arias made it through Xom Bo II without being wounded. Three months later he would once again encounter the 271st Viet Cong Regiment in the battle of Ong Thanh. He would also survive that slaughter. In that battle, he was instrumental in guiding many of the wounded out of the killing zone and back to their base camp.

Another one of Sawtelle's men, Specialist Fourth Class Tom Waldron, from Charlotte North Carolina, also recalled seeing the jets swoop down and drop, what he thought were, 250lb or 500lb bombs around the perimeter. He recalled that they exploded so close that he thought, "They're dropping the bombs right on top of us." If a soldier is laying prone 50 or 60 meters from where a 500lb bomb explodes, he will actually be lifted an inch or so off the ground. Twenty-two-year-old Waldron realized the bombs were certainly a deterrent to the attacking VC, but felt their proximity also added casualties to our ranks. Sergeant Mathis from the Rangers recon platoon, who was wounded during the battle, loved the jets dropping the bombs in their close air support. He was awed at how they appeared almost aerobatic as they swooped low and twisted while they dropped their ordnance. Sgt. Mathis gives credit to those pilots who risked their lives in support of our battle. He felt they had much to do with him staying alive.

The tempo of our battle had changed; the VC seemed less aggressive during this second assault on the Black Lions. It appeared that the Viet Cong were only firing at Bravo's men when they popped smoke. Otherwise, the VC hardly fired on the Black Lions men unless they saw one of them move.

During this skirmish, we were also hit with tear gas. It was delivered by mortars or RPGs. I had a gas mask with me and tried to use it on our first gas attack, but found it soaked and useless. The VC were trying to get us to stand up or run to make us easier targets for their mortars and snipers. When we first got hit with the gas, I had immediately dropped to the ground and landed in a bed of ants. I quickly accepted the fact that a few ant bites weren't that bad compared to being shot or ripped up from shrapnel. Standing at that time would've made me a bigger target for the falling mortars and the hundreds of bullets zipping over my head.

The tremendous amount of adrenaline that pumps through our bodies during a battle stifles a lot of the pain that we would have normally felt. I flung myself to the ground numerous times during incoming mortars attacks, and the adrenaline rushing through me blocked the minor pain from the scrapes and cuts caused by the sharp elephant grass, stones, and sticks that I landed upon. When the eyes see tons of dirt, trees, and debris flung into the air from 750-pound bombs and the sky blotted out by the smoke and fire of artillery, the mind tells the body to disregard minor pain and focus on survival.

Chapter 43
Recon Platoon Attacked

Time: 1:30 P.M., on the southeast side of the clearing.

While the Rangers Alpha Company was engaged with the VC on the northeast quadrant and the Black Lions Bravo Company was engaged with the VC in the northwest sector, the VC launched a simultaneous attack on the Rangers recon platoon. Twenty-two-year-old First Lieutenant Doug Logan was recon platoon's leader. He was from Crane, Missouri. His RTO was twenty-one-year-old Edward Waag from Amelia, Ohio, who had been in-country for about four months.

The recon's positions were spread so far apart that it was impossible to prevent the VC from penetrating the perimeter. Sniper fire was being received by platoon members on the right flank. Then, just south of the perimeter, three VC were spotted and fired upon by recon's men. That was the prelude to the deadly assault on First Lieutenant Logan's platoon.

Suddenly it wasn't just three men but a large force of attacking VC that covered the forty-meter front. The

VC concentrated their attack on two outposts and the platoon's command post, which was protected by an M60 machine gun. The concentrated VC fire on the M60 position took its toll, and the position was overrun. Twenty-two-year-old machine gunner Specialist Fourth Class Sammy L. Holmes of Miami, Florida, was shot and killed, along with his twenty-year-old assistant, Private First Class Leroy Reed from Lake Charles, Louisiana. During the assault, Private First Class Douglas Wallin of Rochester, Minnesota, who was also a machine gun crew member, was hit multiple times with shrapnel from grenades or claymore mines. Severely wounded, he fought on because if he wanted to survive that was his only option. The fighting was intense all around him. He and his comrades were severely outnumbered and the Viet Cong seemed determined to kill all of them.

On the left flank of Recon's area Sergeant Leonard Mathis from Alexander, Alabama was taking fire and was quickly wounded. It was a serious wound that was incapacitating. His RTO was also hit blowing off a hand. The Viet Cong were targeting anyone with a radio. Sergeant Mathis' radio was so shot full of holes that communication with the rest of the battalion was impossible.

Having destroyed the machine gun impediment, the VC concentrated their efforts on the thinly defended recon's command post, which came under heavy automatic weapons fire. Airstrikes were requested, but it would be twenty-one minutes before the first jet arrived.

During the onset of the attack, First Lieutenant Logan was wounded by small arms fire. Medic Ray Gilbert from Henderson Harbor, New York, patched him up on the spot. The wound didn't incapacitate Logan, so he continued to fight and maintain command of his unit.

Sergeant First Class Bajo was the forward observer for recon and was calling in artillery when his team came under heavy fire, resulting in his RTO being wounded and his PRC-25 radio being destroyed by bullets. Twenty-year-old Specialist Fourth Class Dennis Soricelli of Bronx, New York, recalled Bajo's RTO's wounds were far worse than a simple flesh wound. Soricelli also said that virtually every radio in recon was destroyed by bullets or shrapnel. At the end of the battle, he discovered that his radio also was honeycombed with bullets and shrapnel holes. It literally fell apart.

It was soon decided they had to retreat from their position. The firefight was intense. Logan, although wounded by a bullet, crawled from man to man, rallying them and boosting their morale while instructing them on how to escape the killing field they were in. It was decided to first remove the wounded, so platoon Sergeant Gradie E. Sanders, a Korean War vet, Private First Class William Cole, a medic, and the artillery observer Sergeant First Class Bajo left the command post carrying three wounded men. Just as they were retreating, Sanders saw eight to ten VC wearing khaki uniforms, steel helmets, bandoleers, and web gear approaching the CP.

About a few hundred meters north of First Lieutenant Logan's platoon, reinforcements were quickly being assembled by the Rangers headquarters company. Headquarters security squad was assigned the job. One of its members, twenty-year-old Specialist Fourth Class Fred Atkins of Ashland, Kentucky, recalled that his squad of about eight men was being briefed on their mission of assisting the recon platoon when mortar rounds started to crash into the clearing. The men of the security squad were all huddled in a circle, listening intently to the plan of how to best reach the besieged recon platoon. Atkins said there was a sudden flash, and then he and the rest of his squad went flying through the air. A mortar round had fallen right in the middle of the squad. Almost every man in the squad was seriously wounded, dooming the relief mission.

While that was going on, Sanders, Cole, and Bajo were able to get recon's wounded to the Rangers Bravo Company position, close to recon's left flank. Ed Chrisman, the senior medic for the Rangers Bravo Company, rushed to recon's wounded to patch them up. Ed couldn't remember who he treated that day, but guessed it was between fifteen to twenty wounded men. Most were suffering from shrapnel wounds.

Twenty-three-year-old Specialist Fourth Class Chrisman was from Gaylord, Michigan, and was a seasoned medic who just three days before, had treated the wounded from the battle of Xom Bo I, where six men were killed and sixteen wounded. Chrisman was also in the deadly battle of Ap Gu on April 1, 1967, which was fought with the same PAVN 271st Regiment that had ambushed us. He had also seen action in the battle of Prek Klok I back in February 28. In that battle, twenty-five of his comrades were killed and twenty-eight more wounded.

Chapter 44
Recon Platoon Overrun

While the wounded were being evacuated from the battle, First Lieutenant Logan, the recon platoon leader, informed the Rangers commander that his command post group had killed more than 30 VC, saying they were "stacking them up like cordwood." Although wounded, he sounded upbeat and optimistic. However, just after that report was made, radio contact with the recon platoon was lost.

Recon's battle became even more intense. The recon platoon was spread so thinly over the perimeter that its weakness had become evident to the Viet Cong. The VC took advantage of this by concentrating their attack on one small sector of recon's perimeter. They poured men into the center of Logan's perimeter like a human tsunami. I was at the other end of the LZ X-Ray, and I could hear the clamor of the bullets and concussions of RPG's rounds slamming into the remnants of the recon platoon. Their battle was as loud as those going on at the Northern end of the LZ. It was butchery.

Private First Class Wallace Nye was wounded in the shoulder while retrieving more ammo, but he went back to his position and continued to fight as the Viet Cong surged forward. Other members were also taking fire. It suddenly seems like the VC were everywhere.

Twenty-year-old Private First Class David Oshel of Naperville, Illinois, was a very short-timer with recon. He had arrived in Vietnam in June 1966, and when the shit hit the fan at LZ X-Ray, he was virtually counting the hours before the silver bird would take him back to the world. Private First Class Oshel had seen a lot of action during his year in Vietnam and had been wounded twice in previous battles, earning him two Purple Hearts. However, David told me that none of the previous battles were as savage, bloody, or chaotic as what he endured at LZ X-Ray.

The VC fired multiple rocket-propelled grenades at the command post defenders, killing Private First Class Gary Ernst of Perryville, Missouri, and Private First Class Wallace Nye of Minneapolis, Minnesota, along with Specialist Fourth Class Charles Hook of Friendsville, Maryland. All three of them were only twenty years old. Hook was a short-timer with about a month left in-country when he was killed. He was married to Barbara Hook of Confluence, Pennsylvania. They had married during a ten-day leave before he left for Vietnam. His parents Wayne and Grace Hook were notified of his death by a telegram on Monday, June 19, 1967. Charles Hook would leave behind three brothers and three sisters.[10]

The large element of VC was firing a deluge of bullets at the few remaining men in recon platoon. One by one they succumbed to the overwhelming firepower of the attacking VC. Specialist Fourth Class Martin Plotkin of Lynbrook, New York, was shot and killed, along with Private First Class William Cole, of Clairton, Pennsylvania, who was one of the platoon's medics.

Ironically, twenty-one-year-old Plotkin had been just a few days away from moving into a much safer battalion headquarters' job as the official photographer. Plotkin was a well-liked soldier by the men in recon and loved playing cards, according to Specialist Fourth Class William Buonanno. Plotkin was the only Jewish man in the company and sometimes led a few of his comrades in the Jewish folk song "Hava Nagila," which translates to "Let us rejoice." But on June 17, no one would be singing it.

While First Lieutenant Logan was moving among his men in recon platoon, he was hit by multiple pieces of shrapnel from a rocket-propelled grenade. These were mortal wounds, and Doug Logan quickly succumbed to them.

Specialist Fourth Class Ray Gilbert said that Logan was liked by the men of the platoon. Gilbert said First Lieutenant Logan wanted the best for his men and that he didn't shirk danger.

Logan's wife, Sharon, later said she felt a premonition that something bad had happened to Doug. While researching this book, she wrote to me that, "I am not clairvoyant, but I had a personal reaction that something was terribly wrong about the time the ambush occurred.

"I was on edge for the next several days. Back then, the radio would broadcast the units and info about the battles. His unit was specifically mentioned in a broadcast, and because several days had passed I thought he was safe, and I could relax. Unfortunately, that was not the case." In fact, Sharon was visited by a priest at her workplace to inform her of Doug's death. I was moved by something else Sharon, who was a nurse, wrote to me. She wrote, "I have always worried about the other men present that day. I have felt sort of guilty that I wasn't there to give comfort. I know that must be crazy from your perspective because war is not pretty and all tidy, but I just didn't want anyone to be alone."

The massive assault on recon's platoon probably lasted no more than fifteen minutes, but it took nine lives.

Before the VC retreated into their jungle refuge, they searched the dead men of recon platoon. They went through their clothing and took the men's weapons and also mementos.

The Rangers' commander ordered an element of the battalion headquarters company to move toward the recon platoon's sector to provide assistance. An airstrike was also called in, and at 1:41 P.M., twenty-one minutes after the assault started, the first airstrike arrived. The bombs fell about 150 meters east of the perimeter. The VC withdrew a few minutes later at 1:45 P.M., using the same break in the line they had entered through.

Chapter 45
Close-in Artillery and Bombs

More bombs were dropped on the east and southeast side of LZ X-Ray. The close-in artillery was the principal deterrent to the enemy assaults on the Rangers Alpha Company and the Black Lions Bravo Company. The thousands of artillery rounds pouring down acted like a curtain of hot lead preventing the VC from re-engaging with us.

The artillery support was delivered with such fervor that a 175 mm gun firing from a fire base near An Loc got so hot that one of its rounds blew up in the breech, killing two of its crew and wounding five more. Alpha Battery, 6th Battalion, 27th Artillery of the 23rd Artillery Group lost SSG Samuel Lee Modesitt of Manila, Arkansas. He was twenty-five years old and left behind his wife, Shelia, and a young son.

CPL Charles M. Roach of Harvey, Illinois, was also killed. Charles was twenty years old and had been in-country only one month before he was killed supporting our comrades fighting the battle of Xom Bo II. It was this unbelievable and dedicated support that helped us take control of the battle and push back the assaulting Viet Cong.

I was very proud of my parent battalion, the 2/33rd, with its constant delivery of thousands of rounds. To shoot as fast as they were shooting, they must have enlisted every man in their battalion to help uncrate and deliver the rounds to the gun crews. When we asked for "continuous fire for effect," it just kept pouring in. There must have been some sweaty, tired gun crews that evening.

A total of 8,250 artillery rounds were fired in support of the battle. That total included 7,621 rounds of 105mm, 513 rounds of 155mm, 38 rounds of 175mm, and 78 rounds of 8 inch artillery. That's a lot of artillery. In the east and southeast of LZ X-Ray, the airstrikes provided the most effective deterrent against the VC for the Rangers recon platoon. One airstrike, unfortunately, was delivered too close to the Black Lions Bravo line and killed two of its men—at least that was what got reported in the After Action Report. However, Hono Yacapin, a lieutenant with the Black Lions Bravo Company serving as 1st platoon leader, stated that no one was killed during that incident. He said the bomb fell close to them, but not on top of them. Also, Captain John Turner refutes the After Action's report that two of his men were killed by an errant bomb.

First Lieutenant Yacapin distinctly recalls that the bomb exploded just meters in front of his CP. He and his RTO, Specialist Fourth Class Lee, were luckily laying prone on the ground behind a six-foot-tall termite mound. After the dust, dirt and debris settled and the smoke cleared, the termite mound was gone. That termite mound saved the lives of First Lieutenant Yacapin and Specialist Fourth Class Lee. The bomb did wound five men from his platoon, but none fatally.

Chapter 46
The Viet Cong Withdraw

According to the After Action Report, most of the VC assault groups started their withdrawal from the battle at about 1:45 P.M. It was not a quick withdrawal, however, and fighting didn't stop. We kept receiving automatic fire from different locations around the perimeter, and we also received more mortar rounds. The VC, who were left behind continued the battle, but at a reduced scale, allowing the bulk of their comrades to retreat to safer areas. This strategy allowed much of the 271st Regiment to retreat with little threat of artillery barrages or airstrikes following them to their designated rendezvous locations.

Most of us fighting in the battle were unaware that large numbers of the Viet Cong were retreating. We felt that the VC were simply falling back to regroup and then assault us again. They had already fallen back once before, regrouped, and attacked again minutes later. We didn't lessen our resolve during this period, but instead we took advantage of the lull to bring in more ordnance and bomb the areas around us. The bombing consisted of napalm and high explosive bombs that were dropped within an area of 1,000 meters around our LZ. I also continued my artillery barrages.

To most of us, any decrease of the incoming fire was considered a lull in the battle and we continued to reinforce the line and augment any weak spots. Captain Sawtelle at 1:50 P.M. instructed one of his platoons to create another blocking position across the clearing just north of the Rangers recon position.

Around 1:55 P.M., Lieutenant Colonel Rufus Lazzell ordered two gunships to provide additional firepower to the fragile line held by the remnants of the Rangers recon platoon.

At 2:00 P.M., there was still heavy automatic weapons fire pouring in on our troops from the surrounding trees.

Chapter 47
Attack on NDP Rufe

Back at LZ Rufe, many of the men, still at the old NDP, were listening intently to the battalion radio. They heard the desperate cries for help and the background noise of the battle at LZ X-Ray spilling out of their PRC 25 radios. What they heard sounded awful. It was a constant roar of gunfire and men trying to talk over the noises of war. They heard frantic statements of, "we are being overrun." They wanted to help. The fact that they knew the men who were being shot up made it even worse. Then at about 2:03 P.M., the VC launched an attack on them also. It started first with mortars being fired from just outside of their perimeter. An unknown number of Viet Cong were attacking their NDP. The attacking Viet Cong were probably a company from the 272nd Regiment of the Viet Cong 9th Infantry Division. After the Viet Cong lopped a few mortars into the LZ, they followed up with small arms fire on the men securing the NDP. Men from Charlie Company immediately returned fire. It wasn't a concerted Viet Cong attack, but it tied the men down. The NDP was ringed with claymore mines and most of the men had fighting positions constructed with good fields of fire. The attack went on for about 30 minutes and then the Viet Cong just faded away into the jungle. The attack was probably nothing more than a way of keeping the men still located at LZ Rufe occupied, and unable to leave their NDP to reinforce the men fighting at LZ X-Ray. During the battle, the Viet Cong popped about ten 60 MM mortar rounds into the LZ, but luckily they landed in areas unoccupied by the troops. In fact, during this skirmish none of the men remaining at the old NDP were killed. There was no report of how many Viet Cong might have been killed or wounded during the fight either.

Chapter 48
Looking for Wounded and Dead

The attack on LZ X-Ray was winding down and the VC's automatic weapons fire was moving further and further away from us. With the lull in the fighting, we started collecting the wounded and moving them to our evacuation point in the center of the LZ.

Sergeant Greg Murry of the Rangers Alpha Company and his men combed the battle ground for their dead and wounded. They quickly discovered one of their men, Private First Class Robert Maguire from Atascadero, California, sitting on the ground and leaning against a huge termite mound. His eyes were wide open and staring into oblivion, but he was dead. A medic with Greg's men closed Robert's eyes and his comrades carried his body out to the clearing for evacuation.

Specialist Fourth Class Fred Atkins of the Rangers headquarters company was tasked with the job of assisting in the recovery of dead and wounded in the Ranger's recon area. Fred told me it was the worst carnage he'd ever witnessed and the most traumatic job he had during his Vietnam tour. He recounted how he found a dead man with his leg blown off. Fred had to find the leg and load the man and his leg into a black body bag. He came upon another soldier who had part of his face literally blown off. Resting on a sandbag was a grisly mask of skin and hair that had been part of the face. The rest of the head was just a grotesque protrusion of broken bones and bloodied grey goop. This vision was seared into Fred's memories forever. These bodies were his young comrades a year or so removed from high school, some of America's finest who would never grow old.

He also found out that day what dead weight really meant as he carried the many bodies from where they were killed to the evacuation point within the LZ.

One of the recovered wounded from recon platoon was Private First Class Douglas Wallin. He was severely torn up from shrapnel and was bleeding profusely, but the medics were able to stop some of the bleeding and get him on a chopper to a MASH unit where he was patched up more and then shipped off to the USAF Clark Hospital at Clark Air Force Base in the Philippines. For two months Doug fought for his life, but finally on August 28, 1967 he succumbed to his wounds. The news of his death would reach his parents Mr. and Mrs. Dewey Wallin of Rochester, Minnesota a couple days later. Douglas's girlfriend, Jan, the girl he promised to marry when he returned home, would also learn of Doug's death from friends. He was her first big love and his death devastated her. He was her handsome blue eyed blond boyfriend who had touched her heart like no one else ever had.

Most of the VC automatic weapons fire had subsided by 2:45 P.M., but serious sniper fire was still an issue until about 3:00 P.M., when it finally ceased because we had either killed them or they had faded back into the jungle. The few remaining members of the Rangers platoon and its augment of the Rangers Head Quarter members had started the gruesome task of collecting their dead and wounded. They had fifteen men dead and many wounded. Members of the Black Lions Alpha and Bravo companies assisted.

While the Rangers were recovering their casualties and equipment, they found the bodies of thirty-five to forty VC. The majority of these VC were uniformed in khaki, looked well fed, and had new Soviet assault rifles.

Piles of rucksacks and web gear had been stacked up on the field. It told of the many that had become casualties. Much of the web gear was blood soaked and shredded from shrapnel. Sergeant Giles recounted seeing the stacks of bloody webbing and noticing a black holster protruding from one stack. He immediately recognized it as the holster that he had given to his friend, James Elchert. Giles was saddened to see it because it meant that Elchert was badly wounded or dead. Giles would learn later that his friend, James, had been killed.

By 3:00 P.M., the remnants of the Rangers recon platoon had collected their wounded, dead, and equipment and moved them inside the new perimeter formed by the blocking position that one of Captain

Sawtelle's platoons had formed. Medics from our company assisted in doing whatever they could for anyone wounded. The number of wounded was around 150 and our medical supplies were limited so men ripped their shirts into strips for tourniquets and made makeshift litters from ponchos to carry the muddied wounded to the few medics available. According to Doc Ross Philips, with 1st platoon, each medic only carried 5 syrettes of morphine which was hardly enough for our medical nightmare. He also said that each medic carried a bottle of darvocet to give to the wounded to ease their pain. Doc Philips was from Enid, Oklahoma and was only twenty years old during the battle of Xom Bo II. He was tasked with the job of moving the many wounded to their makeshift field triage area. Philips and other medics would give immediate care to the wounded in the field and then move them to the more secure triage area.

James Callahan was one of the medics who worked in the triage area. He worked diligently to save as many men as he could. The wounded were encrusted with mud and blood and soaked from the rain. Many were blackened from the smoke of burning trees and grass. The aftermath of the battle was like a Hans Rudolf Giger surreal landscape, with men missing limbs, men hobbling along with the help of a comrade, men covered with blood, men with pants or shirts shredded, men with their ribs glistening white through a sheen of red, and men with their insides cradled in a poncho tied in front of them. There were men with sucking chest wounds wheezing and drowning in their own blood, men with limbs dangling by a couple sinews, men unconscious and caked in bloody Vietnamese mud, men covered with oozing puncture wounds from shrapnel, men burned from explosions, men blinded from flying debris, and men with their faces ripped apart by bullets or grenade fragments.

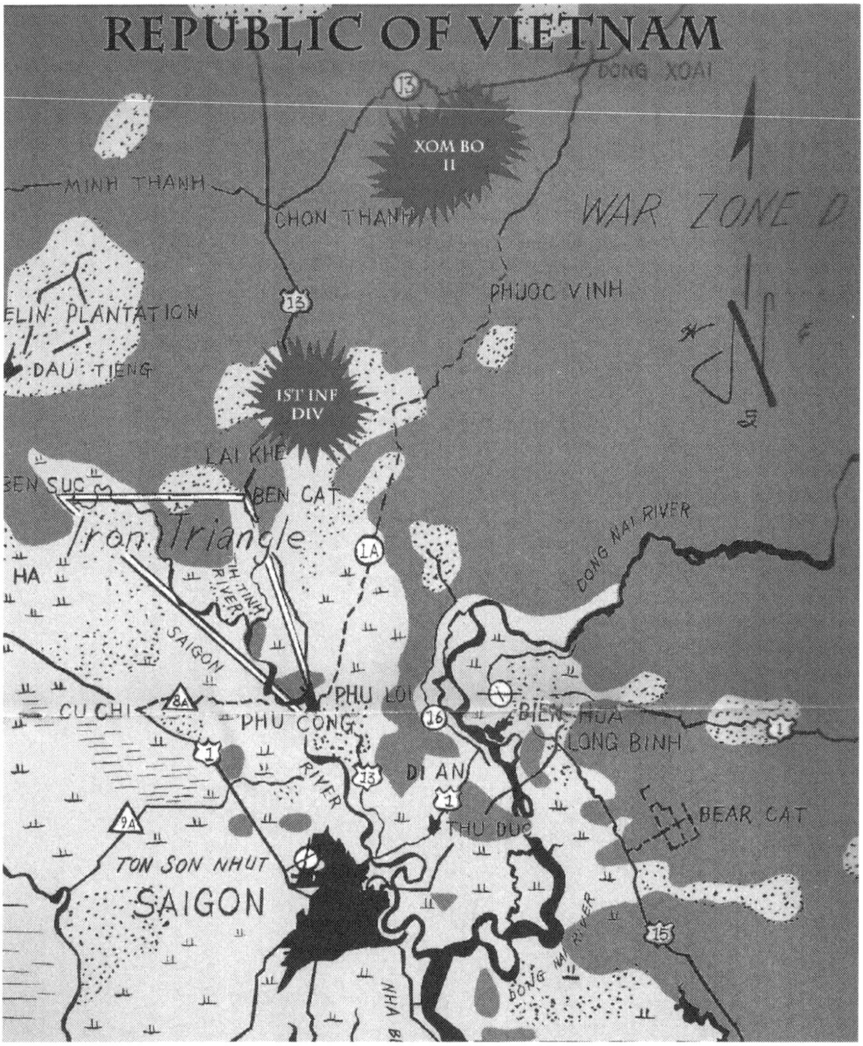

The Battle of Xom Bo II occurred about 47 miles northeast of Saigon. The Rangers and the Black Lions Battalions were based in Lai Khe about 18 miles south of where the battle was fought. These battalions were airlifted into an artillery firebase in the notorious "D-Zone," prior their assault on LZ Rufe. Five days later two undermanned companies from both battalions marched into LZ X-Ray and soon after that the battle started.

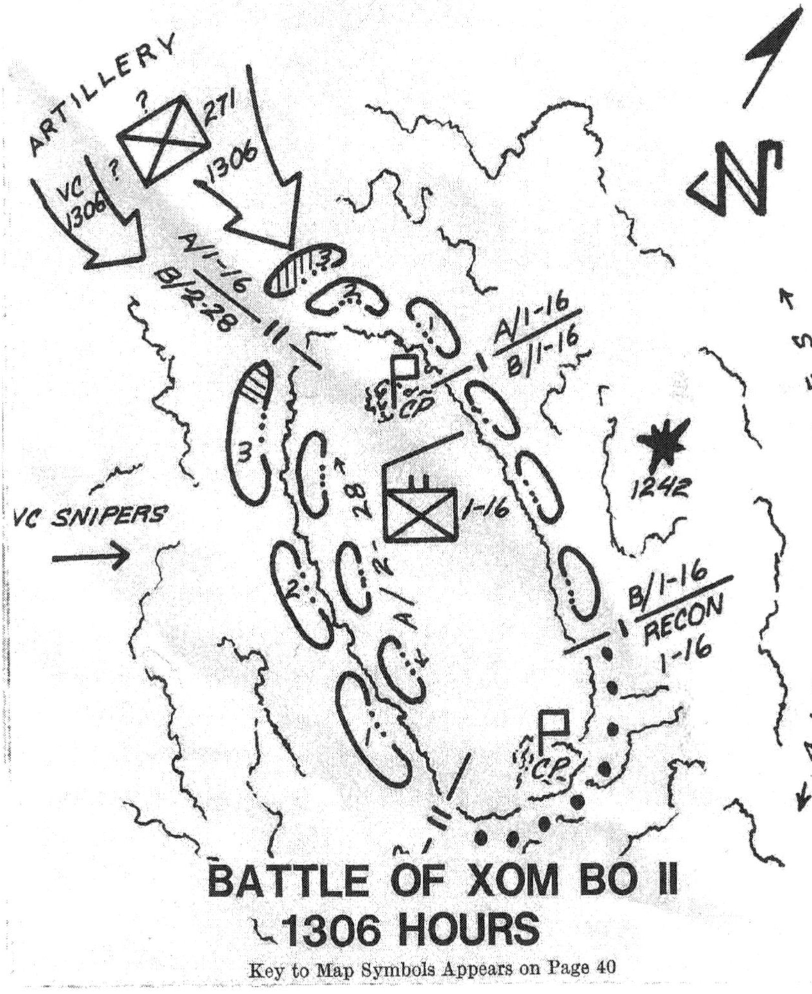

Map of First Assault taken from After Action Report. It should be noted that Alpha 1/16th does not agree with where the map depicts their platoon's positions.

Xom Bo Battle at 1:30 pm

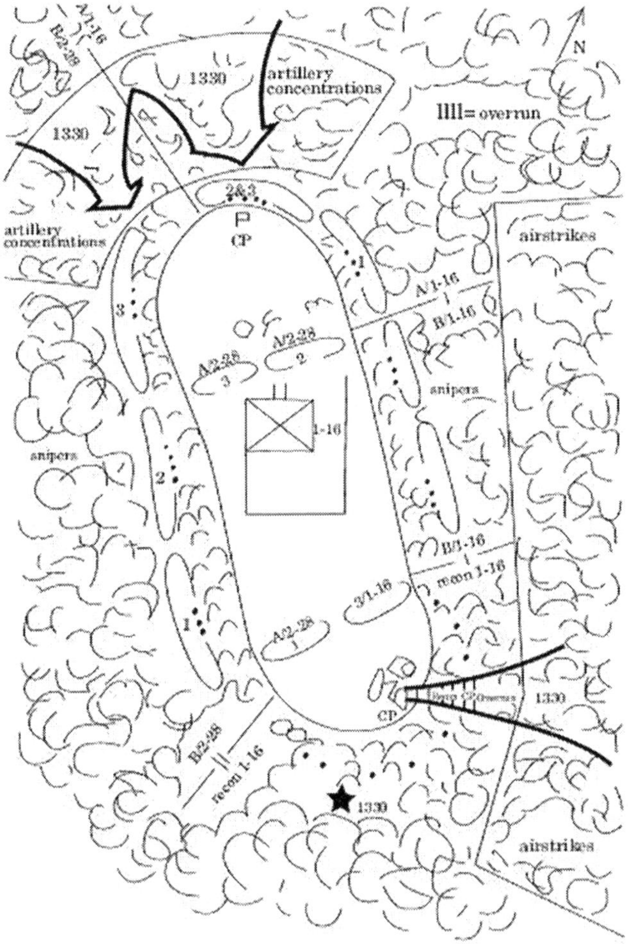

Map of positions of units during the second assault on LZ X-Ray.

LTC Rufus Lazzell was given operational control of the Rangers and the Black Lions during Xom Bo II. Lazzell retired as a Bigadier General. He was born March 29, 1929 and died March 12, 2016.

June 1967 was the Summer of Love and many of those who weren't drafted flocked to the huge concerts held in Monterey, Marin and San Francisco, California. While the battle of Xom Bo II raged, the first day of the Monterey Pop Festival took place. Photo from Wikipedia.

CAMOUFLAGED INFANTRYMEN of B Company, 1st Battalion, 16th Infantry, wait to board helicopters for the air assault into LZ Rufe.

SP4 John Olsen

Getting Ready for our trip to LZ Rufe which preceded LZ X-Ray. Our NDP at Rufe was always wet and muddy. Picture from Danger Forward Volume 2, number 1 – February 1968.

Machine Gunner Jose Garcia waiting for instructions on when to move out on the first day of Operations Billings. Xom Bo II was the last large battle of the operation.

The Rangers loading up to head out for Operation Billings - which ended with Xom Bo II. Picture Courtesy of Jose Garcia.

The Rangers waiting to head out for Operation Billings - which ended with Xom Bo II. Picture Courtesy of Jose Garcia.

SP4 David Litz

The men of the Rangers Alpha Company start to deploy in the northern sector of LZ X-Ray. Picture from Danger Forward Volume 2, number 1 – February 1968.

Picture from Danger Forward Volume 2, number 1 – February 1968

A COMPANY, 2D BATTALION, 28TH INFANTRY, entered the landing zone at 1215 hours and moved north along the positions of its sister company, Bravo. Thirty minutes later the BATTLE OF XOM BO II started.

Picture from Danger Forward Volume 2, number 1 – February 1968.

A wounded 1st Infantry Division trooper crawls to cover as a medic follows him, continuing to apply a bandage. Viet Cong Snipers had shot him. From an old AP report on the battle of Xom Bo II.

Lieutenant Troy Oliver with his motley crew. Their call sign was "Hill Billy." They weren't a platoon you'd want to piss off. The James Berry in this picture became Captain Sawtelle's RTO. The man pictured on the far left is Lonnie Skaggs who was killed April 27, 1967, before the battle of Xom Bo II. Skaggs was a true hero who gave his life to save others. He was awarded the Distinguished Service Cross for his actions. I was there that day - he was our Rambo. I will never forget him.

David Cordeau's Squad (call sign was Outlaw) armed to the teeth; flame thrower, grenade launcher, machine gun – rifles and more. Many of these men were wounded during the battle. Photo courtesy of David Cordeau.

Village of Lai Khe was in the center of our base camp, but we still had Viet Cong within it. Taken by the author.

The place to go to relax. It served food, drink and a lot more. Taken by the author.

Lai Khe Village was located in the middle of our base. The kids always wanted our candy and our C-Rations. Some of our men would create holes in the wire to crawl through, so they could be with their girlfriend.

Lai Khe Vietnam 2016. Courtesy of Troy Bowers.

Bill Williamson (foreground Right) 1/16th Alpha Company CO, Lou Murray, David Hearne (in middle) FO for the 2/28th Alpha Company; Frank John Limiero - RTO who during the battle took command of 3rd platoon of the 1/16th Alpha Company. Donald Sawtelle, CO of Alpha Company 2/28th. Left Front- Jose Garcia, Mrs. & Mr. Gregory Murray – author of "Content With My Wages."

David Hearne was the Forward Observer for the Black Lions Alpha Company. The artillery shot over 8000 rounds during the battle of Xom Bo II.

Richard Dalton was the Forward Observer for the Rangers Alpha Company and took command of the company when Captain Williamson was wounded. Courtesy Richard Dalton.

What does thousands of empty 105 rounds look like? Here is what a few of them look like. We shot over 8000 rounds.

Captain Sawtelle – Company commander of the Black Lions Alpha Company and my boss. Courtesy Jo Sawtelle.

Picture taken of a display at the War Remnants Museum in Ho Chi Minh City. The display shows photographs of the Xom Bo II battle. This set of pictures shows our Medic James Callahan trying to save a man's life. The original pictures were taken by a great photographer, Henri Huet.

General Richard E. Cavazos' wife Caroline with Author David Hearne. Cavazos took over operational control of our battle at LZ X-Ray at about 3 PM June 17, 1967.

General Richard Cavazos was the only living battalion commander of units that were involved in the battle of Xom Bo II as of the time of the writing of this book.

Chapter 49
The Job of a Medic

Medics Felix Vallejo, Mike Stout, James Callahan, Ross Philips, Dwight Krebbs and others went from man to man, doing the impossible. These medics were our doctors, our angels of hope, and our salvation. Their job was immense; they had to make life-and-death decisions that would result in which men of the 150 wounded could be saved and who had the least chance of survival. Men who weren't medics also tried to pitch in and help with the wounded.

The presence of thirty-one-year-old Captain James E. Swink, our battalion surgeon, was an additional blessing for our wounded men as they were pulled out of the wood line. During battalion size operation, Swink would often travel with us to the field. He had been assigned to the Black Lions after a five-month stint at the 12th Evacuation Hospital in Cu Chi, Vietnam. He was there in the aftermath of the battle helping the medics with the wounded.

Jim Swink was from Rusk, Texas. He had been a famed player in his earlier years earning him the moniker "the Rusk Rambler" as he led TCU to consecutive conference championships and Cotton Bowl appearances. In fact, Captain Swink was a two time "All American" halfback who finished second in the Heisman Trophy voting in 1955.

After graduating from TCU, he rejected an NFL career even though drafted by the Chicago Bears. In numerous interviews, Swink stated he had been Inspired by a physician in Rusk, Texas to pursue a medical career.[11] It must have been a difficult decision because Swink had proven himself a formidable football player. He had led the nation in scoring and placed second in rushing in 1955. He got to play against Jim Brown and Swink's team won. He is also remembered for being the object of the University of Texas expression, "Hook em Horns."[12] Prior to the November 12, 1955, game Texas students had come up with the oft-heard phrase in the hopes of unsettling Swink and his team, the Horned Frogs, but it didn't work. Even with thousands of Texas students screaming "Hook em horns," Swink still played one of his best games, rushing for 235 yards on 15 carries for a 15.7-yard average and scored a school-record of 26 points. The Frogs trounced the Longhorns, 47-20 that afternoon.

Captain Swink also fought hard for us, and though he had little in the field to work with, just his presence was comforting to us and especially to the medics. With James Swink around there was someone to go to when a wounded soldier was beyond what a medic felt capable of handling. Captain Swink did whatever he could with the little he had in the field. He said "We can give them some pain medication and start an IV on them or very rarely maybe a system with their airway and breathing." His biggest goal as he stated, "You get them on a helicopter as fast as you can."

In another photograph taken by AP photographer Henri Huet, it shows Captain Swink with his stethoscope dangling from his neck working hard on a wounded soldier. Opposite of him is a soldier with a cigarette hanging from his lips who appears to be assisting. In the background you can see other soldiers, one with his shirt off and two more, probably Jim Callahan and Mike Stout, working on another wounded soldier. The photograph appears to have been taken at a makeshift triage area. The medics liked Captain Swink and he had great respect for them. Ross Philips said Swink was accessible and didn't play the rank game. He said Swink was a fun guy who was always a dedicated doctor. During his tour he was wounded and received a Purple Heart and a Bronze Star metal for his outstanding contribution to the cause.

Chapter 50
Back in the World

Seven thousand four hundred miles away at the Monterey Pop Festival in California, the last act was coming on. It was about 1 A.M. on Saturday morning and Simon and Garfunkel would finish off the night with some of their best songs. Their first song was "Homeward Bound," which was certainly apropos for what we had been enduring. Many men would be homeward bound from the battle of Xom Bo II. Some would still be living, but thirty-seven would just be the empty and broken shells of fallen sons, fathers, lovers, and friends on their final journey home.

Years later, Simon and Garfunkel's "Homeward Bound" still transports me back to LZ X-Ray and that afternoon of blood and gore. It sparks uninvited ephemeral visions. They are hazy and vaporize quickly, but still clear enough to evoke the melancholy memories that creep back into my consciousness.

> Homeward bound,
> I wish I was,

Homeward bound,
Home where my thought's escaping,
Home where my music's playing,
Home where my love lies waiting
Silently for me.
Silently for me.

The last song of Simon and Garfunkel's set was a nonsense song, "I Wish I Was a Kellogg's Cornflake." As the last chords subsided, so concluded the first night of the Monterey Pop Festival. The Summer of Love crowd had loved the music, and participants claimed that a feeling of peace permeated the event. The majority of concert attendees drifted over to the huge camping area near the arena and to the nearby Monterey Peninsula College football field. The crowd was still very much alive with post-concert excitement as they climbed into their sleeping bags, toking on their last joint as music, singing, talking, and just "being" completed the evening.

While they looked forward to a repeat of the same the next day, we hoped and prayed for just the opposite.

Chapter 51
Our First Medevac

At our camp ground at LZ X-Ray, there was no feeling of peace permeating our existence. In fact, we were attempting to bring in new supplies of ammo and evacuate the wounded, who desperately needed immediate medical assistance or they would die.

Our plea for assistance went out and luckily, Captain Paul Wenzel, an aircraft commander of a utility helicopter, was on standby alert. His chopper was fueled and ready to transport and resupply troops. When he heard that our companies were in serious combat with units of the VC 271st regiment and in dire need of ammo and evacuation of severely wounded, he volunteered for the mission. He lost no time—he had his helicopter loaded with the needed ammo and was in the air flying to our hot LZ minutes later.

Our location was easy to spot from the air. He only had to look for large plumes of smoke blackening the horizon. As he came closer to our LZ, he could see the artillery exploding in the northern sector of the LZ and the crisscross of tracers lacing the ground below. He could see trees burning, men scurrying around, and lines of men prone on the ground. Smoke swirled over the muddy landing zone hundreds of feet below.

Before Wenzel could land, other forward observers and I had to pause our artillery fire so he could enter without being hit by the many deadly objects flying through the air. Yellow smoke was popped to indicate where to land.

His arrival was met with intense fire from the VC surrounding the LZ. At his first attempt at landing, he was waved away because a mortar attack started. The VC were probably trying to prevent our resupply. He circled high above, waiting for the mortar attack to end and then came in again for a landing. His chopper was hit multiple times by bullets, but none that disabled it.

He disregarded the imminent danger and successfully landed his helicopter on the east side of the LZ. Once on the ground, he and his crew jumped out and started unloading the ammo. Medics and other men quickly carried some of the worst wounded to his chopper and loaded them aboard. The helicopter and crew were ripe new targets for the VC, and a lot of bullets flew in their direction. Mortars were also being fired, and as soon as the last wounded was aboard, Wenzel lifted the chopper off the ground and flew the wounded men to the nearest medical treatment facility.

That was not his last trip to our LZ; as soon as he delivered the wounded to a field hospital, he returned back to LZ X-Ray. We were still under heavy automatic weapons fire, but he landed his helicopter once more and proceeded to evacuate more of the badly wounded. Captain Wenzel was one of the unsung heroes of the battle. His actions were known to few, but his delivery of ammo and his medical evacuations helped save many lives. Captain Wenzel received a well-deserved Distinguished Flying Cross for his courage and contributions during the battle of Xom Bo II.

Chapter 52
Medevacs Continue

It was right around 3:00 P.M. when Captain Wenzel's chopper arrived to start the evacuation of the wounded.

One of the first wounded men he took out was twenty-year-old Specialist Fourth Class Carl Johnson, one of the many wounded from the Rangers Alpha Company. Carl had been part of Robert Pointer's machine gun crew and had been shot in the throat early in the battle. Unbelievably, even after being shot, he continued to feed Robert's machine gun as they fought desperately to stop the Viet Cong assault.

Johnson died of his wounds soon after he arrived at the field hospital. He was a native of Houston, Texas. It was June 21, 1967 when his wife Rebecker Nell, his sister Elaine, and his brother Steve would receive the devastating news that Carl was killed in the Vietnamese jungle. Carl's heroic deeds, however, would never appear in the Houston papers because of the sensational trial coverage of 25-year-old Cassius Clay, more commonly known as Muhammad Ali. On June 20, 1967, he had been convicted in Houston, Texas of violating the Selective Service laws by refusing to be drafted. Clay was promptly sentenced to five years in prison and fined $10,000, but remained free while his conviction was on appeal. Four years later his conviction was overturned.

Another horribly wounded soldier that had to be immediately medevaced was Private First Class Don Rawls. He had been shot three times earlier in the battle. Two of the bullets had shattered ribs and ripped up his insides. Another bullet had destroyed his left index finger. As the battle raged all around him, Rawls lay virtually helpless on the jungle floor. He was just a few feet away from his dead friend Sergeant Frank Romo. Rawls was pretty sure he would soon be joining him, but he wasn't going to go easily. He had his wife, Shirley, waiting for him back in Maple Hill, North Carolina and he desperately wanted to see her again. He was covered with blood and looked dead, so dead that the Viet Cong soldiers felt no need to shoot him again. Rawls had lost a lot of blood and was constantly in and out of consciousness. Hours later he was finally found behind a termite mound. He was ashen, unable to move and almost bled out. Rawls was quickly rushed to the LZ's evacuation point where medics did their best to stabilize him before they loaded him onto a chopper headed to a field hospital. He spent 12 days in the field hospital before he was strong enough to be transported to the 249th General Hospital in Camp Drake, Japan. There, out of the war zone, he would convalesce for 30 more days. During this time his wife, Shirley, said she received a purple heart medal in the mail which reaffirmed that her husband had been wounded. However, she wouldn't know how seriously until six weeks after the battle when Don finally was there standing in front of her.

Don's visit home was short lived because during the first few days of his leave, he felt terribly tired, nauseous and had zero appetite. He felt so sick that he visited a doctor who diagnosed him as having hepatitis and quickly readmitted him into the military hospital at Fort Gordon, Georgia. Private First Class Rawls spent 9 more weeks there before he was able to return home once more.

Another early medevaced was Sergeant Mathis, one of the survivors of the Rangers recon platoon. He was transported to a field hospital with numerous wounds and then a few days later flown to the 249th General Hospital in Japan. Sergeant Mathis didn't want his wife, Joann, to worry unduly about his wounds, so he requested that the staff let him notify her of his situation. He didn't want her to receive some shocking government telegram stating he had been wounded. In fact, he didn't want her to know about his injury at all until he was sure he was going to be okay, so for a week or more she knew nothing about his injuries. Sergeant Mathis spent a couple of months in the 249th General Hospital before he was well enough to be released and finally return to his home in Alexander, Alabama.

Captain Wenzel and his crew were instrumental in saving many men. After Wenzel successfully completed his mission, more helicopters joined the tedious task of transporting the wounded to MUST and MASH units. The evacuation of the seriously wounded took almost four hours. The task ended at 6:50 P.M.

Chapter 53
Mortar Attack at 3:30 P.M.

During the evacuation at about 3:30 P.M., the VC launched yet another mortar attack on us with the rounds landing within our area. The mortar attack consisted of about thirty-five 60 mm rounds. They were concentrated on the command post of the Black Lions Bravo Company and inside Captain Sawtelle's area within the LZ, which was being used by the survivors of Rangers recon platoon.

"Incoming! Incoming!" was heard from the men around the perimeter. As the first four or five rounds exploded, I couldn't believe it was actually happening again. The lull of the battle had made me feel as if the battle was over, but as more mortar rounds exploded all over the LZ, I realized it wasn't.

The mortar rounds were landing everywhere, but it seemed some were marching down the east side of LZ X-Ray. Those were probably the ones that Specialist Fourth Class Limiero said almost hit him.

Men under trees were the most vulnerable because a mortar round exploding in a tree created a tree burst that showered them with deadly shrapnel. Specialist Fourth Class Fred Atkins of the Rangers headquarters company said he would try to stay as close to a tree as possible, slightly reducing his chance of being hit by shrapnel. I was lucky I was in the clearing away from trees.

Captain Sawtelle and I still had radio handsets in our hands as we hugged the muddy earth, with our RTOs laying adjacent to us. That was all we could do. You just lie there and wait for the incoming mortars to end. Explosion after explosion rained down around us...at least that was how it felt with smoke and dust filling the air. Through the smoke I could see the brilliant flashes of the explosions, hoping those pyrotechnics would come no closer to us. Time was virtually standing still, with minutes creeping by in fractions of seconds—and then suddenly the incoming was over and it was quiet again, a very welcomed quiet.

At about 4:10 P.M., unit commanders were informed that the Rangers Alpha Company would be replaced by elements of the $1/18^{th}$ INF, also known as the Vanguards, and they would also take over the areas of LZ X-Ray that had been Rangers recon platoon and headquarters company responsibilities.

Lieutenant Colonel Lazzell had decided that the survivors from the Rangers Alpha Company and recon platoon would be choppered over to the fire support base at the Chi Linh airstrip. Oddly enough the Rangers Alpha Company was now under the command of First Lieutenant Richard Dalton their FO from Bravo Battery

2/33rd. Captain Williamson, who had been severely wounded and medevaced, had handed command of Alpha Company to First Lieutenant Richard Dalton. Captain Don Ulm stated that 1st Infantry Division had a standard operating procedure (SOP) for combat situation that if the company's executive officer was unavailable to assume command than the FO would take over until another commander could be assigned. Dalton was left with the difficult job of collecting up the remaining survivors of Alpha and getting them choppered to the fire support base a few kilometers away. Their new destination would offer luxury accommodations compared to what they had been accustomed to. They would now have a latrine, no more shitting in the woods. They would have fresh water. They might even get a warm meal that evening or at least a hot breakfast in the morning. Most of them might even get some sleep that evening because Chi Linh was far more secure than where they had come from. Chi Linh was ringed with hundreds of feet of razor sharp concertina wire, 600 Claymore mines, tripflares and 55 gallon drums of Phu-gas, a napalm-like substance that could be detonated by remote control. And in addition, the fire base was protected by infantry units. If the Viet Cong tried to assault this base, they would also be met with 105 mm howitzers firing point blank at them with deadly beehive rounds.

First Lieutenant Dalton's related to me his recollection of his experience as the commander of Alpha Company's when they arrived at Chi Linh Fire Support Base. He wrote:

"We were given an area to bed down at, I received word that Lieutenant Colonel Lazzell wanted to see me at his tent. I went and reported to him as directed and he said 'Glad to have a Redleg commanding one of my companies,' and shook my hand. He went on to say that he wanted a status report of the company referring to the number of soldiers present and the numbers of soldiers dead and wounded."

Dalton also said that Lieutenant Colonel Lazzell told him that come morning Alpha Company would be sent back to Lai Khe, and that the company would be given top priority for receiving new troops arriving in country. Lieutenant Colonel Lazzell told Dalton the company would have a few days to get reorganized into a fighting unit before they would be sent out on another mission.

The night of June 17th there at Chi Linh would be a time for the Alpha Company survivors to decompress and think of their buddies they had lost. For Sergeant Skiles he would wonder why his buddy Frank Romo had been killed. He was so moved by the death of Sergeant Romo that he would later have a tribute to him painted on the side of one of his barns. And yes, Skiles parents were successful in getting him released early from the service. Neil went home just a month after the battle and helped save the farm and as of the time of this writing he is still managing it. He also returned to his love of drag racing. He replaced his old drag race winning 64 Yellow Super Sport Chevelle with a 1969 version.

One guy the Alpha survivors, would think about was Sergeant Edward Heyer. He was a soldier that had developed a lot of friendships with guys from his platoon. The death of Heyer was a tragedy in many ways because he had just lost his father six months earlier and was sent home for the funeral. His father had willed him a sizable estate and Edward's new situation merited him an early out. However, Edward declined the offer and chose to return to his unit and to the guys he had formed such a brotherhood with. He wanted to be with his team while they were still slogging through the jungles, swamps and rice patties of Vietnam. He wasn't going back to Vietnam because of God and Country, but because of the bond that he shared with his squad. These were his brothers who had lived together, fought together, depended on each other and through it all developed a fierce loyalty for one another. He wasn't going to let them down.

Inside the perimeter of Chi Linh, the remnants of 2nd platoon couldn't believe that out of the 42 men who had marched in just hours earlier, only eight of them were still fit for duty. Two of those men, Sergeant Murry and Donnie Gunby, both exhausted from the battle were stunned when they were told to man an ambush patrol for the evening. They did it and luckily nothing happened.

Chapter 54
The Vanguards Are Coming

Back in Lai Khe, Private First Class Wayne Wade was pulling base guard duty with other members of $1/18^{th}$ when they received word to saddle up because they would be replacing units that had been hammered in a battle.

Private First Class Wayne Wade related to me, "When word came for my unit to saddle up, we were some distance from the ambushed $1/16^{th}$. We jumped in trucks and headed for the landing strip, where Hueys were lining up to take us by squads to the LZ. After what seemed like forever, word came to board the Hueys. Within a few minutes of flight, a few moving specks could be seen on the horizon ahead of and below us. The specks grew larger as our formation of weather-beaten helicopters drew closer. They proved to be the F4 Phantom jets that had arrived before us. They were working the area over with napalm, rockets, and Gatling guns. I will never forget the brilliance of the huge, orange fireballs of napalm contrasted against the green of the jungle and the blue of the sky."

Wade was armed with his preferred M14 rifle instead of what he considered the inferior M16. His rifle was cradled in his arms as he sat on the Huey's floor. His legs dangled out of the slick in preparation of stepping out on the landing runner prior to jumping to the ground.

Insertion into a hot LZ was terribly nerve-wracking, because if you started receiving fire, there was nowhere to go. You were packed into a small space and totally visible to the enemy. Door gunners would scan the ground below for any sign of VC taking shots at our chopper.

At about 4:27 P.M., the Hueys formed a single line to make their runs into the center of the landing zone. The seasoned pilots banked and swooped in low and fast over the trees, making it more difficult for the VC to hit their choppers. They would bring the Hueys within a few feet of the ground. As soon as the chopper was hovering close enough, the men would quickly jump off the running boards and dash toward the tree line.

As Wade remembers it, many of his comrades ditched their heavy rucksacks as they dashed into the tree line, hoping to recover them later. Their path to the tree line ran adjacent to the area where mud splattered soldiers were dragging the dead in ponchos and body bags and carrying the wounded to the center of the clearing.

When Private First Class Wayne Wade reached the inside of the tree line, he quickly encountered a member of the Rangers battalion. The man had numerous superficial wounds, apparently from shrapnel. Wade said the soldier claimed that his area was still receiving incoming fire from snipers hidden in large trees east of them. A few seconds after meeting the Rangers soldier, mortar rounds started falling. He and the Rangers soldier both hit the ground and crawled behind a large termite hill. These large termite hills were often a soldier's salvation from incoming. It wasn't the best protection, but it was far better than being in the open. Wade recounted that one round landed within ten meters of his position.

As the mortar rounds exploded around the LZ, new cries for medics could be heard. Unfortunately, medics were scarce, but other soldiers were taking up the slack and helping the wounded. The mortar attack was probably more cover for the VC's 271st retreat rather than a serious attempt at killing our troops. Once the shelling ceased, the men of the $1/18^{th}$ got the orders to dig in. The same choppers that brought in the $1/18^{th}$ troops were used to evacuate the Rangers companies, except for Captain Ulm's Bravo Company.

Chapter 55
Efforts Back in Lai Khe

Back in Lai Khe, Private First Class David Aldridge observed another part of the Xom Bo II events unfolding. He was new in-country and had been assigned to the Black Lions Bravo Company. Since mid-morning he had been sitting around the resupply pad, waiting for a ride out to LZ X-Ray to join up with his unit.

Earlier that morning, after finishing breakfast, Twenty-two-year-old David had hitched a ride to a resupply pad located on the east side of Highway 13 in Lai Khe. When he arrived, resupplies were being prepared for Lieutenant Colonel Lazzell's four companies at LZ X-Ray. Men were quickly stacking sixty- to ninety-pound crates of ammo onto spread out nets. The transfer of the ammo from the trucks to the nets took some time. Finally, they were done, and three Chinook helicopters arrived at the resupply pad to pick up the heavy loads attached to their underbelly.

When that was completed, David watched the Chinooks take off around 12:15, loaded with ammo, C-rations, water, mail, and even cases of beer. Private First Class Aldridge was surprised that beer was part of the resupply. The supplies hung in large nets from the bellies of the Chinooks and swung gently in the air as they were raced to LZ X-Ray. The helicopters were like giant storks flying away with loads of ammo instead of a new baby. The Chinooks arrived at LZ X-Ray just as the battle started and were immediately waved away. They returned back to Lai Khe and dropped their nets and, according to Private First Class Aldridge, flew off empty.

The Jeeps parked on the resupply pad had their radios on, which were chattering away about a battle raging away up near Phuoc Vinh. Private First Class Aldridge quickly discovered that the reports were about the units he was there to join. He heard one of the S-4 guys at the pad saying that the Viet Cong were firing .51 caliber rounds at the LZ. Time ticked by, and finally, a new rumor started that the 1/18th, lovingly called the Vanguards, had been ordered to saddle up and relieve the Ranger companies fighting at LZ X-Ray.

It wasn't a rumor, it was fact, and shortly after that trucks and jeeps rolled up with men laden with combat gear. They jumped off the trucks and were organized to load into the incoming Chinooks. But before that could happen, the wounded and dead had to be removed from the choppers' cargo compartments. Private First Class Aldridge had this to say about what he saw, "As the ramps at the back of the Chinooks lowered, I saw dozens of wounded and dead soldiers come falling and rolling out of the Chinooks onto the ground. Some who were able to walk came stumbling out like they were intoxicated. They had their arms and legs bandaged, and the bandages were all hasty field bandages, half falling off and soaked through with blood. Some of the wounded soldiers who were able to do so assisted others to get out of the Chinooks and onto vehicles. I have never seen blood look so bright in my life. It practically glowed. It was everywhere...on the soldiers, on the Chinook, and on the ramp at the back of the Chinook. All of the wounded had the look of horror and pain across their faces. Medics started showing up in those old box ambulances the army had at the time."[13]

In the Rangers TOC (Tactical Operations Center), located in Lai Khe, twenty-three-year-old Specialist Fourth Class William Buonanno from North Terrytown, New York, was monitoring the radio nets. It wasn't his usual job; normally he would be humping a radio around for Battalion S-3 Tony Jezior. But fate smiled on him that day, and he was assigned the job of covering for an NCO, who had gone on R&R. That got him out of the field for a couple days, giving him some time to write a few letters to his wife, eat some hot chow, take a shower, and maybe drink a couple beers.

That day in the muggy TOC bunker, at about noon, Buonanno was given a message that a man in one of the Rangers units had an emergency back in the world. Whoever that man was, he would need to pack up and be ready to get choppered out of the LZ. The radio reception between Lai Khe and our operation center at LZ X-Ray was very poor, and Buonanno was having a terrible time communicating with Headquarters Company. While he was struggling with the transmission, suddenly a large amount of noise came over the net. There was the distinct sound of AK-47s, M16s, explosions, and men shouting and screaming. The battle had just begun. His message probably never got to the intended recipient.

For the next few hours, Specialist Fourth Class Buonanno stayed glued to the radio in the muggy TOC, listening to the battle of Xom Bo II raging many klicks away. There were frantic transmissions about large numbers of Victor Charlies attacking, need for air support, need for medevacs, need for ammo, and men being overrun. Many of these transmissions were actually coming from Buonanno's replacement, who was serving with MJR Jezior. Lady Luck had smiled at short-timer Buonanno that day, and two months later he would return back to the world.

Chapter 56
The New Perimeter

Back at LZ X-Ray, Lieutenant Colonel Rufus Lazzell moved his Bravo Company from the east side of the LZ to its west side. The entire east side of the perimeter was now the responsibility of Lieutenant Colonel Richard E. Cavazos' Vanguards. His men stretched from the northern tip of the LZ to the southern end, where the Rangers recon platoon had once been. Captain Ulm's Bravo Company now moved into position south of the Black Lions Bravo Company on the west side of the perimeter.

The infantry company I was assigned to, the Black Lions Alpha Company, was given responsibility for the Northwest sector's perimeter. Lazzell had saddled Captain Ulm's company with searching the battlefield the next morning and the arduous task of airlifting the remaining bodies of the dead from the Rangers battalion back to Lai Khe.

During a large battle, some men get killed, and no one is close enough to them to tell the story of what actually happened to them. Three of Captain Williamson's men were killed and their bodies recovered, but the stories behind their deaths appeared to have died with them. One of the soldiers was twenty-year-old Private First Class Robert Taylor Harris of Earle, Arkansas. He had come over three months prior with Private First Class John Brantley, and both were assigned to the Rangers Alpha Company. Both were killed in the battle. A notice of Harris's death showed up on the bottom left, of page twenty-one of the *Northwest Arkansas Times* of Fayetteville, Arkansas. The notice was given an inch of space on the help-wanted page. The notice was titled, "Killed In Action." It read, "Washington (AP) Army Pfc. Robert Taylor Harris of Earle, Ark., has been killed in action in the Vietnam War, the Defense Department said Tuesday."

Robert Taylor Harris had died of a gunshot wound. His parents, Mr. and Mrs. Robert Harris, of Earle, Arkansas, were notified on June 20 that he had been killed in action.

Private First Class James Melvin Elchert, a Medic with the Rangers Alpha Company, was killed by fragmentation wounds. He had just turned twenty a few weeks prior to the battle. James was from Toledo, Ohio. His parents, Mr. and Mrs. Gerald Elchert, were told of their son's death a few days later, and on June 22, 1967, the *Daily Reporter* of Dover, Ohio, listed James's death under a small Defense Department release that was titled "5 Ohioans Die In S. Vietnam." The listing was very succinct; it simply gave his name and where he was from.

Private First Class Emanuel Kris Brickhouse of Brooklyn, New York, was one more of Alpha Company's men killed in action. His death would leave his wife Faye and their two baby girls to fend for themselves. He had been in-country for only three months before his death. The *Detroit Free Press* would list Emanuel Kris Brickhouse in the June 22 issue of their paper. The list appeared on page forty-seven and mentioned most of the Americans lost in the Xom Bo II battle.

After the mortar barrage, large Chinooks began bringing in more supplies. The deliveries consisted of boxes of ammo, sandbags, rations, and more all secured in webbing dangling from the underbelly of the chopper.

It was obvious from all the new supplies that we would be spending at least another night at LZ X-Ray.

Chapter 57
Replacements, Mortars, and Casualties

The replacements from 1/18th Infantry continued to come in till about 5 P.M., when we were again attacked by another barrage of mortars. This attack was the biggest one we endured that day and consisted of around sixty rounds of 60 mm and 81 mm mortars. We returned fire on their positions with counter-mortar fire.

As the battle subsided, the job of collecting the dead and evacuating them to Lai Khe faced the living. One of the battle's casualties was nineteen-year-old Private First Class Ronald David Edenfield, who had been serving in the Rangers Alpha Company. Ronald was a rifleman with four months in-country. He had already been wounded once when a mine exploded under a truck he was riding in. His wounds were minor in that incident, and he returned back to his unit for duty. Ronald was from Grand Ridge, Florida, the son of Ralph N. Edenfield and Lillian S. Rowan. He had unfortunately dropped out of high school in his senior year and soon after that was drafted. By August 1966, he was in the Army and a few months later, in February 1967, he arrived in Lai Khe, assigned to the Rangers Alpha Company. Ronald used to tell his mother that he was his school's official bench warmer, but this time, he didn't sit it out. Instead, he fought hard and his actions saved untold other men.

His father Ralph was notified on June 21 that his son had been shot and killed during the battle of Xom Bo II. His mother Lillian, who affectionately called Ronald "Rooster," was from Chattahoochee, Florida, and was notified at her job at the Florida State Hospital. An officer came to the hospital, and she was led into a private office to receive the horrible news that her son had been killed on June 17, 1967. She said that his funeral was a closed-casket service because of the severity of his wounds. As of this writing, Ronald's mother Lillian was eighty-five and still living in her home town of Chattahoochee, Florida.

Another casualty from the Rangers Alpha Company was twenty-year-old Private First Class Robert Stanley Maguire from Atascadero, California. He was one of our men who planned to go back to school when he got home. He wanted a job where he could help kids at risk. His father had died when he was only sixteen, and Robert had sort of assumed the mantle of the man of the house. Even in Vietnam, he was still giving advice to his younger brother, Chris. He loved his mother, and they corresponded often, but the savagery of Xom Bo II would change everything and on June 20, 1967, Virginia Klee Maguire was stunned at the arrival of uniformed men at her door to announce the death of her son. On the following day, the *San Luis Obispo County Telegram-Tribune* announced Robert's death to the community. The article stated that his body would be escorted home by his brother-in-law Rodengen, who was also serving in Vietnam. Robert had two brothers, Edward and Christopher, and two sisters, Cheryl and Patricia. Cheryl remembers that her big brother, who was seven years her senior, was very protective of her. She remembers all the ribbons he won in diving competitions. Her last recollection of him was at the little airport in Paso Robles, where he turned and waved his last goodbye to her. Her big brother would show the same combativeness and bravery during the battle of Xom Bo II and receive a Bronze Star with a V device for his valor.

Captain Williamson's company had suffered fifteen men killed, including twenty-year-old Private First Class Jerry Robert Cook. He had been a resident of Alpharetta, Georgia, and had been in-country only four months before he was shot and killed by the Viet Cong. His parents, Mr. and Mrs. Clarence Cook, heard of their son's death a few days after the battle, when officers designated to bring the emotional news to the parents of soldiers killed in action visited them.

Chapter 58
Graves Registration Collection Point

The dead soldiers were brought back to Lai Khe, and some member of their unit would be tasked to provide a positive identification of the remains zipped up in a body bag. Usually, the person providing the identification was a friend or a leader who had worked daily with the deceased. Once the body was positively identified, the dead soldier's things had to be collected for shipment back to the next of kin. The job usually fell to one of his fellow platoon members, someone who actually knew him. The task was an emotional one where a soldier gathered together the last remnants of his friend's life. Sometimes a few possessions would be tossed in the trash to avoid shocking a parent with the soldier's collection of girlie magazines or a baggie of dope, but everything else would be packed up. Some of the belongings would be photographs of a smiling wife and children or pictures adorned with X's and O's of a girlfriend or of his mom and dad or even a car. They were the pictures that kept hope alive and were reminders of what was waiting when he'd return home. Now they were sad reminders of a life cut short, of dreams that would never be lived, of love that would never grow; they were just more remains of a life extinguished. Letters written, but not sent would be packed up for the next of kin to read. Just like his remains, these mementos of his life would be put in a box and shipped back to his loved ones. His area would be sanitized and prepared for the next young man to take his place.

The dead soldier's records and personal things would accompany his remains to the Quang Tri Province Graves Registration Collection Point. This facility was close to Tan Son Nhut Air Base, which for many had been their entry point into Vietnam. Now it would be the exit point for the dead.

The men of the Graves Registration Collection Point had the unglamorous task of cleaning the grime, blood, and debris from the bodies. The bodies were thoroughly washed, nails cleaned and clipped, faces shaved, hair cut, and finally dressed in a clean new uniform. It was a hard job because these men saw close up the ghastly wounds, charred bodies, horrible disfigurements and even containers of body parts. They had to sort through this carnage and decide if they all belonged to just one man or several. These macabre visions would haunt them forever.

Sergeant Edward Elias Heyer's body was one of the many they processed before it could be shipped back to

Prichard, Alabama. Heyer had been shot and killed. He had been an NCO with the Rangers Alpha Company. Edward was twenty-two at the time of his death and had four years of service. He had been in-country eight months before he lost his life in the battle of Xom Bo II. His body, clothed in a fresh uniform, along with his personal effects and paperwork, was shipped back to Alabama in one of the Army's reusable aluminum transfer cases used to ship bodies back to the States. It was received by his grief-stricken brother Joseph and sister Mary Ann.

On June 23, 1967, a short statement announcing Sergeant Edward Elias Heyer's death appeared on page two of the Anniston, Alabama, *Star* newspaper.

To accomplish their morbid but noble task of processing the corpses of our dead, the men at the Graves Registration Collection Point wore hospital masks, usually dabbed with vinegar or perfume to reduce the sickening stench emanating from the decaying bodies. The men at these facilities tried to make the dead look as presentable as possible before the bodies or body parts were placed in the aluminum transfer cases used to ship fallen soldiers home to their loved ones. The transfer cases containing these victims of war and their accompanying paperwork would finally arrive at Dover, Delaware, or Oakland, California, depending on the location of the next-of-kin.

As the war continued, the men of the Graves Registration Collection Point near Tan Son Nhut Air Base saw new broken bodies of dead Americans arriving daily at their facilities. Many of the incoming corpses were bloated with maggots still feasting on their flesh.

More than fifty-eight thousand dead Americans would be processed by the Graves Registration Collection Points by war's end.

The men who worked in these facilities are some of the unsung heroes of the Vietnam War. They were surrounded daily with the worst consequences of war, the dead. They viewed the horror of war frozen on the faces of the thousands of dead men who gave everything for a country of many ungrateful citizens.

Chapter 59
Dover Air Force Base

Mr. and Mrs. Julius G. Roese's son Sergeant Alan John Roese's body was one of the casualties from the Xom Bo II battle delivered to Dover Air Force Base in Delaware. Once there, Sergeant Roese's transfer case was moved into a huge hangar and lined up with military precision alongside other similar transfer cases. The hangar was festooned with huge American flags and each case was draped with a smaller American flag. There, the bodies of the dead would quietly wait transportation to their final destination, at which time their flag-draped cases were wheeled out onto a huge cement landing. The facility believed in "Dignity, Honor and Respect" for all the men and women who arrived at their destination.

This same facility was later used by the astronauts of the space shuttle *Challenger* and the hundreds of victims of the 1978 Jim Jones tragedy in Guyana.

Once the American flag–shrouded cases were wheeled on to the cement landing, vehicles would transport them to planes to fly the remains of the dead and their paperwork home to their grieving loved ones and friends.

Sergeant Roese's final destination was to his parents in Lancaster, New York, a small village east of Buffalo. Roese was another casualty from the Rangers Alpha Company. He had been shot and killed during the Viet Cong assaults on LZ X-Ray. Local newspapers paid tribute to the twenty-one-year-old sergeant with short articles. One headline read "NYS Soldier Dies in Vietnam" and mentioned that Alan enlisted in the Army in 1965 and had spent a year stationed in Germany prior to being shipped to Vietnam in October 1966. The articles all mentioned that his parents were notified Monday evening of their son's death. His remains from Dover arrived a couple days later.

Chapter 60
Replacements Still Arriving

The airlift of Vanguards continued after the mortar attack, which ended at about 5:10 P.M. That mortar attack also marked the last large contact we would have with the VC at LZ X-Ray, but of course we didn't know that so everyone was waiting for the next ground assault or mortar barrage.

Private First Class David Aldridge, who had witnessed most of the airlift of Vanguards from Lai Khe and the removal of the many wounded and dead from the returning Chinooks, was finally able to hitch a ride out to the LZ X-Ray. He climbed up the ramp into the Chinooks and saw blood everywhere. There were puddles of blood on the floor and blood on the benches. It was impossible to find a place to sit that didn't have blood stains, David recalled.

Once he was in the Chinook, they flew for about fifteen or twenty minutes before they arrived at the battle site. The companies had again been taking mortar rounds, so the Chinook circled a few times before it attempted a landing. Once David was on the ground, he began his search for Captain Turner and Bravo Company. To his dismay, he was told that Turner's RTO had been killed during the last mortar attack. He had met Turner's RTO, Michael Morrow, and had really liked him. In fact, Morrow was about the only member of Bravo Company he had known.

Specialist Fourth Class Tom Waldron had just reported to Captain Turner's CP minutes before the mortar attack occurred and had engaged Specialist Fourth Class Morrow in conversation. Waldron and Morrow were a couple of the company's old men; they were each twenty-two years old. Both were feeling a little more confident that the battle appeared to be finally over. Morrow was telling Waldron how happy he was that he had just four more months before he would rotate home. He also expressed how he planned to pursue a career in nursing when he returned back to the world. They were still chatting when suddenly they heard incoming mortar rounds. Waldron and Morrow both hit the dirt as fast as they could and listened to the concussions of the mortar rounds landing around them. The rounds were close, too close. One round exploded in a nearby tree, and a piece of its shrapnel hit Michael killing him. The mortar attack that had killed Michael Morrow had also wounded the First Sergeant and the 2nd platoon's leader. Tom Waldron was devastated that his friend, who just moments before, had been talking to him, was now dead.

David Aldridge found Captain Turner and was surprised that his commander actually welcomed him to the field. Turner assigned him to 3rd platoon, which had suffered the most casualties and needed new men. SSG Jiminez told Aldridge to join Specialist Fourth Class Guy Clinger, who was digging his foxhole. Clinger had been in-country since February 28. David pitched in digging the foxhole, and the two talked the night away, smoked a couple packs of cigarettes, and became friends.

The friendship would be short-lived, however.

Chapter 61
Nightfall at LZ X-Ray

Sunset came at 6:17 P.M. in Phuoc Long Province, South Vietnam, that Saturday, June 17, 1967. When not obscured by clouds, the moon was in its gibbous phase, or more than half visible. The remaining trees around the edge of the clearing cast dark shadows over the bloody LZ, but the airlift of Rangers Alpha Company and their recon platoon continued unabated until around 6:30 P.M.

The transfer signaled Lieutenant Colonel Richard E. Cavazos of the Vanguards assumption of the operational command of the situation at LZ X-Ray. He relieved Lieutenant Colonel Rufus Lazzell.

The remnants of the Rangers headquarters company were transported by chopper back to our old NDP Rufe at about 6:55 P.M. They would be welcomed back by their Charlie Company.

At 7:15 P.M., we were still bombing potential enemy areas. The ordnance delivered consisted of CBU, napalm, rockets, plus 250-pound, 500-pound, and 750-pound bombs. The air support also provided 20mm cannon fire. During the battle 43, tactical air sorties had assisted us.

That evening we were all given dire predictions of what probably would happen that night. Specialist Fourth Class Tom Waldron from the 2nd platoon of the Black Lions Bravo Company remembered that during their briefing, they were told that they should expect and be ready for human wave attacks. This was not the inspiring news the men wanted to hear. The expectations for the night were all doom and gloom. Everyone was exhausted, but with another assault on its way, sleep would be impossible.

The evening of June 17, 1967, the entire perimeter was ringed with claymore mines and trip flares. Machine guns were set up, and all the men knew their fields of fire. Ammo had been distributed and everyone had their full standard carrying load.

I had also made my preparations for the expected attack. I had shot in various defensive concentrations (DEFCONs) and registered them with my Fire Direction Officer (FDO) who was located about 5 miles away with Charlie Battery 2/33rd. Once the DEFCON was registered, all I would have to do is call it by its number and Charlie's six 105's would start firing at the registered location. I also made sure we had ample illumination rounds in case the VC did attack, and we needed them to light up the LZ. Illumination rounds create an eerie presence. They slowly drift to the ground by small parachutes, and while that is happening, they cause crazy shadows to dance all over the battlefield. They do, however, light up the enemy and make him much easier to hit.

By nightfall, we felt we were ready for the impending assault.

Chapter 62
It's Nice to Be Alive

In the darkness of the evening, we were subdued and nervous—but a weird sense of security set in as the shock of the battle slowly ebbed away. Men rejoiced at being alive and in one piece. Life feels extra sweet after you have come so close to death that you had accepted it as your fate. Many thanked God for deliverance from death, while less religious men thought about how damn lucky they were to still be among the living.

I know I found it hard to believe that not one bullet had hit me. I was one of those who was sure we were living our last minutes. Jose Garcia with the Rangers Alpha Company was equally astounded at still being alive. He had been a bullet magnet for most of the battle, but he escaped with his life. When you see a body of a comrade blown to pieces, you experience a flood of emotions. You feel horrified, sad, confused, guilty that you are not dead, ecstatic that you are alive, and then guilty again because you're happy. You feel furious at the enemy and at those in command, but at the same time, you are thankful that corpse is not you...but you don't want to admit this even to yourself. The death you witnessed makes your desire to stay alive that much greater than ever before. Death is real. The lifeless bodies all around you wipe away your adolescent belief that death won't visit you because young men don't die, that they are immortal. You are nineteen, twenty, or twenty-one, and you see proof everywhere that you are mortal. You can die. You can be here in the world and then gone in an instant. Who death visits is so random. You could be the most pious soldier or the worst specimen of man, and death doesn't care. Be in the wrong place when that eight-gram bullet punches a hole into your body or you become the recipient of hunks of ragged, red-hot shrapnel, and you're dead. Somewhere deep in each of us is a place where we know all this, and yet we try to tell ourselves otherwise, that the way we live our lives will make a difference in the timing of our deaths. But death doesn't seem to care.

We had lived through a nightmarish plunge into a bloody and masochistic battle that tested us all. We had survived the harshest conditions and the grueling intensity of pitiless violence. Those of us who survived death will forever carry around the guilt, anger, sorrow, resentment, and for some even the regret that we weren't one of the dead. And sadly, for some, the burden would become so heavy years later that they would choose to hasten their reunion with their dead comrades.

Chapter 63
Talking About Those We Lost

The rehashing of the events of the battle began, and all around the perimeter men talked about those who had been killed or wounded. There were many men to talk about. Thirty-five men had been killed outright that day, and 150 men had been wounded. One of the wounded from the Rangers recon platoon would die two months later.

The Rangers Alpha Company suffered the most men killed. Fifteen of its men had died that day in the mud and bushes of the jungle. Their sister company, Bravo, fared better with two men killed. The Rangers recon platoon suffered the largest percentage of men killed, with ten men lost.

The Black Lions Bravo Company lost nine men who would never see their loved ones again. Captain Sawtelle's Alpha Company, to which I was assigned, was the luckiest, with only one man killed. Private First Class Lloyd Wohlford was hit by a Viet Cong machine gun. He was quickly dragged over to an aid station that had been set up by Mike Stout, James Callahan, and Dwight Krebbs.

The station consisted of a slight depression in the ground, but it protected the wounded and the medics from the raking gunfire that crisscrossed the clearing.

At about the same time late in the battle, I was hit in the back with some shrapnel and was instructed to go get patched up. I quickly moved to the aid station and was told to sit next to this man who had lost his arm. The man appeared to be calm, but naturally, he was upset that his arm was gone. I remember him saying that his girlfriend was going to be upset that he had lost his arm.

Around that time, I think medic Dwight Krebbs came over to treat me. He probed around my chest and my armpit and then focused on the entry wound. Quickly he pulled out a jagged one-inch piece of shrapnel from my shoulder, placed a bandage over the wound, and told me I was good to return to the battle. I prepared to stand up and dash away from the aid station, but I wanted to first wish the man next to me good luck. When I looked over at him, he was staring off into space, dead.

When your friends die in battle, you often feel guilt that you weren't able to be there for them. Doc Krebbs felt that way about Lloyd Wohlford. Lloyd and Dwight had been close friends, and Doc Krebbs would carry self-imposed guilt for Lloyd's death for the rest of his life. He felt that if he had been there to treat Private First Class Wohlford when he was shot that Wohlford might not have died. Lloyd had just turned twenty and had three siblings.

While writing this book, I was able to find and talk to Lloyd's brother, Thomas, who was just eleven when

Lloyd was killed. He said his mother Ozzie was the first one to receive the news of his brother's death. His father was away on a job in Minneapolis, Minnesota, and got the horrible news by phone from Lloyd's mother. Lloyd was a bright young man who had taught Sunday school, was the president of his Lutheran Youth League of Decorah, Iowa, and was a decorated member of the Future Farmers of America. Lloyd was no slouch—he was an all-American guy who was an avid baseball player, the proud owner of an iconic white 1959 Chevy Impala, and had been in a long relationship with his high school sweetheart Cathy. He had planned to go into farming when he completed his two years of service.

The people of Decorah came out to honor their first Winneshiek County resident killed in the Vietnam War. It was a shock to the community that their quiet, idyllic town had suddenly lost one of its own in a crazy war being fought eight thousand miles away. Years later, the local Army Reserve Center would be named in honor of Lloyd. It is now known as the Private First Class Lloyd Wohlford Army Reserve Center.

Miraculously, only one of our Black Lions Alpha Company men was killed during the battle. The mortar attacks, the many RPGs that were fired into our area, and the thousands of bullets that flew in our direction had failed their deadly mission. We had our share of men wounded, but by the end of the battle of Xom Bo II, the Black Lions Alpha Company had lost the least dead.

Chapter 64
The Aftermath of Battle

With the battle subsided, we looked to one another for comfort and even salvation. Many of us were still numb to the many dead and wounded. The jungle, littered with the bloodied bodies of our comrades, had become the pitiless testing ground for the young men of the Rangers and Black Lions; it was our crucible of suffering.

Our consciousness was beginning to realize fully how quickly death had entered our world. The horrific events affected our bodies, minds, and hearts—and for many, our spirits and souls. There was a pervasive feeling that things were not real, as though we were all living in a dream. But the dozens of dead and wounded brought back the reality.

Men were comparing notes of who was killed and who was injured. Many men had a buddy who had been killed, and feelings of grief ran high.

Some felt nauseated when they glanced at the rows of poncho-shrouded bodies lying on the wet earth. They could see shattered body parts, congealed blood, and the grotesque shapes of their comrades peeking out from under the ponchos. Even strong men recoiled from the sight. Some of the living men had tried to reassure their dying friends that they would make it. They had held them, offered them water, tried to comfort them, prayed for them, and watched helplessly as their lives ebbed away.

While searching for wounded, Medic Felix Vallejo of Texas came upon his friend, Victoriano Sosa. His friend was in a pool of blood on the ground, dead. Upon seeing his friend's body, Felix stomach clenched up and he had to fight back not being sick. He felt horrible that there in front of him was his bloodied friend, still with his eyes staring blankly out at a world that had just killed him. Felix was not only Sosa's friend, but since he was a medic, he felt bad that he could not have been there to help his friend. They had often talked, shared laughs, and enjoyed each other's company. Now Sosa was gone, and in a few days, his wife Lydia would be greeted by two officers informing her of her husband's death. Sergeant Ronald Moreno also knew Sosa well and remembered that he always had a smile on his face. Moreno was one of the 150 wounded and would be soon medevaced out of the LZ. He spent time in a real hospital on clean white sheets with a beautiful nurse taking care of him.

What we were feeling that evening would soon be felt by hundreds of others. Over the next few days, loved ones would receive the dreaded visits, of officers bringing the news of a soldier's death to a parent, wife, or siblings. It would happen over and over the next few days, and the loved one would call other loved ones, and the grief would spread like some contagion. The loved ones would look at these messengers of death and think it had to be a mistake or untrue, and then they would wonder how did he die, did he suffer and why? Why is my son...why is my husband...why is my daddy dead?

It wasn't happening only in the States; families in Vietnam were also learning of the deaths of their sons, fathers, and husbands. Men on both sides of the big pond had died in the mud that afternoon.

Chapter 65
Dealing with Shock

Most of us felt great exhaustion and fatigue, but because of the underlying fear of another attack, sleep was impossible. For some, the shock left them visibly trembling and nauseated. There was a feeling of numbness. There was a constant nagging feeling of wanting to reach out and comfort your comrades, but at the same time realizing that you had to do your job or more men might be killed.

Some of the macho guys attempted to show unusual reserve, acting as though nothing much had really occurred, but inside they wanted to scream. They experienced hyper-vigilance...watching, listening, unable to rest, and having violent fantasies of what they would like to do with the Viet Cong soldier who had killed their comrades. They would mask their horror of what had happened by referring to their comrades' deaths in macho ways, saying, "Hey, did you hear Rich got offed?" Or maybe they'd say their comrades were "greased" or "dusted" or "fucked up."

It wasn't meant to be disrespectful; it was simply a way to cope. We were John Wayning it. A soldier might have been asked about a comrade and he would respond back, "You didn't know he was waxed?" We had a whole list of words we used to hide our real feelings about those bloody and mud-caked corpses wrapped in ponchos scattered about the LZ. We used terms like "KIA," "lit up," "wasted," "zapped" and other macho phrases.

We couldn't grieve; feeling real emotions was dangerous. We had a job to do, and that was to stay alive until the freedom bird would fly us home. However, we would grieve about our dead comrades later, and for many, it would be years and years of grieving. Later, we could say he was killed or slaughtered and let the emotions well up in us, let the anger burn in our souls. We wouldn't have to be Rambos anymore. We could cry if we wanted to, but we still had to be careful because we were soldiers. Among our own kind, it was okay; we could stop acting and be real and display human emotions.

One of our very own, Black Lions' Medic Felix Vallejo, would become a Texas Licensed Professional Counselor (LPC) after his army discharge. He would dedicate most of his life helping veterans with PTSD and other combat related issues. I got a chance to talk with him about his views on how our men coped with their Vietnam experience.

Felix said, "Combat veterans coped in various ways with their experiences in Vietnam. Most simply refused to talk about it when they arrived stateside, this suppressed their feelings."

Felix stated that, when Vietnam veterans returned home, there weren't any centers set up nationwide to provide professional counseling services. The veteran was left to integrate back into society by himself. Second, the media chose to support the anti-war movement's narrative, which further exacerbated the public's negative view of veterans. Job placement and job training services were also lacking. In fact, the returning veteran was shattered by multiple traumas, public opinion, the media and the lack of support by politicians.

Chapter 66 Remembering Some that We Lost

The names of the dead were whispered around the perimeter. The Black Lions had nine men killed during the battle. Captain Turner's RTO, Specialist Fourth Class Michael J. Morrow, from New York City was killed by shrapnel. Turner was right beside Morrow when he was hit with a small but deadly piece of shrapnel behind the ear and instantly killed. Specialist Fourth Class Morrow was awarded a Bronze Star with a V for his valor. He was a young man who was well liked, both in his unit and those he left back in the world. His old classmates from Good Shepherd School would grieve over his death, and one would write, "I honor you for fighting to protect this country of ours. I hope we are worthy of your sacrifice." A girl named Pat, who was in the third grade when Michael was killed, remembered his funeral almost fifty years later and the furor his death created in the Inwood community of New York City.

Machine gunner, Private First Class Alan J. Farhat of Lansing, Michigan, another member of Bravo's third platoon, was killed by fragmentation wounds while trying to hold back the VC onslaught that rainy afternoon. Private First Class Joe Hare missed twenty-year-old Farhat immensely. In the past, Joe had talked Alan into playing barber and had been astounded at Farhat's ability to make him look handsome.

Private First Class Alan W. Denney of Phoenix, Arizona, who loved motorcycles, was another casualty from the Black Lions Bravo Company third platoon. He is recorded as dying of fragmentation wounds, but it was rumored that he was killed accidently by fire from a gunship. His friends back in Phoenix had nicknamed him "Swede." He was actually born in Seattle, Washington, but he moved to Phoenix with his parents, Mr. and Mrs. Paul E. Denney, and lived there for six years, attending Phoenix Union High School. Alan was only twenty years old when he was killed on June 17, 1967, and had only been in-country for three months. His parents, brothers Roger and Keith, and his sister Paulette learned of his death on June 22, 1967. Four days later, they laid him to rest at Resthaven Cemetery with full military honors.

How I felt that day so many years ago is still very vivid. I walked around the LZ and heard the names of the men killed or grotesquely wounded and felt my stomach clench up. No sound could escape my lips, but I wanted to cry out. I wanted to yell some guttural howl that would banish the pent-up anger, hate, and confusion that filled my mind. My mind was going crazy trying to disregard the horrible vision of the many dead men and the field of wounded soldiers in front of me. Men bleeding, men half dead, men missing limbs, men dazed and just waiting for death to deliver them from their pain and hell on Earth. I would see the poncho-wrapped remains of someone who had once been one of our young soldiers and hoped that his death had been quick. I hoped he had been hit with something hard enough that it turned off his life switch so fast that he was dead without him even knowing he had been hit. Most men did die that way. They were with us and then an instant later they weren't.

That was one of the bizarre things I thought about as I heard of men like thirty-one-year-old SP5 John H. Stout of Luxora, Arkansas, who was killed by fragmentation wounds. He was a Radio Telephone Operator (RTO), which unfortunately was a prime target for the Viet Cong. His death would deprive Vicky, Sheila, and Rodney of their father and his wife, Nora, of a loving husband. He had loved his three children and wrote to them often, prompting them to write back. He was defiantly thinking of the future and trying to provide his family with a good life. In fact, he had just moved his family into a new house, and he wanted to know how they liked it. He would never get to enjoy it himself. The 1st Infantry Division would remember SP5 John H. Stout as a good soldier and father. A year after his death they would award his young son Rodney a $1,500 scholarship.

Then there was twenty-three-year-old Sergeant Bobby Minton, from Elizabeth, Indiana, who was killed by small arms fire during the battle. Bobby was a family man and had a wife named Georgia and two sons and a daughter. His sister, Lucy, was devastated by his death and would honor him often throughout her life. She would outlive him by over half a century.

Bobby was buried at New Albany National Cemetery. Sergeant Minton's father, Milton, was notified of his son's death on June 20, 1967, three days after the battle. Four years prior, on February 11, 1963, Bobby had lost his mother Kizzie, and now his father Milton, of Louisville, Kentucky, would struggle to accept the death of his wife and son. Life would go on for Bobby's wife, Georgia, who six months later on December 9, 1967, married Lorenzo L. Peck.

Many of the men killed at LZ X-Ray had been in-country for just a few months. Twenty-year-old Private First Class James Edward Starks was from Cameron, South Carolina and had only enjoyed two months in sunny Vietnam before he was killed. His mother Rosa C. Starks was notified on June 20, 1967, of her son's death. A few days later, James's remains were buried at St. Paul Cemetery in Cameron, South Carolina, with full military honors.

Private First Class Paul Kelly of the Rangers Bravo Company had been in country 124 days before he was killed. Less than a year before he'd been enrolled in Albany State University in Albany, Georgia studying to be a physical therapist. The news of his death was delivered to his family on June 20th. At 7 AM a military sedan stopped in front of 93 North Knoll Road in Smyrna, Georgia and two uniformed officers alighted. They walked up to the door and knocked loudly. Paul Kelly Senior responded to the knocking and saw the two Uniformed Officers standing there. They didn't need to say anything; he knew what their visit meant. He invited them in and went down the hall to get his wife, Evelyn. She was still in bed. He didn't tell her what was wrong, but just to come to the living room. When she entered and saw the two uniformed officers standing there, she started to scream waking up Cynthia Kelly, Private First Class Paul Kelly's younger sister. Cynthia was only sixteen, but remembers well that morning, like it was yesterday. She remembers her sobbing mother breaking down emotionally and how hard her father struggled with the terrible news. She remembers how difficult it was for her dad to inform Paul's fiancé, Sandra Martin of his death. It couldn't be a face to face, and it would be void of comforting hugs because Sandra lived in Dayton, Ohio.

Paul was loved by his family and especially Cynthia who described him as a wonderful brother, a man who tried to resolve issues, a peace maker, and a great athlete. She would never forget him neither would the community he came from. Today, Paul Kelly's picture is proudly hung in the foyer of the American Legion, Paul E. Kelly, Jr. Post-Auxiliary #296 in Marietta, Georgia.

Chapter 67
Some Men Die as Heroes

Some men died as heroes. In reality, we had many heroes, but some men did things that were noticed as considerably beyond the normal call of duty, and we honored them for what they did.

Black Lions Bravo Company had its share of them; some lived, and some died. Twenty-year-old Private First Class John J. Rieck Jr. was a hero who died. In fact, the headline of his hometown paper in Cleveland, Ohio, read, "He died so others could live." John was posthumously awarded a Silver Star and a Bronze Star with a V device for Valor. His parents, Mr. and Mrs. John J. Rieck Sr., accepted the awards at a ceremony in Cleveland on September 1, 1967. Preceding the ceremony, the announcement in the paper read, "Hero's parents to get medals."

Private First Class Rieck was one of the few unwounded during the initial VC assault in the northwest sector of LZ X-Ray. When things quickly went to shit, Private First Class Rieck found himself in the dilemma of needing to take command of a sector of the perimeter to stop an onslaught of Viet Cong swarming his area or just give up and be instantly killed. He chose to fight on.

During the ensuing battle some of Private First Class Rieck's comrades were wounded and John unhesitantly rushed out to their aid exposing himself to heavy fire. He dragged the men back to the cover of a small berm and did what he could to stop their bleeding. The battle was still raging, however, and he joined the few men that were able to fight back.

Captain Turner moved reinforcements up to where John's men were struggling to hold back the assaulting Viet Cong. By this time the Black Lions 3rd Platoon had suffered numerous men dead and wounded. Private First Class Rieck again took time to apply field dressing to a couple more of the wounded. The Viet Cong were as close as thirty meters to their position and had superior numbers. The incoming fire was intense. Bullets were hitting everywhere. When incoming is this thick, Murphy's law kicks in, "It's not the one with your name on it; it's the one addressed 'to whom it may concern' you've got to think about." Sometime during this assault John was hit by incoming. He was seriously wounded, but he continued to fight until he was finally medevaced from the LZ. He didn't give up easily and fought death for another day, but finally succumbed to his wounds on June 19, 1967.

His parents, Mr. & Mrs. John J. Rieck SR., were notified of his death on June 20, 1967. His funeral was a large affair, with many former students from his

Collinwood High School Class of 1965 coming to pay their respects. He was honored with a twenty-one-gun salute.

Chapter 68
Who Was the Enemy?

The battle we had just experienced was not fought with some poorly trained local militia, but with the hard-core, well-trained, and heavily armed 271st Regiment, which had just replenished its forces in Cambodia. They were part of the 9th Infantry Division under the control of General Thanh. The Viet Cong elements were determined to make the life of the soldiers of the Big Red One as miserable as possible.

This was the second year of the Viet Cong's decision to fight big-unit warfare with American units. General Thanh's objective was to have his soldiers kill as many American and ARVN soldiers as possible. He had sent the 271st Regiment, commanded by Colonel Vo Minh Triet, to the D Zone to secure the area and destroy any American or ARVN units they encountered. The news that the 271st Regiment was in the D Zone and the Long Nguyen Secret Zone caused Major General Hay to launch a preemptive operation to wipe them out. This operation was given the name "Billings."

The Viet Minh, during their resistance war, divided South Vietnam into nine regions. War Zone D was in Region 7, which was often called Eastern Nam Bo. The view in 1967 that the Vietnam War was being waged against guerilla combatants was far from the truth. By 1967, the battles were much larger. We were fighting against huge, well-trained battalions or larger units.

There were still guerilla units all over South Vietnam, but those local, small units primarily acted as the eyes and ears of the larger VC units, keeping them abreast of what was going on with the ARVN and American units. At night, they set out booby traps and tried to kill unwary American or ARVN soldiers. They were usually older men or very young boys who could not serve in units like the 271st Regiment. These fighters fit the profile of the Westernized caricature of Viet Cong combatant, a “shoddily armed farmer by day, guerilla by night,” as author Warren Wilkins described in his book, *Grab Their Belts to Fight Them*.

In fact, the hooch boy who cleaned our officer’s quarters in Lai Khe was supposedly our friend during the day and our enemy at night. I was told he was killed in a firefight outside the Lai Khe perimeter a short while after I left Vietnam.

Then there were the local forces, which were poorly trained but well-armed.

Finally, there were the main forces, which were well trained, well-armed, and organized in the same fashion as American units. They had companies, battalions, regiments, and divisions. A Viet Cong battalion was usually around 350 men; a regiment was about 1,750 soldiers; and a division had an operating strength of 7,350 men. They were well-trained men who would stay together as a fighting unit for long periods of time, unlike the American fighting forces.

The Viet Cong practiced what was referred to as the "triad system," which translated to having three men to a cell, three cells to a squad, three squads to a platoon, and three platoons plus a heavy weapons platoon to a company. A battalion typically consisted of three companies plus a heavy weapons company. The Viet Cong were well armed with AK-47s, Soviet Degtayrev 7.62 mm light machine guns, rocket-propelled grenade launchers and Soviet DKZ-B 122 mm rockets.

Chapter 69
Major General Hay Visits Our LZ

Our battle had been followed intently by all of our staff back in Lai Khe and by the 1st Infantry Division commander, Major General Hay. As soon as the battle quieted down, Major General Hay flew into the LZ with his entourage. He came with congratulations for our accomplishments.

One very surprised soldier was Private First Class Ben Walker from the Black Lions Bravo Company, who had been summoned by Sergeant First Class Gilbert to immediately report to the command post. When Walker got there, he was greeted by Major General Hay, who praised him for bravery and courage and then pinned a Silver Star medal on his chest. When Walker returned to his fox hole, he still had his Silver Star medal pinned to his shirt.

Chapter 70
Viet Cong and Their Dead

While we were working on evacuating our wounded and dead, the Viet Cong were also attempting to evacuate their wounded and dead from the battle site...but not by helicopters.

The Viet Cong would drag their dead from the site to a location where they could be buried. Locals, women, and the elderly often assisted in the collection of the dead Viet Cong. They would drag the bodies away from the site for burials. They would attempt to identify the dead and give the names to the appropriate officials so the dead soldier's family could be notified and the soldier's death could be recorded in the battle records.

Usually, weeks if not months later, an official notification of death would be delivered to the parents, giving some details of the death along with praise for the soldier's bravery and loyalty to the cause of reunification of the fatherland. During my time in-country, these notifications bore the signature of the soldier's commander. These yellowing documents, smudged and crinkled, are treasured by family members and served as a tearful reminder of the dead soldier during the Vu Lan Festival, the second most celebrated Vietnamese holiday. Many Vietnamese believed that if a soldier is killed in combat and his remains are not returned to the family, his soul will be left to wander, frantically searching for his loving family. The Vietnamese holiday of Trung Nguyen, also known as Wandering Soul's Day or the Vu Lan Festival, helps the soul find its family and finally rest. If the soul can't find its family, it is doomed to wander helplessly as a spirit sitting on black clouds high above the earth, floating over rivers and trees for eternity.

The U.S. Army's psychological operation units incorporated this superstitious fear into the ghostly recordings of pleading Vietnamese wife and child calling for their lost soldier to come back home to them. In the background, Hollywood spooky sound effects were added to make these ghostly recordings even eerier. These chilling tapes were played over huge speakers from helicopters in an attempt to get Viet Cong soldiers to desert their units. More often than not, the recordings simply infuriated the VC, who would try to blast the evil messenger out of the sky.

It is believed that some three hundred thousand bodies of North Vietnamese and Viet Cong soldiers were never recovered. Some of the soldiers were vaporized by B-52 bombs; others were buried alive in collapsed tunnels and bunkers; others were so badly mangled they were unrecognizable; and others were simply buried unrecorded somewhere in South Vietnam, or their records were lost.

Chapter 71
Politics Behind the Battle

There was a lot more behind the battle of Xom Bo II than just the accidental ambush that we happened into. The engagements in the D Zone during the summer of 1967 were very much a result of North Vietnamese hard-liners' desire to bolster their bargaining position at the negotiation table with U.S. President Lyndon B. Johnson. They wanted some major military victories, and their April 1967 directive from the NVA General Staff promoted a "Talk-Fight" strategy. This strategy entailed severely damaging American forces and shattering ARVN units while carrying on negotiations for America's troop withdrawal and cessation of the bombing of North Vietnam. In fact, they sat the lofty goal of killing 150,000 American soldiers and 300,000 ARVN soldiers between the summer of 1967 and 1968.

The NVA General Staff wanted to create as much chaos in South Vietnam as possible, hoping to affect the outcome of the September 1967 South Vietnamese presidential election and the potential 1968 reelection of President Johnson. The NVA General Staff felt that both candidates would welcome a negotiated settlement to end the war—but if such a settlement was to be favorable to North Vietnam, the NVA had to win some big-unit battles. They thought that America needed to bleed so we would realize that the VC and NVA were capable of sustaining the war and had the ability to seriously hurt American forces.

Interestingly enough, President Johnson decided not to run for another term. He worried that he would die in office if he ran again. His father and grandfather had both died when they were sixty-four, the same age Johnson would have been in his last term in office. He also wanted time to participate in family life with his wife, his daughters, and grandchildren. The prosecution of the Vietnam War was draining him of energy. He was a passionate commander-in-chief who wanted to conclude the Vietnam War honorably, but he fretted daily at the losses America sustained. He often got up in the middle of the night to peruse the daily casualties report; he worried about the safety of his son-in-law, Chuck Robb, who was a Marine officer in the thick of heavy combat; he felt a personal sense of responsibility for the men he was sending to Vietnam; and he had a growing sense of the futility for achieving total victory. All of this had taken a toll on his vitality.

President Johnson was right with his death prediction.[14] He died at age sixty-four.

To succeed in the diplomatic talks with President Johnson, Hanoi's diplomat General Tran Do cautioned that it was critical that the NVA win numerous big-unit battles against the Americans. It was also at these strategy sessions that General Van Tien Dung and Mr. Le Duan, who succeeded Ho Chi Minh at his death, argued for a full-scale, implacable prosecution of the war against South Vietnamese and American forces, which resulted in the 1968 Tet Offensive.

Chapter 72
Life of a Medic in the Field

The work for the medics was massive. We had around 150 men wounded, with all kinds of wounds. Many men had multiple wounds, either from shrapnel or being sprayed by bullets at close range. These wounds were dirty, with mud and debris embedded in them. Our medics had to make life-and-death decisions under great pressure. It wasn't only about patching up holes and pushing men's guts back where they should be—it also meant crawling up to a wounded man who was in the crosshairs of some VC's AK-47. It took insane courage to hover over a wounded man and try to focus on his wounds, disregarding their own danger as the bullets cracked around them.

Sometimes the medics were lucky and could drag the wounded out of the killing zone to safety, but sometimes they became one of the wounded or, worse, one of the killed in action. In fact, two of our medics were killed during our battle as they worked on the wounded. It was bad enough to be wounded and remember your fear of dying in the Vietnamese mud, but it was a much heavier burden to also carry the memory of another man being killed trying to save your life.

Specialist Fourth Class Stephen "Doc" Noggle was with the Rangers recon platoon. He was shot and killed while administering aid to a badly wounded soldier. Noggle was only twenty years old. He was married and had been in Vietnam for less than six months. His wife Sue, who he married September 10, 1966, while on leave, was living in Mason City, Iowa, when she got the dreaded knock on her door and learned that her husband of nine months and ten days had been shot and killed. It was June 20.

She wouldn't know until later that he died trying to save another man's life. In his short time serving in Vietnam, he had already been wounded once and had returned to active duty only a short time before the battle of Xom Bo II. Stephen's younger brother Stanley was also informed. Now he would have to cope with another death in a family that had already suffered the death of their father, Ivan Benjamin Noggle, who had died of a heart attack in March 1957, and his mother, Catherine Lucille, who died soon after that from cancer. After their parents had died, Stephen and Stanley became orphans and lived at Boys Town in Nebraska. This was the same orphanage depicted in the 1938 movie "Boys Town" starring Spencer Tracy. The movie was a hit and made Boys Town famous and won an Academy Award for Spencer Tracey for his portrayal of Father Edward Flanagan, the orphanage founder.

Boys Town's has a statute depicting a boy carrying a younger boy on his back and on its base is the inscription "He ain't heavy, Father ... he's m' brother." Those words became a phrase synonymous with the burden of the soldiers who fought in the Vietnam War. The song "He Ain't Heavy, He's My Brother," sung by the Hollies, Neil Diamond, and Olivia Newton John presented a powerful statement about brotherhood: carrying one another, bearing someone's burdens and sharing another's load. The song certainly fit Stephen Noggle's persona. He had been the big brother who had to shepherd his younger brother Stanley into Boys Town. Stanley, just ten years old then, held Stephen responsible for him being in the orphanage. The anger lingered for years and prevented the brothers to really get to know one another. The fact that they were a few years apart in school and didn't hang out that much at Boys Town also added to the distance. In fact, that separation continued even when Stephen got married to Sue Seeberger. The wedding was conducted minus his family members. Stanley, his twin sister Sharon, and his other sister, Mary were soon informed of Stephen's new marital status and of his new destination-good old Vietnam.

Stanley and his two sisters would really never know much about their brother Stephen until years later, when some research by another relative and the help of Minnesota Senator Al Franken enlightened them about who Stephen really was and how he was killed. Senator Franken made sure that Noggle's family finally received Stephen's posthumous Purple Heart medal, which he had earned June 17, 1967. Stephen was also awarded and received a Bronze Star with a V for valor for his willingness to put his life on the line to save the lives of his comrades. The presentation of Specialist Fourth Class Stephen Doc Noggle's Purple Heart prompted his brother Stan to say, "It has brought Steven Michael Noggle back to life. It has made him real again. It had made his selfless sacrifice scream out and say, 'Hey, I'm not dead. I'm still here, still vital. After all these years I'm still in the hearts and minds of my family and friends. After almost 50 years, they still remember who I am and what I've done.'"

Stan was correct, because Doc Noggle was the kind of medic other medics aspired to emulate and the kind of medic who made wounded soldiers feel safer and more hopeful.

Imagine yourself as a medic patching up the wounded during combat, with bullets and shrapnel slicing through the air all around you. Fear invades your mind, and all the training and practice fades in and out of your consciousness as you try to focus on what you must do to save your wounded comrade. At the same time, you know one of the bullets whizzing around is going to slam right into your head, and your brains will spew out, and you'll be gone. You don't have a chance in hell of surviving. The bullets are thicker than flies around a day old corpse. In front of you is a man begging you to save his life. He's saying, "I don't want to die, Doc, help me."

You respond with something like, "You're going to be okay. Don't worry, stay calm."

But your heart is beating like a jackhammer as you try to stay calm, stay focused, and plug his holes. He's been hit with shrapnel from a grenade and is leaking from all over the place. You've got to get him out of there, but you've got to worry first about shock and splintered bones that might rip open a lung or an artery and cause him to bleed internally. You have to check him out before you move him. So you bend over him and start examining his wounds. You just do your job, you have no choice, and you wait for a bullet to take you out. You can smell his blood and the Vietnamese mud and the burning woods behind you. You hear the artillery crashing down and someone else yelling for a medic, and you wonder who will help you if you get hit.

He asks, "Doc, am I going to die?"

"Shit no, you just got a couple million dollar wounds," you say. "You'll be taking the Freedom Bird home real soon, just stay calm. I'm going to patch you up and get you a medevac out of here."

You're not wearing a big red cross on your helmet or on your arm because they stopped that farce for the Vietnam War. The only thing the red cross did was make a medic a more visible target. Rules like "Don't shoot a medic in war" never seemed to work very well with the enemy.

Your eyes burn from sweat and smoke, but you squint through the haze and apply another compress and wonder how soon it will be before you are laying in the mud, also staring up at the gray and sullen sky yelling, "Medic, medic, I'm hit!"

If you can really imagine that scenario, you will know how hard it was for the medics that we affectionately called "Doc" to do their jobs.

Medics often had to rein in their emotions and work on men who had just tried to kill them. As Medic Ed Chrisman reminded me in one of our conversations, medics were often tasked with saving the lives of Viet Cong soldiers. When that happened, the medic had to put aside his anger and dislike of the enemy and treat the VC with the same compassion as they would an American casualty. The medics were some of the smartest and courageous men in our units.

Private First Class William Cole was another medic who was killed while trying to save lives. He was with the Rangers recon platoon when they were overrun. He had already evacuated some wounded to a more secure area and returned to the platoon's command post to help others. Doc Cole was trying to hold the line, but they were out-gunned and he was killed. He was from Clairton, Pennsylvania, the son of William A. Cole. His bravery earned him a Bronze Star with a V device for valor.

Doc Cole's actions and death was noticed by Carol Haberchak, a wonderful woman who submitted stories and posted tributes on the website vvmf.org/Wall-of-Faces about the fallen men of the Vietnam War.

On February 22, 2012, she wrote, "PFC Cole, you are not forgotten and remain in the hearts of many all these years later. You have been designated to be one of God's special angels, along with the love of my life, who also sacrificed his life during this war. God bless you, Bill, for being who you were and for all you did."

She had lost the love of her life, Warren Muhr, in Vietnam on February 26, 1967. He was her inspiration to become a Vietnam veteran's advocate. On July 24, 2012, just a few months after posting her comments about William Cole, Carol died...but her legacy of good lives on.

Chapter 73
Hard Decisions for Medics

The number of men wounded and dead from the battle of Xom Bo II was so great that it's hard to comprehend. In all, there were 189 dead and wounded men. This would fill a large 707 airliner, which can only hold 189 passengers, to capacity.

Our many wounded sat in the Vietnamese mud or sprawled out on ponchos. Medical attention was urgently needed to prevent them from going into shock or bleeding to death. The few remaining medics had to make difficult decisions about who they would care for next. Which man needed medical help the worst, the man missing a leg, the man with his intestines piled in an obscene mess in his lap, the man bleeding from a gunshot wound to the chest, the man with his face blown away by shrapnel, or one of the other men broken and bleeding?

There were more than 150 of these life-and-death decisions facing the handful of medics as they tried to treat and prepare our wounded for evacuation by medevacs. Some of the attempts of saving the wounded were recorded by AP photographer Henri Huet, who was with us that day. He immortalized Medic James Callahan on film trying to resuscitate a dying soldier. Medic Mike Stout from Oklahoma is also visible in another of Huet's photographs, as Callahan and Stout attempted to save a young wounded soldier. You can see the desperation and helplessness on Callahan's face as he looks up with sadness and loss, knowing he must move on to his next wounded comrade. There is no time to mourn for the dead.

I knew Callahan. He traveled with our command group, and since he was a damn Yankee from Pittsfield, Massachusetts, we had things in common to talk about. I was another Yankee from Charlestown, New Hampshire, about a hundred miles away from Callahan's hometown. He was one of the few men I connected with while serving with the Black Lions Alpha Company. He and Medic Stout were two of our real heroes. They tried to save men while bullets cracked about them. They were able to comfort and save most of the wounded men they worked on. Luckily, they were not the only two medics left. Medic Felix Vallejo was another medic who tried to mend the broken.

These medics would see and remember some of the most horrific visions of what war is all about. They would remember the glassy, wide-open eyes of the dead staring up at them and the eerie silence of the dead after they gulped their last breath of smoke filled muggy air. They would remember those vacant faces staring up at them forever.

War is about killing, spilling another man's blood, snuffing out life, stealing a man's future, terrorizing, the grotesque maiming of men, reducing men to snarling bloodthirsty animals or cowering defeated wrecks of mankind. The shared horrors these medics had seared into their brains might explain why Mike Stout of Glencoe, Oklahoma, and James Callahan of Pittsfield, Massachusetts stayed friends until they both died years later.

In fact, James Callahan was on his way to see his dying colleague Mike Stout on July 29, 2008, when he was killed in a motorcycle accident. His daughter Cheryl, a Pittsfield police officer, was one of the first to answer the emergency call and arrived at the scene of her dead father. Six days later, on August 4, 2008, Mike followed his buddy James out of this world.

Wherever the other side is, I bet they both are enjoying each other's company.

Chapter 74
Doing Our Jobs as Usual

While the medics and others were caring for the wounded, the rest of us were trying to do our jobs as usual. Most of us were still in some sort of mental shock. We still didn't know or feel that the battle was over. We did feel better that 1/18th was there to add more security to the LZ.

While wounded men were being carried out of the jungle on makeshift stretchers made of bamboo poles and ponchos, others were working at finally digging their fighting positions or preparing to go out on a night ambush or man a listening post.

The night of June 17, 1967, had a moon that was less than full, casting an eerie light on the LZ and into the jungle's small clearings. Like any other night, men for ambushes, patrols and listening posts were sent out beyond the perimeter to interdict any VC reconnoitering or preparing to attack the NDP. But this evening wasn't like any other night; it was the night after a terrible battle with a regiment of VC from the NVA 9th division. Where were the survivors of the eight hundred or more VC soldiers we fought earlier?

Sergeant Mike Stubbs of the Black Lions Alpha Company recalled how that night some English speaking VC would yell from their jungle hiding places fake cries for medic. These ploys to trick our men were easy to detect because of their heavy accented words and the fact that Alpha Company had already accounted for all its men. It was disconcerting, however, to know that our enemy was still out there in the dark jungle, taunting us and trying to draw our few medics into a killing zone.

As the night wore on, the majority of us continued to wonder how many more VC from the 271st Regiment would be creeping back in the dark to look for their comrades' bodies lying cold on the muddy ground surrounding LZ X-Ray?

Chapter 75
Manning a Listening Post

Brand new to the country, Private First Class Douglas Ikerd was one of the soldiers manning a listening post on the evening of June 17, 1967. He had already been baptized in the ferocity of the earlier battle, and the vivid images of the dead and wounded were burned deep into his brain. He had seen broken men crawling out of the woods with shattered limbs, leaving trails of blood behind them, their young faces contorted in pain, eyes bulging in disbelief, choking on their own blood and mucous as they called for help. He had seen soldiers rush to help the wounded because, in combat, time is extra precious because death creeps right behind the wounded.

Douglas was eighteen years old. He didn't want to be on the KIA or WIA list, because he knew exactly what the men on those rosters looked like—but an even more powerful fear was that if he hesitated or balked, his comrades would see his fear or, even worse, think of him as a coward. That fear—the fear that your anxiety over dying would show—was more powerful for most of us than even the fear of dying. It was true for me, and it was true for Douglas and every soldier who was true to his feelings. In an interview of Captain Swink our Battalion Surgeon he said, "There is just something about being in a combat unit that is like nothing else. You just as soon see someone shoot you, if you thought you were going to be [seen as] a coward. There're some things worse than death, and that would almost be worse. I didn't see many shirkers. I didn't see many guys get shot in the back."[15]

After all that had happened earlier, Douglas knew he would be killed out on the ambush that evening. At least he was pretty sure of it. But he accepted it, because death was easier than the shame of people seeing you were afraid of what might happen out there in the dark. He already knew how random being hit was because he had been hit in his ammo pouch. Just another inch and it would have been in his stomach or chest.

There was a piece of moon glowing, but the trees blocked its few rays of light, so the jungle was dark.

Private First Class Douglas Ikerd set out that night with two other soldiers to man their listening post. After they left the perimeter, they slowly moved through the brush, listening intently for any strange sound around them. They all knew they would most likely walk right into a VC ambush that would kill all of them, probably before they even had time to set up their listening post.

It was muddy, and water dripped from trees and bushes as they picked their way through the woods. No flashlight or illumination could be used to light the way, because it would make them a highly visible target to the

VC who they knew were right at that moment watching their shadowy figure. They could feel the eyes of Viet Cong staring at them. They could even sense the rifle barrels being leveled at their faces. It was going to be quick. They were all going to catch a bullet right in the forehead and fall to the ground dead. They would never even hear the shots because bullets travel faster than sound. After they lay dead on the Vietnamese earth, the sound of the shots that killed them would echo through the jungle and three Viet Cong would creep up to where they lay on the ground and slit their throats to make sure they were dead.

But they were not dead. In fact, they had not heard anything yet that sounded like another living creature. They finally reached their listening post. It was a place where a clump of bushes and shrubs overlooked a clearing illuminated by the half moon. They set out their trip flares and claymore mines, making sure that the "Front Toward Enemy," warning on the convex side was facing away from their hiding spot. Then they moved back into the shadows to wait.

They could still smell the sweet scent of the napalm that had been used earlier, mixed with the smell of the burned jungle and probably even the smell of burned flesh of the VC who died on this devastated piece of land. They could feel the stickiness of their own sweat against their dirt-encrusted shirts. They could even feel the rivulets of sweat trickling down from their armpits. The night was going to be very long. None of them could sleep, because too much had happened already and they didn't know what would happen before dawn. The constant buzz of mosquitoes was the loudest noise they heard. Mosquitoes crept over their faces and lit on their hands, sucking blood.

Then suddenly the sound of mortars drowned out the buzz of the mosquitoes.

The sound of the mortars firing was close and made their hearts beat faster. The attack was starting again. They stared into the small clearing in front of them, waiting for the VC to come creeping in. Their rifles were on automatic and unlocked. They were ready.

The mortars suddenly stopped. Now the VC would be coming...but they waited and waited, and nothing happened. They hunkered down and waited. They were wet and their eyes burned from being up since 5:30 A.M. the day before, as well as the ash particles still filling the air. In fact, they would be blowing out black snot for another day, if they lived to see that day.

The night ticked away slowly, and horrible visions played out in Douglas's mind about what had happened the day before. When the moon was hidden behind clouds, it was so dark that he could not see his hand in front of his face, which only added to the fear.

Waiting in the dark to kill someone after a day of death and mayhem makes you more susceptible to hearing or imagining things that aren't real. The breeze blowing cooling air over your sweaty body becomes the spirits of the dead telling you that they are still there. Maybe it was the spirit of an American dead or maybe it was a VC dead. If there were spirits of the dead, there would have been a lot of them floating about. There would have been the lost souls of thirty-six Americans and a hundred or more VC.

One man who was in the battle told me that he feels spirits of the dead still haunting him. He said they visit him often. I didn't ask if they were spirits from both sides or just the men he knew.

As the sky started to turn from black to the gray of dawn, it happened. Private First Class Douglas, who was still awake and waiting for the attack, heard movement. There was real movement in the brush immediately in front of the listening post. It was more than one of them. Douglas could hear them brushing against the bushes. He heard a limb snap. He steadied himself for the assault and his imminent death, but he told himself he would take a few of them with him. Surely they knew he was there. Then, before they could kill him, he opened fire. He raked the brush with fire, and to his surprise, a bunch of monkeys scampered out of the leaves.

It was time to pack up for Private First Class Douglas Ikerd. He could reel in his Claymore mines and trip flares and get back behind the perimeter where it was safer. Douglas had made it through the night and was still alive.

Chapter 76
A New Morning and Revenge

With the coming of dawn, the LZ became a flurry of activity. Men gazed at the rising sun, the trees, and the mist hovering over the swaying grass. They breathed in the humid air and gave thanks they were still alive to see the mud, puddles, and burned spots of the LZ. Some still had legs that felt rubbery, maybe from lack of sleep or maybe still from shock of what they endured. It still felt surreal, and even with a temperature of 90° Fahrenheit, chills ran through our bodies.

There was an extremely odd silence. It wasn't total silence, but it felt like it because there were no calls for medics, no rattle of machine guns, no sharp cracks of AK-47s or the steady thunder of the artillery and explosions of bombs. We were alive, and it was a new day.

While we were eating breakfast, reading our mail, and preparing to face the new day, the remnants of the 271st were hastily retreating to Cambodia again. General Thanh wanted to ensure the survival of the 271st Regiment. He was sure that Major General Hay, the 1st

Infantry Division commander, would carpet bomb areas that seemed likely avenues of escape for the 271st.

As Thanh predicted, Hay ordered B-52s to carpet bomb areas of the D Zone and C Zone where he thought the 271st might try to regroup or use as escape routes to Cambodia. A B-52 bombing run was feared because a single run was capable of destroying everything within an area as large as a kilometer long and about a half a kilometer wide. The B-52s could carry up to 110 750-pound bombs. These bombs would demolish most of the VC tunnel systems and virtually disintegrate any troops caught in the open. The concussion alone could turn VC bodies to mush. Even VC located a klick away could lose their hearing from the concussions. The B-52s were also deadly because they flew at thirty thousand feet, making them silent and invisible to the naked eye.

As frightening as these bombers were, they were unable to kill very many Viet Cong soldiers. This was because of the tremendous number of spies the NVA had infiltrated into the ARVN and Military Assistance Command Vietnam (MACV) infrastructure. Bombing runs would be communicated to MACV prior to any bombing to make sure there were no American troops in the area. The bombing coordinates were seized by KGB-trained NVA agents and quickly communicated to the targeted Viet Cong divisions. The VC units would skirt the targeted areas as much as possible, greatly reducing the devastation they could have encountered.

Another simpler source of this information was the divisional radio nets and specifically the air liaison net, which was primarily used for medical and special aviation support, but also transmitted information about pending air strikes, artillery barrages, and B-52 strikes to the units they supported. After intercepting a B-52 strike warning from one of these sources, the VC would have ten to twenty minutes to dispatch a runner to the closest radio station to transmit warnings to Viet Cong units in the targeted area.[16]

Chapter 77
General Thanh Plots to Save the 271st

General Thanh used numerous tactics to divert US forces from pursuing the 271st Regiment. He ordered the VC 7th Division to take the offensive and attack An Loc, and at the same time ordered the 141st PAVN Regiment to attack and seize the hamlet of Xa Tan Hung.

Thanh's plan worked well enough to allow the 271st to regroup, rearm, and replenish their forces. Just a few months later, on October 17, 1967, the 271st, under the command of Colonel Vo Minh Triet, would again engage the Black Lions in the battle of Ong Thanh, where they would kill sixty-four Americans and seriously wound seventy-five.[17] The company I had been attached to, Alpha Company, was mauled. Captain Sawtelle's replacement, Captain Jim George, was wounded. My replacement, First Lieutenant Paul R. Kay, was also seriously wounded.

By the time of the battle of Ong Thanh, I had moved up the ladder and was a fire direction officer with the 2/33rd. Oddly enough, during this battle, I was supporting my old Alpha Company with our 105 mm howitzers. It was heart wrenching trying to deliver artillery to a unit that was being overrun, constantly losing radio contact and vividly imagining what they were going through.

The VC had wanted to fight big unit battles and bring some victories to the negotiation table, and now they had a couple. They damaged Alpha Company and Delta Company of the Black Lions so severely during the battle of Ong Thanh that both units were considered combat ineffective.

Similarly, in the battle of Xom Bo II, Alpha Company of the Rangers and the massacre of most of its recon platoon caused the remnants of those two units to be considered combat ineffective. The Black Lions Bravo Company was also designated combat ineffective.

General Thanh had accomplished a few of the goals that the NVA General Staff's "Talk-Fight" strategy had saddled him with. General Hay, meanwhile, was also claiming victories. American newspapers trumpeted that "1st Infantry Division forces chase VC from jungle battle site." According to an AP article about the battle of Xom Bo II, 196 Viet Cong were killed in the five-hour firefight. In the 1st Division After Action Report, it claimed 222 VC killed during the June 17, 1967, battle. The numbers were questioned by many, however, because officially only three small arms, four machine guns, seventeen grenades, and fifty-seven RPG-2 rounds were recovered from the battlefield. In the book *Combat Operations: Taking the Offensive October 1966 to October 1967 – Part 3*, the author stated that the low weapons count cast suspicion on the high body count claim.[18]

What the true Viet Cong body count really was will never be known, but those of us who fought in the battle and survived knew what we had endured and that we had survived, and that was what mattered the most to us. We learned to make the best of the situation. If the brass wanted a battle to smell like roses instead of stinkweed all they had to do was up the Viet Cong body count. In my mind our battle of Xom Bo II could be likened to a couple of pugilists beating one another up so badly that they both end up in the intensive care ward, with both of their managers declaring their boxer the winner. In Xom Bo II, there were no real winners just a bunch of dead and wounded on both sides.

Back in the states that evening, thousands of men were watching the longest Double Header being played at the Tiger Stadium in Detroit, Michigan. It was between the Detroit Tigers and the Oakland Athletics. The first game was won by the Tigers in a close 7 to 6 run game. The game lasted 3 hours and 25 minutes, but the second game went on for 19 innings. Finally won by the Oakland "A's" by one run. The Athletics ended with six runs to the Tigers five runs, and the game concluded at 12:17 A.M. Sunday. The game started with 14,871 fans in the stadium, but by the time the deciding run was hit there were only 200 still in the stadium.

Other big events were happening that evening; 135,000 concert-goers converged on Central Park to listen to Barbra Streisand entertain. On the west coast, the second night of the Monterey Pop Festival rocked on. Our battle would be relegated to a third-page snippet, if we were mentioned at all, in newspapers the following day. Top of the news was, of course, China's entry into the elite group of countries with nuclear capability. The lights at the White House and at the Pentagon would stay on late June 17.

One other event occurred that day to titillate the public. Two Border Patrol officers—twenty-five-year-old Theodore L. Newton Jr. and twenty-one-year-old George F. Azrak—went missing. The two were supposed to be at their assigned checkpoint just seventy-five miles north of the Mexican border near Oak Grove, California. When their shift ended that morning, they didn't report in, causing their superior to fear foul play. Over four hundred FBI agents, police, and Border Patrol agents started a huge manhunt for the missing men.

It wasn't long before their deserted jeep was located. A few days later, the missing officers' bodies were discovered. They had been shot numerous times in the head. The public fixated on the gruesome murders, and for months the search for the murderers grabbed headlines. Finally, based on tips from the public, the guilty parties were arrested. This was a double murder of police officers in a time when criminals didn't find it prudent to kill police officers. It was the kind of crime that was easy to comprehend, and the public wanted the perpetrators caught and punished. Today, the two murdered officers are recognized for their sacrifice and have a medal named after them, called the Newton-Azrak Award. This award is given to border agents who demonstrate unusual courage and bravery.

Chapter 78
Big Brass Visitors

Major General Hay, 1st Infantry Division's commanding general, flew in to see what the battle site looked like and how the troops were doing. If he ventured out about thirty meters from the tree line, he would have discovered the wasteland Sergeant Don Koch described as, "It looked like a tornado went through the jungle. A person could stand and look all around. Nothing in that area was over five feet high."[19]

First Lieutenant Hono Yacapin from the 1st platoon of the Black Lions Bravo Company searched the area also and found it difficult to navigate because of all the downed trees and other debris blanketing the jungle floor. In one of the few standing trees, Hono discovered a dead VC hanging upside down. The man had wrapped vines around his ankles and legs to prevent falling out of the tree, but now, almost a day later, the vines just left him dangling high up in the tree like some ripening vulture feast.

When Major General Hay arrived, men were still having breakfast, taking a morning smoke, listening to rumors, and hoping that the new day would be boring and quiet. Some guys were still totally drained from the day before and wanted to stay hidden in their bunkers. Medic Mike Stout was one of them. His friend, Doc Callahan, had harassed him about getting up and grabbing a bite to eat, but Stout just wanted to be left alone.

Finally, an event much more demanding than a request from a friend caused Stout to leave his bunker: nature called, so Stout crawled out of his bunker and headed to the five-star shit trench. While he was taking care of business, a messenger from the battalion interrupted his defecation and told him he was immediately needed at the command post. Stout, with his trousers around his ankles, responded that he was taking a shit and would come once he was finished.

The messenger left, but 1SG Ford, better known as "Top," told Stout that he better cut his shit short and get his ass up to the command post or he would be in a shit-load of trouble. Stout semi-finished his business, pulled up his britches, and walked over to the command post with Top Ford. He was afraid he had fucked up somebody he treated the day before and was going to pay for it. Or maybe some brass wanted him to work on another wounded soldier. Then he remembered he had badgered a full bird colonel into helping him the day before and had not used military decorum with him. Stout thought, "Shit, I am going to get my ass chewed out or worse."

Sawtelle also joined Stout and Top on their way to the command post. Captain Sawtelle asked Stout what had he done to warrant being summoned by the division commander, Major General Hay. Sawtelle looked serious and a bit glum. Stout was astonished to see that the division commander was really there waiting for him with a very sour look on his face. Stout saluted, and Major General Hay asked Stout if he thought he had been playing doctor the day before. Stout replied, "Sir, I wasn't really playing doctor. I was just trying to do my job." The general looked sternly at Stout, and then broke into a grin and reached over to pin a Silver Star on Stout's chest.

Stout was dumbstruck—but not so much that he forgot his friend and fellow medic, James Callahan. Stout actually protested that if Callahan wasn't receiving a Silver Star, then he shouldn't. He actually told Major General Hay it was bullshit that Callahan wasn't also receiving a Silver Star. The major general was a little taken aback, but his aide, a captain, told Stout that he would look into Callahan receiving a Silver Star later. Top cautioned Stout to quit protesting and accept the medal and honor bestowed on him. Stout reluctantly thanked Major General Hay, saluted him, and then did an about face and marched off. When Captain Sawtelle and Top left the CP, they couldn't help but laugh that Stout had actually used the word "bullshit" with the general. [20]

Chapter 79
Another Encounter with General Hay

On June 18, 1967, men continued to search the battlegrounds for other dead or wounded. The Rangers Bravo Company, commanded by Captain Ulm, would soon leave the LZ X-Ray and return to Chi Linh Special Forces Camp. There, Ulm's men would also encounter Major General Hay, who thanked them for their valor and professionalism. One of Captain Ulm's men told Major General Hay that they needed ice cream. Major General Hay replied that they might like ice cream, but they didn't need ice cream. Captain Ulm grimaced as he heard his soldier talk to the major general, but about an hour later a chopper flew in with gallons of ice cream. The major general had come through.

Captain Ulm would remain in the army after Vietnam and retire as a major in 1980.

Chapter 80
General Westmoreland Visits Our LZ

Another visitor, General William Westmoreland, flew into our LZ the morning of June 18, 1967. He brought a camera crew to record the aftermath of the battle. The Black Lions Bravo Company's commander, Captain Turner, was saddled with the job of escorting the entourage around the battlefield.

About an hour and a half into the visit, Specialist Fourth Class Guy Clinger, David Aldridge, SSG Jiminez and Sergeant Glover and his RTO were told to check out a trail to the right front of the group's position. With Specialist Fourth Class Clinger in the lead, the squad moved down the trail. Then suddenly, a deluge of bullets and RPGs were fired at them. Specialist Fourth Class Clinger was immediately hit. Fire was returned, and more men from the LZ X-Ray joined the battle to kill the attackers. Sp4 Thomas Waldron was one of them. He raced up to where the action was and attempted to administer first aid to the man he saw on the ground.

While the firefight continued, Waldron, David Aldridge and a couple of other men succeeded in pulling Clinger's body back to safety. By the end of the ten-minute firefight, however, Clinger had succumbed to his wounds.

Aldridge was so traumatized by the death of his new friend that years later he visited Clinger's family in Pennsylvania and told them how brave Clinger had been. David said he tried to convey to them how courageous Clinger was to walk point in Vietnam.[21]

Chapter 81
Some Who Survived?

In a battle of the ferociousness of Xom Bo II, even men who survive without a mark are often damaged. I think hundreds of men from the Rangers and Black Lions who witnessed the carnage, the savagery, and the brutal violence that day would forever think of June 17 as the most transformative day of their lives. They will remember the panic, the fear of becoming the victim of a killing machine that was not just the Viet Cong, but also our own deadly power. We learned that some lives would be sacrificed to save lives of others. We experienced the anger of what many felt was the incompetence of some who brought harm to our brothers-in-arms and the horrible feeling of utter impotence as we accepted the fact that fate and luck decides so much of who lives and who dies in battle.

We had casualties after the battle. One soldier committed suicide years later because the carnage of the battle haunted him constantly. One of our best medics stabbed his wife to death in a fit of jealous rage that most believe was partially a result of the trauma he endured after Xom Bo II and his guilt over those who died. Major General Troy Oliver told me that this particular medic carried a tremendous amount of guilt for those who died in the field that day and that his day of rage was totally foreign to his normal demeanor. He had been a healer, not a killer.

Many medics carried the weight of the horror they had been so much a part of into their civilian life. For them, there was always the agony of self-doubt lingering somewhere deep in them. It would rear up when they reflected on the hard decisions they were forced to make trying to save the wounded. Mistakes were always inevitable and irreversible. Specialist Fourth Class James Callahan, after leaving the service, at first tried to drown his demons in liquor. When I knew him prior to the battle of Xom Bo II, he rarely drank. What he endured as a medic cursed him for years. He suffered emotionally from the horrors of the battle. Finally, after he became active with local Vietnam veterans, he was able to shake his demons. In fact, Callahan became a founding member of Chapter 65, Vietnam Veterans of America, of Pittsfield, Massachusetts. He and other members of the chapter became instrumental in helping other veterans who had endured the trauma of death. Upon his tragic death in 2008, they renamed Chapter 65 the Vietnam Veterans, James E. Callahan Chapter 65. He had endeared himself to not just his fellow veterans, but to the Pittsfield community as a whole. In recognition of his contribution, the town showed its love and appreciation by naming the

Hubbard Avenue Bridge after him. The bridge is now called the James E. Callahan Memorial Bridge.

First Lieutenant Hono Yacapin, who was almost vaporized by an errant 250-pound bomb during the battle of Xom Bo II, remained in Vietnam for about eight more months. On January 25, 1968, while playing pool at the Lai Khe Officers Club, he suddenly found himself rocketing over the pool table as a bomb exploded that was probably planted by Viet Cong sappers. The warrant officer who was playing pool with Hono actually tossed Hono out a window, and they both scurried away from the club. Once they were a short distance away, they stopped and watched smoke pouring out of the ruined officer's club. There was silence for a couple of minutes, and they headed back to investigate the damage. Before they took ten steps, however, the place totally blew up. The concussion was so great that Hono was again knocked to the ground, still unharmed. Six men died in that sapper attack and many more were wounded. Major Roland Davis, Major Francis Gercz, First Lieutenant Raymone Caswell, Second Lieutenant Michael Romano, Specialist Fourth Class Kenneth Trier, and Silver Star recipient SP5 Julius Morris were all killed.

Simultaneously, a short distance away the colonel's villa blew up. This all happened just days before the Tet Offensive.

First Lieutenant Hono Yacapin told me that in spite of the danger he enjoyed the Army and returned to Vietnam for another tour in 1969, this time serving with the special forces. He was one of the untouchables; Hono walked away from bomb blast after bomb blast without a scratch. Hono retired in 1986 to Damascus, Oregon.

I returned from my tour in Vietnam after the Tet Offensive and was shocked at the change in America. I was accosted by jeering young men and women when I first arrived back in the States. I flew into Sacramento or Oakland, I actually don't remember which, and somehow got to Lawton, Oklahoma, where my wife was living. There was a lot to look forward to; I was going to see my son, Scott, who had been born five months prior to my return, as well as my wife, who I had not seen in over a year. I desperately hoped that the woman I left behind, would still find me the same guy she was so in love with when we married. She had written to me virtually every day while I was in Vietnam. They were sweet love letters that got me through a lot of hard times and gave me real reasons to want to survive and return home.

But the welcome home was not as special as I had dreamed it would be. In fact, there was a perceptible coldness as we finally made love and cuddled my first night back. I dismissed the strangeness to the fact that we had not been together for over a year. In fact, we had been apart longer than we had known each other before I left to Vietnam. This story was similar for many returning soldiers.

During the next few days of my leave, Gayla found herself needed every day by her brother, sister, or another relative in Lawton, taking her away from home. I was left home alone with Scott and my stepson Donnie, giving us time to supposedly bond. Something was wrong;

I could feel it. The crazy love she once had for me was gone and the relationship felt hollow and forced. The time we spent together was filled with almost palpable tension. At first, I tried to push my mounting fears out of my mind and enjoy the other things that were important to me, including spending time with Scott. I had never really been around a baby before, and it was exciting to be around this little guy.

My wife was young, pretty, and had a wonderful mother named Frances, who helped her while I was away. She was there when Gayla gave birth to Scott, and she was around when I returned home from Vietnam. One major issue that I faced back home was the fact that we were virtually broke. While I was in Vietnam, I received combat pay and didn't have to pay taxes. Gayla had forgotten to factor that in when figuring our budget and had overspent on a brand new trailer home and a sports car based on my higher Vietnam pay. The car she bought was a red Triumph Spitfire that she said was for me.

I had reassignment orders for Fort Hood, Texas. So during my thirty-day leave, I had to get us packed and moved from Lawton, Oklahoma, to my new duty station. However, Gayla was making no effort to get packed and ready to go.

One afternoon while I was taking care of the kids alone in our trailer, my mother-in-law Frances called. We exchanged pleasantries, and then she said she had something she hated to tell me., but it was something I needed to know. She proceeded to tell me that Gayla was having an affair with another soldier and that she didn't think Gayla would be moving to Fort Hood with me. I was shocked, betrayed, and hurt.

I was with the kids in our new trailer trying to think what I should say. Finally, she walked in and I told her I knew about her affair. She didn't deny it and told me she didn't know what she wanted to do. She thought we should split up so she could figure out what she really wanted. She was going to go back to her mother's house to live with her. Oddly, she wanted me to have Scott. I accepted the arrangement, and a couple days later we parted.

As soon as I got to Fort Hood, I tried to find a woman to help me take care of Scott, who was just a few months old. I asked my younger sister to come out and help me. Her answer was a resounding no, an answer that affected our relationship for years to come. So I went about searching for a live-in housekeeper/nanny and finally found a wonderful Mexican lady who became Scott's surrogate mother for a few months.

Just when I felt things were totally finished between us, Gayla showed up on my porch with my stepson Donnie in tow. She wanted to get back together and see if things could go back to the way they were. We tried, but the love and the magic we once shared never returned. The relationship was shattered and a few years later we divorced.

The same story played out between many, many returning vets and their spouses. It was a problem that came from rushing into marriage before leaving for Vietnam. In many cases, we got married so we'd have someone to love us from afar and someone to live for. Our wives and girlfriends were our connection to the world we left behind.

Some of our comrades had big relationship surprises when they returned home. Sergeant Richard Ancira got back to his home town of Austin, Texas, after racking up three purple hearts. He had lived through grueling combat and now he was going to get married. He had one lady that he couldn't wait to see. It had been a long time, since he had been home and this was going to be a big surprise for her. He got to her home and knocked on the door. The smile and the tears of happiness that he had envisioned didn't happen, instead a guilty and angry young woman suddenly opened the door and Richard quickly discovered his sweetheart was already married. That night Sergeant Ancira drank a bottle of whiskey to ease his broken heart, but he was home, alive and that was a blessing.

In 1967, our generation was living the Summer of Love and peace. Many were also living out the lyrics of Stephen Stills's song, "Love the One You're With." The song's chorus goes, "Sometimes you can't be with the one you love. Honey, love the one you're with. You gotta love the one you're with."

The song wasn't released till 1970, but the lyrics expressed the feelings of many young people in 1967 waiting for their loved ones fighting in a war thousands of miles away. It was a year of rock concerts, smoking dope, doing LSD, and rebelling against our parents and society in general. Our women were wearing miniskirts, going braless, being hippies, and shocking their parents with the altered morals of the time. They were seduced by the sights, sounds, and passions of an era of psychedelia and free love, when for but a brief moment in time everything seemed possible.

The seduction of the Sixties touched all elements of society. Lieutenant Colonel Terry Allen, the son of famed World War II hero General Terry Allen, fell victim to his wife's betrayal. While he was in Vietnam fighting a war, she was having an affair with a rodeo clown.[22] Losing the battle on the home front is devastating to your will to stay alive and fight in a war. Coincidence or not, Lieutenant Colonel Terry Allen was killed in the bloodbath of Ong Thanh just about three months after returning from his failed mission back home to revive his marriage. In fact, while we were battling Viet Cong in LZ X-Ray, Lieutenant Colonel Allen was home in El Paso fighting for his marriage.

Just as many or more marriages survived the trials and tribulations of war. Captain Sawtelle's marriage to his wife Jo stayed strong, and they are still together as of this writing. Medic Mike Stout and his wife were together right up to the day he died in 2008. Machine gunner Jose Garcia stayed true to his high school sweetheart Janie, who he married after his return to the States. Their marital bonds weren't broken until she died in April 2014. My own father, CWO4 James Hearne, a career soldier, sustained his marriage through World War II, the Korean War, and two tours in Vietnam. It is hard sometimes, but it can be done.

In Lockport, NY, another story was playing out about the same time that I was trying to live my life as a bachelor Captain and dad with a six-month-old son. It was the spring of 1968 and David Ward, who had been so seriously wounded in the battle of Xom Bo II had finally shed his body cast, completed multiple surgical procedures and was now living at home. One of his neighbors had introduced him to this young college student, Patricia Cook. Quickly David and Pat Cook became inseparable. She was his reason to live; her love, his medicine to make him whole again. Patricia said she saw David with his black eye patch as this tall, dark and mysterious young man. She described him as being like the Energizer Bunny, never wanting to quit and always with a big smile that was so bright that it would light up the world. In September of 1970 they married.

David was still receiving physical therapy in 1970 and on the way to the VA Clinic, he would often have to drive thought anti-war protest. It didn't get him down; he felt proud of what he had participated in and never complained about his situation. David just kept living. He went back to school and in 1974 graduated from Niagara University with a degree in accounting. He got a job as an accountant and when not working enjoyed his family, friends, golf and skeet shooting. When David died from combat related issues in 2006, he and Patricia had shared 35 years together and raised two boys, Andrew and Matthew. The soldier we all thought had died was as his wife had described a real life Energizer Bunny who would go on and on and on.

Chapter 82
Where Would They Be?

One thought that has often entered my mind since that fateful afternoon on June 17, 1967, is what would my thirty-seven dead comrades in arms be doing now? What would those men have become? Even now, so many years later, I still feel this pain and guilt over the lives that were stolen from them. They died for some obscured belief, some failed policy, for greed, and for the glory of a bunch of old men who had forgotten how important being young and alive had once been to them.

I think it is safe to assume they would have gone on in life as the rest of us did. They would have returned to a fractured America, a country torn apart over the Vietnam War with its cities under siege by race riots. Their return would not have been a triumphant one, but simply a welcome home by a loving family and friends. In 1967, a total of 475,000 men were serving in Vietnam, and the peace rallies were multiplying, as was the number of war protesters. It was hard not to notice them upon our return to America. Anyone who returned right after our battle would have heard about boxer Muhammad Ali being stripped of his boxing world championship title for refusing to be inducted into the U.S. Army. Once again in the summer of 1967, cities throughout America exploded in rioting and looting. The worst was in Detroit on July 23, where seven thousand National Guard were brought in to restore law and order on the streets.

The returning soldiers would have been entranced with the way young women were dressing. In England, a new model by the name of Twiggy became a fashion sensation, and miniskirts continued to get shorter and shorter. Returning soldiers would also have encountered the loud discotheques and singles bars that suddenly appeared in cities across America. History records the summer of 1967 as the Summer of Love, when the youth of America got friendly and smoked pot and grooved to the music of Janis Joplin, the Grateful Dead, Jefferson Airplane, and The Byrds.

The soldiers would have been entertained with movies that were produced to appeal to the younger audience, like *The Graduate*, *Bonnie and Clyde*, and *Cool Hand Luke*.

Color television had become affordable in 1967, and TV shows were produced to take advantage of the great new technology. Now shows like *Gunsmoke*, *The Fugitive*, *Bonanza*, *I Love Lucy*, and *The Monkees* were all in color.

Men coming back from the war got to see what they had left behind reported in living color on the evening news. Chet Huntley, David Brinkley, and Walter

Cronkite reported the events of the war, usually juxtaposed against scenes of the mounting war protests spreading across the nation.

Returning veterans would learn more about how the public viewed General Westmoreland's strategy of attrition. They would hear about his gamble that our war machine could kill more Viet Cong soldiers and create intolerable grief and hopelessness for their nation than the Viet Cong could do to us. A kill ratio of 10:1 or 20:1 was what Westmoreland considered an acceptable level and one that would be tolerated by the American public.[23]

But the American public disagreed with the proposition that one American soldier's life was worth ten dead communists. Truthfully, Westmoreland and his successor General Abrams had few options in the prosecution of the war because the politicians in Washington and the Pentagon had saddled them with herculean restrictions in the war's prosecution. They could not chase or attack the enemy when they fled to Cambodia or Laos, and it was not permissible to launch ground attacks into North Vietnam. Those were but a few of the rules of engagement.[24]

A 1969 *Life Magazine* featured a large fold-out pictorial section depicting all the American dead for that week. It was a total of 242 young men. The article emphasized that a kill ratio of 12:1 was an unacceptable way of measuring the success of a war.[25]

Westmoreland's war of attrition wasn't only unacceptable to the American public; it was also terribly inaccurate. The number of killed Viet Cong we reported was almost always a fictional value that was given to appease our superiors and help us get promoted. Official body counts were usually calculated by attempting to first count the physical bodies. Once that was done, a few more were added to make up for those that must have been dragged away or would die later. After that number was tallied up, if it was still too low, a few more bodies would be added to represent those bodies that were probably hidden in the bush or up in trees. If that number looked pretty good, it was radioed into headquarters.

Headquarters would then look at the body count, compare it to the number of Americans killed during the conflict, and decide if maybe the enemy body count should perhaps be "corrected" a bit more to make sure all possible dead were accounted for. In the battle of Xom Bo II, we had thirty-seven killed, and the official report stated that we killed 222 communist soldiers. It also stated that the VC likely removed a large number of their dead.

In Xom Bo II, we had failed to maintain Westmoreland's acceptable 1:10 ratio. To meet that measurement of combat success, we would have had to kill at least 150 more enemy soldiers. And of course, we failed miserably to meet the greater challenge of the 1:20 ratio. To meet that ratio, we would have had to of killed at least another 498 Viet Cong.

In 1967 as we fought General Westmoreland's war of attrition, he reported to President Johnson and Congress that we were fighting an army of around quarter of a million men. Our strength at that time was close to half a million. However, after he reported those numbers to the President and the public, his report was challenged by his own intelligence officer, Major General Joseph McChristian. It was also disputed by Colonel Gains Hawkins and CIA officer Sam Adams, but Westmoreland made the decision to disregard their estimates and stick with his much lower enemy strength counts. General Joseph McChristian's estimates were around six hundred thousand versus Westmoreland's of two hundred and fifty thousand.

It seems insane that our figures of our enemy's strength were so far removed from reality. We had come to believe our own skewed numbers even though we knew that most of our body counts of the enemy were contrived.

General Westmoreland in the movie "Hearts and Minds" (directed by Peter Davis) commented that "The Oriental doesn't put the same high price on life as does the Westerner," Westmoreland famously said. "Life is plentiful; life is cheap in the Orient." Peter Davis was criticized for putting Westmoreland's statement juxtaposed to a Vietnamese woman crying over her dead soldier, but the fact remains that Westmoreland did utter those words. I have often wondered how precious our lives were regarded by those civilians running the war from a desk across the big pond in the Pentagon. Were we also a cheap commodity?

The men who passed through the Graves Registration Collection Points became our attrition count on the big Vietnam War scoreboard. Which side had the biggest pile of dead soldiers was supposed to be the loser.

Maybe their desks should have been located in a Graves Registration Collection Point so they could be more aware of the reality of war.

In short, returning soldiers would come home to a country damaged, in turmoil, yet moving forward with vigor and exuberance.

Afterword

We had participated in a war that could have been totally avoided if our leaders at the end of the Second World War had upheld the promises embodied in the Allies' Atlantic Charter of 1941, signed by Franklin Roosevelt and Winston Churchill. This charter stipulated that, among other things, there would be no territorial changes that did not accord with the freely expressed wishes of the peoples concerned.[26]

The Atlantic Charter of 1941 also said that Allies would respect the right of all peoples to choose the form of government under which they lived, and that Western governments wished to see sovereign rights and self-government restored to those who have been forcibly deprived of them.[27]

The Vietnamese Declaration of Independence was declared on September 2, 1945, and eloquently demanded that the triumphant Allies honor their self-determination promises expressed in the Atlantic Charter. That day, September 2, 1945, also coincided with the formal Japanese surrender ceremony aboard USS

Missouri in Tokyo Bay. It was the day President Harry S Truman declared as VJ Day.

An October 1943 an OSS (Office of Strategic Services – CIA's predecessor) memo proposed that the United States "use the Annamites, which were essentially Ho Chi Minh's Viet Minh forces, against the Japanese troops." The memo also suggested that the "Annamites should be led to believe that their help in the fight against the Japanese would bring about their independence upon an Allied victory."

The Viet Minh were successful in their battles against the Japanese, and by September 1945 the Viet Minh had captured most of the major cities across Vietnam and declared Vietnam's independence. Ho Chi Minh called it the Democratic Republic of Vietnam, with Ho Chi Minh as its first president.

Within a few weeks of this declaration of independence, the West decided that Vietnam should be returned to France, which had been Vietnam's colonial master prior to the Second World War. The problem, however, was that France was too weak to take control, so the Western powers decided that England should occupy the southern part of Indochina and return it to France when they were strong enough to govern it. The United States also sought the assistance of Nationalist China under Chiang Kai-shek to govern the northern part of Indochina until France was able to take control of that portion of Vietnam. During the following year, military units from England, India, and Japan fought the Viet Minh to wrest control away from them.

Between October 1945 and February 1946, Ho Chi Minh wrote eight letters to President Truman, reminding him of the self-determination promises of the Atlantic Charter. One of the letters that was sent both to President Truman and to the United Nations read:

I wish to invite attention of your Excellency for strictly humanitarian reasons to following matter. Two million Vietnamese died of starvation during winter of 1944 and spring 1945 because of starvation policy of French, who seized and stored until it controlled all available rice....Three-fourths of cultivated land was flooded in summer 1945, which was followed by a severe drought; of normal harvest, five-sixths was lost....Many people are starving....Unless great world powers and international relief organizations bring us immediate assistance we face imminent catastrophe.

President Truman never replied, nor did any representative of the United Nations.

By December 19, 1946, the French and the Viet Minh were struggling over control of Vietnam. The Battle of Hanoi was the first battle of France's war, which lasted from 1946 to 1954. This war ended with the climactic battle of Dien Bien Phu on May 7, 1954, when the Viet Minh defeated France's forces, killing 2,293 and capturing more than 8,000 men.

During the battle, the French artillery commander, Charles Piroth, committed suicide because of his failure to mount any sort of counter-battery fire against the Viet Minh's massive bombardment, which lasted days and killed so many.

The battle of Dien Bien Phu was a planned ambush by the French that turned into the ambushers being ambushed. This scenario was repeated many times over during our war with Vietnam, started on November 1, 1955, and finally ended on April 30, 1975.

America's ground involvement in Vietnam ended on March 29, 1973. After that, the South Vietnam government and the ARVNs stood alone. In accordance to the Paris Peace Accords, the fighting should have ended—but fighting continued to rage in South Vietnam. In January 1974, President Thieu publicly stated that the Paris Peace Accords no longer applied.

After the passage of the Foreign Assistance Act of 1974 by the US Congress, which cut off all military aid to Saigon, and President Richard Nixon stepping down from the presidency, the situation in South Vietnam worsened dramatically. Shortly after the act's passage, North Vietnam decided to test if a large attack would cause America to alter its support policy toward South Vietnam. They began a limited offensive in Phuoc Long Province, which proved to be the true beginning of the end for South Vietnam.

Within just a few weeks, the Viet Cong defeated the South Vietnamese military. The battle started on December 12, 1974, and ended on January 6, 1975. It was a decisive battle that proved the ineptness of the South Vietnam government and President Nguyễn Văn Thiệu's failure as commander-in-chief. He was more interested in his own power than the needs of his army and their ability to fight. He refused requests from his generals on the battlefield and as a result, the Battle of Phuoc Long was lost. The aftermath of the battle resulted in the Viet Cong capturing about 2,444 ARVN soldiers, which included twenty-six officers. The quick retreat of the South Vietnamese forces left behind thousands of small arms and about 100,000 rounds of ammunition.

The battle also signaled Hanoi that America would not come to the aid of South Vietnam. America's executive branch was still in turmoil. Nixon had resigned in disgrace, and Gerald Ford was dealing with a country fraught with racial strife and a public that had no interest in re-engaging in Vietnam. This hands-off political climate in America and the decisive defeat of South Vietnam forces opened the floodgates for North Vietnam to go forward with its offensive. Rivers of troops from North Vietnam flowed into South Vietnam and immediately began to take control of large swatches of land. Virtually every engagement against South Vietnamese forces was won by the Viet Cong, who were now using tanks, heavy artillery, and well-trained troops.

Buôn Ma Thuột was the next big prize that fell to the Viet Cong. The battle resulted in the near-total destruction of the entire ARVN force in the central highlands. Total anarchy spread across South Vietnam. The confusion, fear, and turmoil prevented any coherent defense and led to the utter collapse of ARVN's forces and the loss of the northern two-thirds of the country.

Hanoi was surprised by the speed and success of its assault and decided to change its strategy and steamroll straight down to Saigon in hopes of capturing the capital of South Vietnam just in time for the birthday celebration of the late President Ho Chi Minh and the end of the war. North Vietnam had to move its forces 350 miles south to accomplish this feat. The NVA started its march, and soon Kon Tum and Pleiku fell.

President Nguyễn Văn Thiệu wanted his troops to fall back around Saigon and make a last stand against the Viet Cong juggernaut. The problem was that the Viet Cong controlled most of the roads, so to return to Saigon the units would have to fight their way to the capital. Those South Vietnamese, who tried to use the roads discovered that the Viet Cong had most of them registered with their artillery, so using a road meant the virtual annihilation of your unit. The future looked so bleak to many of the ARVN units that entire battalions shed their uniforms and retreated to their villages.

Unless America came to the rescue, the Viet Cong would soon roll into Saigon and reunify the country, as Ho Chi Minh had dreamed back in 1945. Cities and villages continued to fall under the Viet Cong onslaught as Huế, Da Nang, and Qui Nhơn were decimated. The battle in Da Nang was so chaotic that ARVN soldiers removed their uniforms, dropped their arms, and fled with the civilians in an exodus that filled the roads around the city. Thousands of civilians and soldiers died during the fight for Da Nang. Ships were used to help evacuate the city, but seventy thousand ARVN troops were taken as prisoners. After the fall of Da Nang, towns and cities fell like dominoes.

The Viet Cong juggernaut soon fought its way to the area that in 1967 was the home of the 1st Infantry Division. General Dũng used Ben Cat, which was just south of Lai Khe, as his new forward command post. It was here where he prepared plans for the final battle for Saigon. He had at his disposal about 130,000 men, plus supporting artillery and armored units to encircle Saigon. He launched his attack on April 26. His divisions struck Biên Hòa and the sprawling logistical complex at Long Binh from the south and southeast. Three days later, Vung Tau was under assault.

With the enemy nearing Saigon, President Gerald Ford ordered the evacuation of American personnel and embassy staff. In addition, efforts were made to remove as many friendly South Vietnamese refugees as possible. These missions were accomplished through a series of operations in the weeks and days before the city fell.

On April 28, Viet Cong forces fought their way to the very outskirts of the city. At the Newport Bridge just three miles north of the city center, ARVN soldiers battled the Viet Cong troops for control of the span. The bridge was the last overland connection to downtown Saigon. Later that afternoon, as the new South Vietnam President Minh finished his acceptance speech, a formation of four A-37s, captured from the South Vietnamese Air Force, bombed Tan Son Nhut airbase. News of Biên Hòa falling to the Viet Cong was delivered to the new president, who realized the fate of the South Vietnam was sealed.

As total chaos paralyzed the defense of Saigon and its surrounding area, the top ARVN leadership recognized the inevitable and resigned themselves to defeat. Some officers and ARVN troops committed suicide to prevent being captured by the Viet Cong. The Viet Cong's defeat of the South Vietnam happened weeks sooner than Hanoi had planned. They had hoped that victory would come a little before or on Ho Chi Minh's birthday, but their commanders had succeeded almost three weeks before Ho Chi Minh's birthday.

On April 30, 1975, Viet Cong troops captured Saigon. What was left of South Vietnamese government and military forces surrendered the same day. After thirty bloody years of conflict, Ho Chi Minh's vision of a united, Vietnam had been realized.

Much could be said about how we fought the war, and how so much of the American public failed to support the troops, but that is not the purpose of this book. The lesson of Xom Bo II and the thousands of other battles and skirmishes that our military forces fought is that a war of attrition as the main strategy of a war is not a strategy at all. Attrition, unfortunately, is simply part of the very nature of war. There must be more logic applied to the prosecution of wars and more thought of what our actions will cause. Our strategy in Vietnam under General Westmorland was like a witch hunt of old, with us going around searching for Viet Cong and destroying villages that harbored them. We uprooted thousands and thousands of people from their land and relocated them to refugee camps. We devastated their land with defoliants and peppered their forest and farm lands with thousands of unexploded ordnance that to this day still kill or maim people.

After a few years of this strategy, General Abrams decided to try to win the hearts and minds of the people. It was just a little too late because we had already alienated ourselves from the majority with Westmoreland's search-and-destroy policies.

The Vietnam War remains for many Americans a scar and a haunting metaphor for political disasters and tragic consequences. It evokes memories of napalm, carpet-bombings, burnt-out villages, dead civilians in black pajamas, and army helicopters hovering over wounded GIs in rice paddies.

As soldiers, we did our duty and did it well. The Vietnam War was fought during a time of tremendous strife in America. We had to deal with the assassination of President John F. Kennedy; we had tremendous race issues exacerbated by the assassination of the civil rights leader Martin Luther King Jr.; and we had a president whose questionable actions forced him to step down from the Oval Office in disgrace. And after the death of more than 58,000 American soldiers, 303,000 wounded, and $150 billion spent on the prosecution of that war, the people of our nation finally said we just don't care what happens in that far-off land called Vietnam; we just want you to bring back our boys.

I hope that our nation, our politicians, and our bureaucrats will concede that war has to be the absolute last resort used to settle differences with our adversaries. Our motive to go to war should be completely clear and justifiable to the people of our nation and to those of our allies.

Another lesson that should be obvious is that we should never enter a war without an exit strategy. The Vietnam War raged on for so long because nobody really knew what the end goal was. Now it seems the same philosophy is being used in Iraq and Afghanistan. If there is no clear goal, then it will never be reached.

The third and perhaps the most important lesson is that we cannot impose our ways, customs, and values on people of other beliefs, religions, and customs. It has been proven over and over that the use of military force does not endear the people of another nation to our way of life.

The world needs a new way to resolve its issues, because war just doesn't work very well. It's a killer.

As President Kennedy said, "Mankind must put an end to war before war puts an end to mankind."

Appendix 1
Official After Action Report

Official After Action Report
The Battle of XOM BO II (LZ X-RAY)
17 June 1967

The Battle of XOM BO was the result of Viet Cong plans to ambush US troops conducting a heliborne assault into landing zone (LZ) XRAY (XT958680). Operating in War Zone D 1st Infantry Division units had found a limited number of clearings suitable for LZ's and night defensive positions (NDP's). The thickness of the jungle surrounding clearings in War Zone D provides a shield from aerial observation to Viet Cong (VC) units waiting in ambush. The enemy found a profitable tactic in predicting the site of a US troop assault and positioning ambush units around it.

The 271st VC Regiment, operating in the TRANG DA1 area where the battle took place, knew that US troops were also in the area and that LZ XRAY was likely location for a heliborne assault. The US troops, however, moved into LZ XRAY by foot. The VC attacked without the advantage they would have had over US troops arriving by helicopter. Nevertheless, the VC conducted a well-planned attack on the NDP which resulted in US losses of 35 killed and 150 wounded. The VC inflicted the heavy losses on the Americans with a series of brief, well-coordinated assaults. By the end of the day, however, the concentrated US fire power had returned the blow and overwhelmed the enemy by inflicting losses which included 222 VC killed.

Background:

On 13 June 1967 the 1st Battalion 16th Infantry (1-16 Inf) conducted a heliborne assault into LZ RUFE (XT955663) and secured the LZ for the landing of the 2d Battalion 28th Infantry (2-28 Inf). A two-battalion NDP was established, and the units conducted search and destroy patrolling from the LZ in the days that followed. At XT935658 on 141215H June 1967 Company A, 1-16 Inf (A/1-16 Inf) engaged 5 VC who fled but were identified as belonging to the 271st VC Regiment. At 141412H June 1967 B/1-16 Inf in the vicinity of XT937669 engaged what was estimated to be a battalion of the 271st VC Regiment, resulting in 6 US killed, 12 US wounded, and 60 VC killed.

Interrogation of a VC soldier who was captured on 17 June 1967 revealed that on 16 June 1967 four companies of the 271st VC Regiment prepared an ambush site at the battle area around LZ XRAY. No ambush resulted that day, and when the VC returned on 17 June 1967 the US troops were already there, and the fighting began.

On 17 June 1967 the two-battalion NDP at LZ RUFE was to relocate to LZ XRAY. At 0730 C/1-16 Inf was placed under the operational control (OPCON) of 2-28 Inf to secure the 1-16 Inf portion of the NDP at LZ RUFE. At the same time B/2-28 Inf was placed under the OPCON of 1-16 Inf to move with elements of 1-16 Inf to LZ XRAY and help to secure the area for the later transfer of the two-battalion NDP from LZ RUFE to LZ XRAY. The first march unit was, in order of march, A/1-16 Inf, B/-16 Inf, the reconnaissance platoon of 1-16 Inf (recon 1-16 Inf), and B/2-28 Inf. It departed from LZ RUFE about 0800 with the mission of moving to LZ XRAY and securing it for the insertion of supplies to be transferred from LZ RUFE to LX XRAY by CH-47 aircraft. At LZ XRAY it was planned for the 1-16 Inf units to take the eastern portion of the perimeter, from XT958682. A/1-16 Inf would deploy in the north, B/1-16 Inf in the center, and recon 1-16 Inf would secure the C/1-16 Inf sector in the south until C/1-16 Inf arrived. B/2-28 Inf was responsible for the west side of the LZ.

Artillery fire was directed in front of the unit as it marched. The "marching artillery" was discontinued after reaching LZ XRAY. At 1030 A/1-16 Inf arrived at LZ XRAY, and the second march unit, A/2-28 Inf, departed from LZ RUFE. To avoid exposing themselves in the clearing, the units began to deploy around it by making their way through the jungle that surrounded LZ XRAY. Approaching the LZ from the south, A/1-16 Inf led the 1-16 Inf units around the east side of the LZ, and B/2-28 Inf moved up the west side.

CH-47 helicopters arrived at LZ RUFE about 1100 to extract supplies. At 1115 A/1-16 Inf discovered some freshly dug positions in front of their sector of the perimeter. The holes were only a few inches deep and looked as if they had received one rainfall. At 1125 A/1-16 Inf and B/2-28 Inf linked in the north, completing the securing of LZ XRAY. Movement of supplies from LZ RUFE began immediately.

In deploying, B/2-28 Inf spread itself thinly over the west side of the perimeter. There were 15 to 30 meters between individual positions, 30 to 70 meters between platoons, and 50 to 75 meters between the linked positions of B/2-28 Inf and A/1-16 Inf in the north. Contact was to be maintained between the two battalions in the north by patrolling the 50 to 75 meters between the two end positions. A/2-28 Inf, en route to LZ XRAY, was to take over the northwest sector of the perimeter, B/2-28 Inf would then deploy all of its men in the southwestern sector, in positions that were closer together.

Captain William R. Williamson, 094018, the commanding officer (CO) of A/1-16 Inf, deployed his 3d platoon in an overwatch formation in the extreme north, linked with B/2-28 Inf. Captain Williamson tied the 1st platoon in to the right of the 3d platoon; that is, there was the same distance between the two platoons as there was between the positions within the platoon. There were 25 meters between each forward position in A/1-16 Inf. Captain Williamson was in the process of deploying his 2d platoon as a reserve unit behind the 1st and 3d platoons when the engagement started. At the same time B/1-16 Inf had tied in with A/1-16 Inf and deployed in the center sector of the eastern side of LZ XRAY. South of B/1-16 Inf, recon 1-16 Inf divided into nine outposts, called "strongpoints", covering the southeast sector from B/1-16 Inf to the end of B/2-28 Inf in the southwest. There were two men at each outpost and 60 to 150 meters between positions. The platoon command post (CP) was set up in the clearing under a few trees, in the southeast near the tree line.

The 1-16 Inf CP was located near some trees in the east-center of the clearing. Elements of the command group of 2-28 Inf set up a forward CP in the clearing nearby. At 1200 B/2-28 Inf returned to the OPCON of 2-28. At this time the units at LZ XRAY occupied a perimeter made up of positions from 30 to 50 meters into the tree line from the clearing. They were in triple-canopy jungle consisting of tall trees and thick bamboo. The visibility was 15 to 20 meters. Visual contact between US defensive positions was generally non-existent. Immediately on deploying, the units sent out "cloverleaf" patrols. Before the men started digging defensive positions or set up Claymore mines in front of the perimeter, the patrols had revealed the enemy's presence, and the engagement was started.

The Engagement:

At 1215 Captain Donald W. Sawtelle, 093924, CO A/2-28 Inf, stopped his company after his 2d platoon, the lead element, had entered LZ XRAY, from the southwest.

Captain John A. Turner, 094727, CO B/2-28 Inf, discussed deployment instructions with Captain Sawtelle, and Captain Sawtelle then started his company moving north along the B/2-28 Inf positions. B/2-28 Inf's first cloverleaf patrol was re-entering the perimeter, and the second one was starting out. Then, at 1225, one man in the northernmost platoon of B/2-28 Inf, the 3d platoon, spotted 5 VC walking north. They disappeared before fire could be brought on them. At the same time, 3 VC were spotted climbing trees in front of another 3d platoon position. Two M-79 rounds were fired at the VC, and the VC ran. The VC were wearing black "pajamas". B/2-28 Inf's second patrol, having reached about 50 meters from the perimeter, was called back in. Captain Sawtelle, figuring that B/2-28 Inf was about to become engaged in the northwest, pulled his company A/2-28 Inf, out of the tree line and began to march them northward in the clearing toward positions where they could provide rear support for B/2-28 Inf.

At ____ one man in B/1-16 Inf spotted 2 VC east of the perimeter and shot them. A few minutes later he shot two more. At the same time a B/1-16 Inf patrol received two sniper rounds about 100 meters in front of the perimeter. The CO of B/1-16 Inf notified his battalion's CP of the activity, but it was already clear that a heavy engagement was imminent. The intensity of sniper fire was increasing. Patrolling units rejoined the perimeter in the sectors of A/1-16 Inf, B/1-16 Inf, and B/2-28 Inf; recon 1-16 Inf had not sent out patrols from its sector. At about 1245 a CH-47 resupply helicopter received several small arms rounds over the LZ and returned to LZ RUFE, where it landed in a disabled condition. At 1255 B/2-28 Inf and A/1-16 Inf were receiving heavy automatic weapons and small arms fire from the north. The 2d platoon of A/2-28 Inf (2/A/2-28 Inf) was immediately pinned down in the clearing behind 3/B/2-28 Inf. The heaviest enemy fire was brought on the two northernmost platoons, 2/B/2-28 Inf in the northwest and 3/A/1-16 Inf in the northeast.

Artillery and light fire team gunship helicopters were requested, and response was immediate. Tactical air support was requested at 1252. With 105mm Howitzers of the 2-33 Artillery providing principal support, the artillery fire arrived about 1300. The first rounds were directed to fall about 200 meters north of the perimeter, and the artillery gained effectiveness as it was adjusted closer. Two gunships arrived and began providing continuous support to the units in the north.

At 1306 at least three groups of VC began simultaneous ground assaults on the left flank of 3/A/1-16 Inf and the end position on the right flank of 3/B/2-28 Inf. The US troops used ant hills and clusters of bamboo for cover. Sixty or seventy VC in two orderly groups moved toward 3/A/1-16 Inf throwing hand grenades and firing automatic weapons. RPG's and anti-tank weapons were also used against the US positions. The VC concentrated on the left flank of the 3d platoon. The M-60 machine gun position there was knocked-out immediately when an RPG round hit the position, wounding the men and leaving the gun inoperative. The VC killed or wounded all of the left flank of the 3d platoon of A/1-16 Inf. It was reported by troops in the action that the VC used a chemical agent, probably a type of tear gas, on the 3d platoon positions. The right flank of the platoon was able to move back and join the 2d platoon line about 40 meters to their rear. The dead and the wounded who were unable to move had to be left forward. The new line formed by the 2d platoon and men from the 3d platoon was about 15 meters from the clearing, and directly behind the original 3d platoon positions. At the beginning of the engagement of A/1-16 Inf, support from the company's two 81mm mortars was requested in addition to the artillery fire. Both arrived immediately, but the company mortars could place close-in fire on the enemy during the time the artillery was being adjusted into the area near the perimeter, where it would be most effective. After about 10 minutes, effective artillery was falling, two gunships were firing into the area, and heavy US automatic fire was delivered from the newly-formed line with the 2d and 3d platoons. The attacking VC had reached the original 3d platoon positions then ended their first assault. This was at about 1315.

In the meantime, a group of VC attacking B/2-28 Inf had killed the two men in the northernmost position of that company at the start of the assault from the north. Two VC occupied the position and started firing from it, using the US bodies as a shield. Other small groups of VC approached the northern positions of 3/B/2-28 Inf, wounding several of the men on the platoon's right flank. The platoon sergeant, SFC Billie J. Dodd, RA16526378, took four of his men toward the end position that had been taken by the VC. The VC fired on the group, killing two and wounding SFC Dodd. PFC Ben Walker, US56824413, the radio operator Dodd had chosen to help retake the lost position, was unwounded and moved to his right, where he found some cover from enemy fire. He stayed in this spot, about 30 meters from the VC and isolated from US positions, until the VC finally withdrew. He used his radio to report on the battle and direct artillery. The other unwounded men, PFC John J. Rieck, Jr., US51825322, gave first aid to SFC Dodd and returned to the platoon CP to get a medic. Another member of the 3d platoon, SP4 Dannie Smith, US526315325, occupied the position next to the end one that had been overrun and held his position alone through most of the engagement. He could not see the US positions on either side of his. Three VC approached his position from 50 to 75 meters away. They were black "pajamas" and had among them one AK-47 and two carbines. Smith moved behind a small tree and stayed there throwing grenades and firing his M-16 at the three VC, who fired and threw grenades at Smith from behind an ant hill. Smith left his position when an enemy round hit one of his smoke grenades, which made his clothes start to burn. Smith ran back to the clearing where men of A/2-28 Inf put out the fire and gave first aid to his burns.

At about 1325 a 60mm mortar barrage was directed against the northern elements of A/1-16 Inf and B/2-28 Inf. The barrage consisted of 15 to 20 rounds and ended at 1330. The rounds were most effectively placed around the left flank of A/1-16 Inf and accounted for the majority of that company's wounded. The assault at 1306 had been responsible for most of the company's killed. The enemy attack in the north was coordinated so that as soon as the mortar rounds stopped falling, at 1330, the VC were in front of the 2d-3d platoon line of A/1-16 Inf and began a second large ground assault. It was coordinated with increased pressure on the B/2-28 Inf right flank as well as a simultaneous assault on recon 1-16 Inf in the southeast.

The 1330 assault on A/1-16 Inf consisted of apparently the same groups of VC attacking the same area that had been hit in the first assault. This time, however, A/1-16 Inf had a stronger left flank, with the 2d and 3d platoons' lines consolidated, and artillery was already falling close in front of the US positions. During the second VC assault from the north, fifteen minutes of continuous artillery fire fell in front of A/1-16 Inf. Though the enemy was next to the perimeter before the ground attack even started, they could not again overwhelm the US with their heavy automatic weapons and RPG fire. The VC got within 30 meters of the tree line, or 15 meters from the 2d-3d platoon line. A rifleman in the 3d platoon, PFC Daniel J. Phelps, RA16929631, saw a group of 10 VC assaulting his two-man position. The VC wore black "pajamas" and were walking and firing at the same time. They got within 25 meters of Phelps' position, which was behind an ant hill. With about 2 minutes of automatic M-16 fire Phelps and his partner killed the 10 assaulting VC. Then the other rifleman with Phelps was hit and killed, probably by a sniper. Phelps stayed at this position through the entire engagement. He could see no other US position from his. Phelps saw and shot VC crawling toward his position one at a time. He saw VC bodies being dragged away, but the bodies of the 10 VC who assaulted remained in front of Phelps' position. The A/1-16 Inf CP had been moved from the center of the company's sector to the area that was being assaulted so that the CO could have better control of the action, and the forward observer could adjust the artillery close to the area that was being attacked. Soon after 1330 the radio operator of A/1-16 Inf reported that he and the company commander were wounded and that he could see two VC entering the perimeter. These were apparently the only VC that broke through the A/1-16 Inf perimeter on the second assault, and they were killed immediately. With a medic attending his wounds, Captain Williamson continued to command his company throughout the battle. The US artillery barrage was so close to the perimeter that occasional pieces of shrapnel reached the friendly positions through the trees. Still hot after filtering through the umbrella of bamboo, the shrapnel sizzled on the men's wet clothes. It was largely a result of this massive, close-in artillery support that the VC were unable to reach the US positions as they had in the first assault on A/1-16 Inf. The VC withdrew suddenly at 1345.

At the same time as the second assault on A/1-16 Inf started, at 1330, the VC moved in on the right flank of B/2-28 Inf, which was next to A/1-16 Inf in the north. Artillery fire was then heavy and effectively holding back the VC. The artillery fell within 30 meters of the perimeter. The 2d platoon of A/2-28 Inf, pinned down in the clearing behind B/2-28 Inf's right flank, crawled south toward some trees near the center of the LZ. Because of heavy automatic weapons fire they were unable to stand up in the tall elephant grass in order to open fire. At about 1335 they formed an east-west line across the clearing sealing off the two battalions' CP's from the north. They then stood up and fired into the tree line, aiming high to avoid hitting US positions whose locations were unknown. The 2-28 Inf's caliber .50 machine gun was set up there and was used effectively against snipers in trees.

It appeared to the men of B/2-28 Inf that the VC could not see their line, as the VC fired at smoke grenades whenever they were thrown. Otherwise the VC did not fire unless they saw a US troop move. It was reported by men of A/2-28 Inf that tear gas was in the air in the northern portion of the IZ on two separate occasions during the battle.

Apparently coordinated with the attack on the US positions in the north, at 1330 a large group of VC assaulted recon 1-16 Inf in the southeast. The VC assault covered a 40-meter front. Two outposts were engaged by the assault group, but the fire was concentrated on an M-60 machine gun position and the platoon CP. The CP was located in the clearing directly behind the M-60 position. The machine gun position was immediately overrun. The US positions were too far apart to prevent the VC from penetrating the perimeter at that point. The positions on the platoon's right flank were receiving sniper fire. Three

VC were observed south of the perimeter and were engaged, with unknown results. At the platoon CP the artillery observer had just finished making initial adjustments on supporting fire for in front of the perimeter when his radio operator was hit and the radio destroyed. The CP was receiving heavy automatic weapons fire, and it was decided that the CP group could not hold the position. The wounded had to be evacuated first, so the platoon sergeant, SSG Gradie E. Sanders, RA14723897, the artillery observer, and a medic left, carrying three wounded men. Before he left, SSG Sanders saw 8 to 10 VC approaching the CP. The VC wore khaki uniforms, steel helmets, bandoleers, and web gear. The wounded were carried to a point on the left flank of the platoon, near the B/1-16 Inf positions. The platoon leader, talking by radio to the CO of 1-16 Inf, reported that his CP group had killed more than 30 VC, saying they were "stacking them up like cordwood." Radio contact with the recon platoon CP was then lost. The VC killed all of the group at the CP and frisked their clothes. The CO of 1-16 Inf ordered an element of the battalion headquarters company to move toward the recon platoon's sector to provide assistance. At 1341 the first airstrike arrived, about 150 meters east of the perimeter. The VC withdrew at about 1345, using the same break in the line through which they had entered.

Continuous air support was provided east and southeast if LZ XRAY. The fire coordination line ran north and south through the NDP. Artillery was the principal deterrent placed on the enemy assaults on A/1-16 Inf and

B/2-28 Inf in the north and northwest; airstrikes provided the most effective support for recon 1-16 Inf in the southeast. Part of one airstrike, however, was delivered on the west side of the LZ, killing 2 men in B/2-28 Inf.

Although the enemy assault groups all withdrew from around LZ XRAY at about 1345, the US positions continued to receive heavy automatic weapons fire. By 1350 a platoon of A/2-28 Inf had formed a line of blocking positions across the clearing just above the recon 1-16 Inf sector. At 1355 two gunships were called to provide additional support in front of the recon platoon sector. At 1403 the elements of 1-16 Inf and 2-28 Inf located at LZ RUFE received 10 60mm mortar rounds and small arms fire lasting for about one-half hour.

Around LZ XRAY the sources of the enemy automatic weapons fire were moving farther from the US positions. All units at LZ XRAY started their efforts to collect the wounded and move them to the evacuation point in the center of the NDP. By 1445 most of the VC automatic weapons fire had stopped. Sniper fire from a distance continued until about 1500, when all incoming rounds stopped. By 1500 recon 1-16 Inf had moved all its men, casualties, and equipment within the perimeter formed by the A/2-28 Inf blocking positions. Helicopter evacuation of casualties from LZ XRAY began after 1500 and lasted until about 1850.

At about 1530 a barrage of 30 to 35 60mm mortar rounds was concentrated on the B/2-28 Inf CP area in the west and the area newly occupied by recon 1-16 Inf in the south.

After US casualties and equipment had been removed from the recon 1-16 Inf sector, there was no other police mission conducted in that area until the following day. The search of the battlefield in the north covered a maximum of 100 meters from the US positions. Recovering US casualties and equipment, A/1-16 Inf found 35 to 40 VC bodies in front of their positions. Most of the VC bodies wore khaki uniforms, looked well fed, and had new Soviet assault rifles. A/2-28 Inf also conducted a limited search of the area in front of the northern sector of the perimeter. They found 2 VC bodies and shallow depressions in the ground that looked as if they had been dug under fire. A large amount of communication wire ran on trails between most of the enemy positions.

Initial interrogation of a captured enemy soldier was very limited because the prisoner was wounded and had to be evacuated. In subsequent interrogation the prisoner stated that he was one of a group of 30 to 50 North Vietnamese infiltrators who had recently been assigned to the 2d Battalion of the 271st VC Regiment. His unit moved to the battle area on 7 June 1967. On 16 June the 1st and 2d Battalions of the 271st VC Regiment had prepared the ambush site at LZ XRAY because they knew that US troops had entered the area on 13 June. Each company had three 60mm mortars and a Chinese heavy machine gun of unknown type. The VC had spent the night of 16 June at another location and returned to LZ XRAY on 17 June after the US troops had arrived.

At 1610 1-16 Inf was notified that the 1-18 Inf would replace Company A, the headquarters company, and the recon platoon of 1-16 Inf at LZ XRAY. 1-18 Inf began arriving at LZ XRAY by helicopter at 1627. The helilift was stopped at 1700 when LZ XRAY received a 50 to 60-round barrage from 60mm and 81mm mortars. After 1710 there was no further enemy activity. Counter-mortar fires were employed, and the lift of 1-18 Inf was subsequently completed. The lift of A/1-16 Inf and recon 1-16 Inf to CHI LINH was completed at 1830. The lift of the headquarters company of 1-16 Inf to LZ RUFE was completed at 1855.

The last airstrike was delivered at 1915. There was a total of 43 tactical air sorties in support of the action at LZ CRAY. Ordnance requested was CBU and napalm. Ordnance delivered was CBU, napalm, rockets, 500-pound and 750-pound bombs, and 20mm cannon fire. A total of 8,250 artillery rounds were fired in support of the battle. There were 7,621 rounds of 105mm, 513 rounds of 155mm, 38 rounds of 175mm, and 78 rounds of 8 inch artillery.

On 18 June 1967, 1-18 Inf conducted a search of the battle area. They found 26 bodies, which brought the body count of enemy killed to 222. It is likely that the VC removed a large number of their dead.

Appendix 2
Citations from Xom Bo II

Citation for Posthumous Award of the Silver Star for John James Rieck, Jr

The President of the United States takes pride in presenting the Silver Star Medal (Posthumously) to John James Rieck, Jr. (US51825322), Private First Class, United States Army, for gallantry in action against a hostile force while serving with Company B, 2d Battalion, 28th Infantry Regiment, 1st Infantry Division, on 17 June 1967, in the Republic of Vietnam. On this date during Operation BILLINGS, Private First Class Rieck was serving as a rifleman. While moving through the dense jungle near Chu Linh, his unit came under attack from a reinforced Viet Cong battalion. Both Private First Class Rieck's squad leader and team leader were wounded in the opening moments of the battle. Private First Class Rieck immediately took command of the squad and with effective direction of his men, repulsed a massive Viet

Cong human wave assault. Later in the battle, an insurgent squad moved to within 10 meters of the friendly lines in an effort to capture weapons and equipment from the wounded soldiers. With complete disdain for the vicious enemy fire, Private First Class Rieck led his squad to meet the insurgents. The Viet Cong were soon forced to withdraw after minutes of violent fighting. The enemy fire was still intense when Private First Class Rieck saw a wounded squad member lying within the hostile kill zone. With complete disregard for his personal safety, he crawled to the casualty, administered first aid and then pulled the soldier from the open terrain to the cover of a small berm. When reinforcements had arrived, Private First Class Rieck again exposed himself to enemy fire to bring medical aid men to the friendly casualties. He then returned to his squad to lead them in aggressive counterassaults against the enemy. Due in large measure to the courage and calm demeanor Private First Class Rieck displayed in the face of enemy fire, the lives of many fellow soldiers were saved and a large hostile force defeated. Sergeant First Class Rieck's unquestionable valor in close combat against numerically superior hostile forces is in keeping with the finest traditions of the military service and reflects great credit upon himself, the 1st Infantry Division, and the United States Army.

Citation For Award
Of Army Commendation Medal with "V" for Valor
to Thomas W. Waldron

Waldron, Thomas W Private First Class E3 United States Army
Company B 2d Battalion 28th Infantry

Awarded: Army Commendation Medal with "V" device
Date of Action: 18 June 1967
Theater: Republic of Vietnam
Reason: For heroism: On this date, during Operation Billings, Private First Class Waldron was serving as a rifleman on a search and destroy mission. He was in the lead element when it was suddenly subjected to intensive fire from a large Viet Cong force. During the initial barrage, his platoon sustained several casualties and it was ordered to withdraw to rejoin the main body of the company. The company then formed into a cordon around the insurgent positions and called for artillery fire to be placed on the enemy. As the artillery rounds began hitting, it was discovered that one wounded soldier was pinned down by enemy fire. With complete disregard for his personal safety, Private First Class Waldron ran through heavy enemy fire and the debris and shrapnel from the incoming rounds to administer first aid and drag the casualty to safety. His undaunted courage and bold initiative were directly responsible for saving his comrade's life. Private First Class Waldron's actions are in

keeping with the finest traditions of the military service and reflect great credit upon himself, the 1st Infantry Division, and the United States Army.

Authority: By direction of the Secretary of the Army, under the provisions of AR 672-5-1.

FOR THE COMMANDER: Frederick C. Krause
Colonel, GS
Chief of Staff

Citation For The Posthumous Award Of Bronze Star Medal with "V" for Valor to Charles P. Kelly

Kelly, Charles P. Specialist Four E4 United States Army Company A 1st Battalion 16th Infantry

Awarded: Army Commendation Medal with "V" device
Date of Action: 17 June 1967
Theater: Republic of Vietnam
Reason: For heroism in connection with military operations against a hostile force: On this date, during Operation Billings, Specialist Kelly was serving as an automatic rifleman while participating in a search and destroy mission. As they moved through a dense jungle area near Chua Hoa, Specialist Kelly and his comrades came under intense fire from a Viet Cong regiment. Specialist Kelly immediately position himself behind a small berm and began to place suppressive fire onto the advancing enemy. His fire was so effective that time after time the insurgent assaults were turned back. Once he had expended his ammunition, he moved in the direction of the supply point to obtain additional rounds for his weapon. Enroute, he saw a wounded comrade lying exposed to enemy cross fire. With complete disregard for his personal safety, he crawled to the soldier, administered first aid and pulled him to cover. He then procured ammunition and returned to the battle line to once again engage the enemy. Suddenly, the Viet Cong

began a massive human wave attack. Specialist Kelly calmly remained in place and directed devastating fire into the insurgent ranks. In this manner, he killed many Viet Cong before he was mortally wounded. His comrades, inspired by his demonstration of courage, fought with increased determination until the enemy was defeated. Specialist Four Kelly's outstanding display of aggressiveness, devotion to duty and personal bravery is in keeping with the finest traditions of the military service and reflect great credit upon himself, the 1st Infantry Division, and the United States Army.

Authority: By direction of the President, under the provisions of Executive Order 11046, 24 August 1962.

Citation For Award
Of The Bronze Star with "V" for Valor
to David J. Hearne

Hearne, David J. First Lieutenant Artillery United States Army Battery C 2d Battalion 33d Artillery

Awarded: Bronze Star Medal with "V" device
Date of action: 17 June 1967
Theater: Republic of Vietnam
Reason: For heroism in connection with military operations against a hostile force: On this date during Operation Billings, Lieutenant Hearne was serving as an artillery forward observer with an infantry unit which was conducting a search and destroy mission deep in a Viet Cong infested area of War Zone D. While establishing a night defensive position they were subjected to intense small arms and automatic weapons fire from an estimated Viet Cong battalion. Disregarding the heavy hostile fire, Lieutenant Hearne unhesitatingly moved along the friendly perimeter calling for and adjusting artillery fire on the approaching enemy. When the Viet Cong assault had been repelled, Lieutenant Hearne's unit was subjected to an intense mortar barrage. With complete disregard for his personal safety, Lieutenant Hearne ignored the exploding mortar rounds as he moved to an exposed position from which he called for and accurately adjusted artillery fire on the enemy emplacements until the Viet Cong had been routed from

the area. First Lieutenant Hearne's outstanding display of aggressiveness, devotion to duty, and personal bravery is in keeping with the finest traditions of the military service and reflects great credit upon himself, the 1st Infantry Division, and the United States Army.

Authority: By direction of the President, under the provisions of Executive Order 11046, 24 August 1962.

Citation For Award Of The Bronze Star with "V" for Valor to Edward N. Skiles

Skiles, Edward N Sergeant E5 United States Army

Awarded: Bronze Star Medal (First Oak Leaf Cluster) with "V" device
Date of action: 17 June 1967
Theater: Republic of Vietnam
Reason: For heroism in connection with military operations against a hostile force: On this date during Operation Billings, Sergeant Skiles was serving as a weapons squad leader as his battalion was preparing a night defensive position near Chi Linh in War Zone D. In the late afternoon hours, they were subjected to a heavy volume of mortar, small arms and automatic weapons fire from elements of the Viet Cong 271st Regiment. Several of Sergeant Skiles' men were wounded in the initial barrage, and he immediately ran through a hail of fire to reach them. After administering first aid to the wounded soldiers, he remained in the open and assisted in evacuating all the casualties from the area. With complete disregard for his personal safety, Sergeant Skiles later moved along the perimeter resupplying his men with ammunition. When an entire gun crew was medically evacuated, Sergeant Skiles assumed the duties of gunner and placed a devastating barrage of fire onto the insurgents until they were forced to retreat. The bold initiative and exemplary courage demonstrated by

Sergeant Skiles significantly contributed to the overwhelming defeat of the Viet Cong force. Sergeant Skiles' outstanding display of aggressiveness, devotion to duty, and personal bravery is in keeping with the finest traditions of the military service and reflects great credit upon himself, the 1st Infantry Division, and the United States Army.

Authority: By direction of the President, under the provisions of Executive Order 11046, 24 August 1962.

**Citation For Award
Of The Silver Star
to Frank John Limiero, JR**

Limiero, Frank John Specialist Four E4 United States Army Company A 1st Battalion 16th Infantry

Awarded: Silver Star Medal
Date of action: 17 June 1967
Theater: Republic of Vietnam
Reason: For gallantry in action against a hostile force while serving with Company A, 1st Battalion, 16th Infantry Regiment, 1st Infantry Division. On 17 June 1967, during Operation BILLINGS, Specialist Limiero was participating in a search and destroy mission in War Zone D. As his company was preparing a defensive position, they were subjected to intense automatic weapons and small arms fire from the numerically superior 271st Viet Cong Regiment. During the initial barrage, the unit sustained numerous casualties, including two rifle team leaders. Specialist Limiero immediately assumed command and deployed the squad into the most advantageous firing positions from which they could deliver maximum fire power upon the advancing Viet Cong. With complete disregard for his own personal safety, Specialist Limiero exposed himself to the heavy volume of fire as he moved from position to position, encouraging his men and personally ensuring that they were supplied with sufficient ammunition to repel the

repeated Viet Cong assaults. Ignoring the heavy fire, Specialist Limiero moved forward of his defensive line to a position from which he called for and adjusted artillery fire with devastating accuracy upon the enemy until the insurgents were forced to withdraw. Maintaining the offensive, he adjusted the artillery to cut off the enemy's retreat. Although he was still receiving sporadic sniper fire, Specialist Limiero moved throughout his unit searching for and evacuating casualties. Specialist Limiero demonstrated exemplary leadership and undaunted courage and significantly contributed to the defeat of a large Viet Cong force. Specialist Fourth Class Limiero's unquestionable valor in close combat against a numerically superior hostile force was in keeping with the highest traditions of military service and reflects great credit upon himself, the 1st Infantry Division, and the United States Army.

Authority: By direction of the President, under the provisions of Executive Order 11046, 24 August 1962.

Citation For Award
Of The Bronze Star with "V" for Valor
to Jose Garcia JR.

Garcia, Jose JR Specialist Four E4 United States Army
Company A 1st Battalion 16th Infantry

Awarded: Bronze Star Medal with "V" for Valor
Date of action: 17 June 1967
Theater: Republic of Vietnam
Reason: For heroism in connection with military operations against a hostile force. On this date, during Operation BILLINGS, Specialist Garcia was serving as a machine gunner on a search and destroy mission near Chi Linh. The unit was preparing a field defensive position when it was suddenly subjected to heavy small arms and automatic weapons fire from a numerically superior Viet Cong Force. Specialist Garcia immediately placed highly effective fire on the advancing insurgents until they were forced to withdraw and regroup. Simultaneously, his position was subjected to an intense Viet Cong mortar barrage. Ignoring the hail of debris and shrapnel from the incoming rounds, Specialist Garcia continued placing suppressive fire on the insurgents until he was wounded by shrapnel. Despite the fact that he could not fire his weapon, Specialist Garcia refused medical evacuation and served as an assistant machine gunner until the Viet Cong were forced to retreat.

His undaunted courage and bold initiative significantly contributed to the defeat of a large Viet Cong force. Specialist Four Garcia's outstanding display of aggressiveness, devotion to duty and personal bravery are in keeping with the highest traditions of military service and reflects great credit upon himself, the 1st Infantry Division, and the United States Army.

Authority: By direction of the President, under the provisions of Executive Order 11046, 24 August 1962.

Citation For Award Of The Bronze Star with "V" for Valor to Stephen M. Noggle

Noggle, Stephen M Specialist Four E4 United States Army Company A 1st Battalion 16th Infantry

Awarded: Bronze Star Medal with "V" for Valor
Date of action: 17 June 1967
Theater: Republic of Vietnam
Reason: For heroism in connection with military operations against a hostile force. On 17 June 1967, during Operation BILLINGS, Specialist Noggle was serving as a medical aid man on a search and destroy mission. As his unit prepared night defensive positions, they were suddenly attacked by a large hostile force. During the opening moments of the battle, Specialist Noggle learned that both medical aidmen from an adjacent platoon had been wounded by the hostile fire. With complete disregard for his personal safety, he moved through a vicious enemy cross-fire to the area being held by the adjacent friendly unit. Specialist Noggle immediately began to administer first aid to the wounded men. Several times he placed his body over that of a fellow soldier to protect the casualty from the relentless Viet Cong fire. Despite the increasing intensity of the battle, Specialist Noggle continued treating his fellow Soldiers until he was mortally wounded by the hostile fire. His great courage and selfless regard for the welfare of his comrades doubtlessly saved many lives and distinguished

him as a combat Soldier of the highest caliber. Specialist Four Noggle outstanding display of aggressiveness, devotion to duty and personal bravery are in keeping with the highest traditions of military service and reflects great credit upon himself, the 1st Infantry Division, and the United States Army.

Authority: By direction of the President, under the provisions of Executive Order 11046, 24 August 1962.

Citation For Award
Of Distinguished Flying Cross
to Paul J. Wenzel

Wenzel, Paul J Captain United States Army

Awarded: Distinguished Flying Cross
Date of action: 17 June 1967
Theater: Republic of Vietnam
Reason: For heroism while participating in aerial flight on 17 June 1967. On that date, during Operations Billings, Captain Wenzel was serving as aircraft commander of a utility helicopter transporting and resupplying troops engaged in a search and destroy operation in War Zone D. While on standby alert, he received word that a friendly battalion had received intensive hostile fire and human wave assaults. They urgently needed a helicopter to bring in more ammunition and to evacuate several seriously wounded men. Captain Wenzel immediately volunteered for the mission. He supervised the loading of his aircraft with ammunition, then flew directly to the scene of the battle. He landed amidst intensive hostile fire, receiving several hits. Once on the ground, he got out of the aircraft and, disregarding the hostile fire aimed directly at the helicopter, supervised the unloading of the ammunition. He helped to place the most seriously wounded soldiers onto the helicopter. After evacuating the wounded men to a medical treatment facility, he returned to the battle site and, again under heavy automatic weapons fire, landed his helicopter to evacuate

more casualties. His courage and determination under fire contributed significantly to the friendly battalion's success in repelling the Viet Cong assaults and saved the lives of many seriously wounded men. Captain Wenzel's actions are in keeping with the finest traditions of the military service and reflect great credit upon himself, his unit, and the United States Army.

About the Author

Author David Hearne served as an artillery officer in Vietnam during 1967 and finished his tour a week after the 1968 Tet Offensive. During his tour, his eyes were opened to the true savagery of war and its aftermath.

David is an award-winning author, who has written two novels, a collection of short horror stories, and a non-fictional book on computer programming. His fictional work has been described as fast paced thrillers that weave fictional characters into events mirroring problems facing contemporary society.

His literary awards have come from local, national, and international book competitions and events. His novel The Christmas Special has won awards at the New England Book Festival, Midwest Book Fest, and from book competitions in Florida and California. He also received an international award for The Christmas Special at the British Library in London, England. His book of short horror stories, Bloodstained Tales of Sin and Sex, won awards both from Press Club of Southeast Texas Excellence in Media Awards and from the 2014 Halloween Book Fest in Hollywood, CA. David's work has received five other awards from the Press Club of Southeast Texas Excellence in Media Awards.

As the son of a career Army officer, David enjoyed growing up in many different places, along the east coast of the United States. Early on, David developed a love for traveling and learning about different places and diverse cultures. His life experiences are many; he has served in the Army as an Artillery Officer, ran numerous companies, lived in San Francisco and Berkeley California during the "Age of Aquarius", an age of love, light, and humanity, worked as a software engineer, founded a successful construction company and more. Now David and his wife, Stacie, own and operate the eclectic bed and breakfast, Book Nook Inn located in the golden triangle of Southeast Texas.

Glossary of Military Terms and Acronyms

ARVN
Army of the Republic of Vietnam; the South Vietnamese Regular Army

CP
Command post

CWO4
Chief Warrant Officer, 4th Grade

FO
Forward observer; a person attached to a field unit to coordinate the placement of direct or indirect fire from ground, air, and naval forces.

KIA
Killed in action

LZ
Landing zone; usually a small clearing secured temporarily for the landing of resupply helicopters. Some become more permanent and eventually become base camps.

MACV
Military Assistance Command / Vietnam. The main American military command unit that had responsibility

for and authority over all U.S. military activities in Vietnam; based at Tan Son Nhut.

MARS
Military Affiliate Radio Station. Used by soldiers to call home via Signal Corps and ham radio equipment.

NDP
Night defensive position

OSS
Office of Strategic Services

RTO
Radio telephone operator; the man who carried his unit's radio on his back in the field.

TOC
Tactical operations center

WIA
Wounded in action

Index

O

P

R

S

T

U

V

W

Y

Endnotes

[1] China explodes its first thermonuclear bomb, (https://www.ctbto.org/specials/testing-times/17-june-1967-chinas-first-thermonuclear-test)

[2] Battle of Ap Gu Battle of Ap Gu https://en.wikipedia.org/wiki/Battle_of_Ap_Gu

[3] Danger Forward volume Two, Number one --- February 1968, Billings pg. 24

[4] George L. MacGarrigle, (Taking The Offensive October 1966 to October 1967) MilitaryBookshop.co.uk, page 329

[5] Where's My Army by Reggie Pennington page 17 published by Xulon Press.

[6] https://en.wikipedia.org/wiki/Battle_of_Prek_Klok_I Preparation of the battle of Prek Klok.

[7] Letter dated 6-21-1967 from SP4 Thomas Waldron to his parents

[8] Dec 17th 2015 Phone Call conversation with Ronald Moreno about recollections of XOM BO II

[9]

http://freepages.military.rootsweb.ancestry.com/~realmccoy/billings.html article by Fred Hill and Don Koch see map

[10] Cumberland Evening Times, Cumberland Maryland Page 17 – Garrett Area GI Killed in Vietnam

[11] Stephen F. Austin Website, by Deborah Burkett http://www.sfasu.edu/heritagecenter/9005.asp

[12] http://magazine.tcu.edu/winter-2015/jim-swink-1936-2014/

[13] Black Lion Newsletter, Last Foxhole for Clinger by David Aldridge

[14] Why LBJ bowed out by James Jones LA Times March 30, 2008

[15] Oral History Project for James Swink http://www.oralhistory.ws/tpl/index3.php?view=audio_clips&client=4889&free=1&total=2

[16] Military Communication A Test for Technology, By Center of Military History Page 403

[17] https://en.wikipedia.org/wiki/Battle_of_Ong_Thanh

[18] George L. MacGarrigle, (Taking The Offensive October 1966 to October 1967) MilitaryBookshop.co.uk, page 343

[19]

http://freepages.military.rootsweb.ancestry.com/~realmccoy/billings.html article by Fred Hill and Don Koch

[20] Combat Medic Vietnam, Chapter 2. Written by Craig Roberts published by Pocket Books a division of Simon & Schuster Inc. in August 1991

[21] Black Lion Newsletter, Last Foxhole for Clinger by David Aldridge

[22] The War at Home, by David Maraniss, Oct 2003 http://www.texasmonthly.com/articles/the-war-at-home-2/

[23] Battle Notes: Music of the Vietnam War By Lee Andresen page 42

[24] The Vietnam War in Context (Enquiring History... (Paperback) by Dale Scarboro page 35

[25] Ibid

[26] http://www.duhaime.org/LawMuseum/LawArticle-1600/1941--The-Atlantic-Charter.aspx 1941 - The Atlantic Charter

[27] Ibid

37566999R00215

Made in the USA
Middletown, DE
03 December 2016